The Psychology of Grandparenthood

The majority of people will now spend about one-third of their lives as grandparents, yet developmental psychologists have largely ignored the nature of the grandparental role, and the influence which grandparents can have on grandchildren. Originally published in 1991, this book redresses the balance and uses life-span evolutionary and psychodynamic theoretical frameworks to provide a comprehensive analysis of the phenomenon of grandparenthood from cross-cultural perspectives.

Much recent work in developmental psychology has disregarded the extended family in favour of the two-generational nuclear family of parents and children. But grandparents do have a significant role in family relationships and children's development. This volume contains detailed discussion of inter-generational transmission of parenting skills, cooperation and conflict in three-generational families and the ways in which grandparents and grand-children perceive one another.

The importance of considering social and cultural contexts of development applies to grandparents just as much as to other areas of human development. Kinds of family structure, social policies regarding employment, health and housing, attitudes to marriage and even particular historical events all have an impact on the position and role of grandparents and on stereotypes of old age. These factors vary considerably from country to country. Our understanding of grandparenthood can only be enriched by learning about the variety of ways in which it is expressed in different cultural settings. Most previous research has been confined to the USA. This book is truly international containing contributions from Britain, Canada, Finland, Italy, the Netherlands, Poland, West Germany and the USA. International comparisons enable us to see which elements are essential to grandparenthood and which are culture dependant. In most Western countries the population is ageing and this sort of study is becoming vitally important. *The Psychology of Grandparenthood* is required reading for anybody who is professionally involved with the elderly and for psychologists interested in development, the life-span and family systems.

T0386181

The Psychology of Grandparenthood

An international perspective

Edited by
Peter K. Smith

Routledge
Taylor & Francis Group

LONDON AND NEW YORK

First published in 1991
by Routledge

This edition first published in 2018 by Routledge
2 Park Square, Milton Park, Abingdon, Oxon OX14 4RN

and by Routledge
711 Third Avenue, New York, NY 10017

Routledge is an imprint of the Taylor & Francis Group, an informa business

Publisher's Note
The publisher has gone to great lengths to ensure the quality of this reprint but points out that some imperfections in the original copies may be apparent.

Disclaimer
The publisher has made every effort to trace copyright holders and welcomes correspondence from those they have been unable to contact.

A Library of Congress record exists under ISBN: 0415047307

ISBN: 978-1-138-30007-1 (hbk)
ISBN: 978-0-203-73360-8 (ebk)
ISBN: 978-1-138-30036-1 (pbk)

The Psychology of Grandparenthood

The majority of people will now spend about one-third of their lives as grandparents, yet developmental psychologists have largely ignored the nature of the grandparental role, and the influence which grandparents can have on grandchildren. This book redresses the balance and uses life-span evolutionary and psychodynamic theoretical frameworks to provide a comprehensive analysis of the phenomenon of grandparenthood from cross-cultural perspectives.

Much recent work in developmental psychology has disregarded the extended family in favour of the two-generational nuclear family of parents and children. But grandparents do have a significant role in family relationships and children's development. This volume contains detailed discussion of intergenerational transmission of parenting skills, cooperation and conflict in three-generational families and the ways in which grandparents and grandchildren perceive one another.

The importance of considering social and cultural contexts of development applies to grandparents just as much as to other areas of human development. Kinds of family structure, social policies regarding employment, health and housing, attitudes to marriage and even particular historical events all have an impact on the position and role of grandparents and on stereotypes of old age. These factors vary considerably from country to country. Our understanding of grandparenthood can only be enriched by learning about the variety of ways in which it is expressed in different cultural settings. Most previous research has been confined to the USA. This book is truly international, containing contributions from Britain, Canada, Finland, Italy, the Netherlands, Poland, West Germany and the USA. International comparisons enable us to see which elements are essential to grandparenthood and which are culture-dependent.

In most Western countries the population is ageing and this sort of study is becoming vitally important. *The Psychology of Grandparenthood* is required reading for anybody who is professionally involved with the elderly and for psychologists interested in development, the life-span and family systems.

The Psychology of Grandparenthood

An international perspective

Edited by
Peter K. Smith

London and New York

First published 1991
by Routledge
11 New Fetter Lane, London EC4P 4EE

Simultaneously published in the USA and Canada
by Routledge
a division of Routledge, Chapman and Hall, Inc.
29 West 35th Street, New York, NY 10001

Phototypeset in 10pt Times by
Mews Photosetting, Beckenham, Kent
Printed and bound in Great Britain by
Biddles Ltd, Guildford and King's Lynn

British Library Cataloguing in Publication Data

The Psychology of grandparenthood: an international
    perspective.
    1. Grandparenthood
    I. Smith, Peter K.
    306.8745

Library of Congress Cataloging in Publication Data

The Psychology of grandparenthood: an international perspective/
    edited by Peter K. Smith.
    p. cm. – (The International library of psychology)
    1. Grandparent and child–Congresses. 2. Grandparents-
    Psychology–Congresses. 3. Grandparenting–Psychological aspects-
    Congresses. I. Smith, Peter K. II. European Conference on
    Developmental Psychology (3rd: 1988: Budapest, Hungary)
    III. International Society for the Study of Behavioural Development.
    Meeting (10th: 1989: Jyväskylä, Finland) IV. British
    Psychological Society. Developmental Section. Meeting (1988:
    Harlech, Wales) V. Series.
    BF723.G68P79 1990
    155.6'46–dc20   90-40037
                                                              CIP

ISBN 0-415-04730-7

Contents

Contents

Illustrations

Figures

Tables

Contributors

Dr Piergiorgio Battistelli
Universita degli Studi di Urbino, Istituto di Psicologia, Via Saffi 15, 61029
Urbino, ITALY

Dr Rita Benn
Merrill Palmer Institute, Wayne State University, Detroit, MI 48202, USA

Dr A.J.L.L. de Brock
Institute of Family Studies, University of Nijmegen, Erasmusplein 1, 6525
GG Nijmegen, THE NETHERLANDS

Dr Alessandra Farneti
Universita di Bologna, Dipartimento di Psicologia, Viale Berti Pichat, n. 5,
40127 Bologna, ITALY

Dr Helena Hurme
Åbo Akademi, Pb 311, 65101 Vasa, FINLAND

Ms Maria Leek
Department of Psychology,
University of Sheffield, Sheffield S10 2TN, UK

Dr Daphna Oyserman
Baerwald School of Social Work, Hebrew University, Mt Scopus,
Jerusalem, ISRAEL

Professor Norma Radin
School of Social Work, University of Michigan, Ann Arbor, MI
48109, USA

Professor Isto Ruoppila
University of Jyväskylä, Department of Psychology, Seminaarinkatu 15,
SF-40100, FINLAND

Professor Martin Sherer Smith
Psychology Department and Child Studies Program, Brock University,
St Catherines, Ontario, CANADA L2S 3A1

Dr Peter K. Smith
Department of Psychology, University of Sheffield, Sheffield S10 2TN, UK

Dr Elisabeth J. Sticker
University Children's Hospital, Bonn, Adenauralle 19, 5300 Bonn 1,
WEST GERMANY

Dr Maria Tyszkowa
Adam Mickiewicz University, Instytut Psychologii, u. Szamarzewskiego 89,
60–568 Poznan, POLAND

Dr A.A. Vermulst
Institute of Family Studies, University of Nijmegen, Erasmusplein 1, 6525
GG Nijmegen, THE NETHERLANDS

Professor Emmy E. Werner
Division of Human Development and Family Studies, Department of
Applied Behavioral Sciences 123 AOB IV, University of California, Davis,
CA 95616, USA

Dr R.A.H. van Zutphen
Institute of Family Studies, University of Nijmegen, Erasmusplein 1, 6525
GG Nijmegen, THE NETHERLANDS

Preface

This book has provided an opportunity to do two things: first, to make a contribution to a relatively neglected area; second, to bring together contributors from a number of different countries, working on a broadly similar theme.

All the contributors to this book would probably agree that grandparents have had a relatively poor deal from researchers in developmental psychology. Until recently, the topic of grandparents and their relationships with children and grandchildren has been neglected, with developmental psychologists mainly being interested in infancy and childhood and only rarely considering periods of the lifespan after early adulthood. Many of the contributors for this book met for the first time at the Third European Conference on Developmental Psychology, in Budapest in June 1988; some others were at the Tenth Meeting of the International Society for the Study of Behavioural Development, held at Jyväskylä, Finland, in July 1989. So far as we are aware the papers presented were the first on grandparenthood at these series of conferences. I had a similar experience at the Developmental Section meeting of the British Psychological Society, held at Harlech, Wales, in September 1988, at which an earlier version of the material in the first chapter was presented; this was the only paper on grandparents and one of only two or three relevant to the latter half of the lifespan.

The balance has been redressed most thoroughly in North America. Over the last decade (as documented further in Chapter One) there has been a spurt of research on grandparenthood, and several notable contributions have appeared. These include books by Cohler and Grunebaum (1981), Kornhaber and Woodward (1981), Bengtson and Robertson (1985), and Cherlin and Furstenberg (1986), as well as many journal articles and theses. This work has clearly influenced many of the European contributions featured in this book.

However, the importance of considering the social and cultural context of development applies to grandparents and grandchildren just as much as to other areas of human development. The kinds of family structure, social policies regarding employment, health and housing, divorce rates, as well as traditions and stereotypes regarding older people, and even particular historical events such as war or revolution, will all have an impact on the position and role of grandparents; and these vary considerably from country to country. Our understanding of grandparenthood can only be enriched by learning more about the variety of ways in which it is expressed in different cultural settings. There also appear to be important commonalities in the role of grandparent across cultures, however, several of which will be apparent in reading through the book.

This volume contains contributions from Britain, Canada, Finland, Italy, the Netherlands, Poland, the USA, and West Germany. This is a variety of modern urban societies in Europe and North America but it does not, of course, include contributions from societies in Asia, Africa, South America or Australasia. Another restriction is disciplinary; the volume is very much on the psychology of grandparenthood and grandparent–grandchild relations. Disciplines such as sociology, anthropology and gerontology are not represented. There will surely be much to be gained from cross-disciplinary as well as cross-cultural comparison and cooperation. The different chapters do, however, present some variation in theoretical perspective, in particular incorporating ideas from psychoanalysis (Chapter Nine) and evolutionary biology (Chapters Ten and Eleven), as well as lifespan development, the perspective which broadly lies behind the other chapters in the book.

References

Bengtson, V.L. and Robertson, J.F. (eds) (1985) *Grandparenthood*. Beverly Hills, CA: Sage.

Cherlin, A.J. and Furstenberg, F.F. (1986) *The New American Grandparent: a Place in the Family, a Life Apart*, New York: Basic Books.

Cohler, B.J. and Grunebaum, H.U. (1981) *Mothers, Grandmothers and Daughters: Personality and Child Care in Three Generation Families*, New York: John Wiley & Sons.

Kornhaber, A. and Woodward, K.L. (1981) *Grandparents/Grandchild: the Vital Connection*, Garden City, NY: Anchor.

Chapter one

Introduction: the study of grandparenthood

Peter K. Smith

About 70 per cent of middle-aged and older people become grandparents. Since the average age of becoming a grandparent, in Western societies, is approximately 50 years for women, and a couple of years older for men, they are likely to remain grandparents for some twenty-five years or more; about a third of their lifespan. Grandparenthood is thus an important part of the life cycle for most people. It is important both as a personal experience and for its impact on others. For many, the role is very much a positive one. It is common for grandparents to report at least weekly contact with their grandchildren, and to have satisfying relationships with them.

In the light of this, it is perhaps puzzling that the topic has had relatively little attention from developmental psychologists; not least since child development has been an active and flourishing field of study since the 1920s; and grandparent–grandchild relations, the main theme of this book, would appear to be an integral part of the developing child's experience. An analysis of original publications mentioning grandparents or grandchildren, via bibliographic sources[1] reveals only five publications prior to 1950; five in the 1950s; four in the 1960s; and seventeen in the 1970s. This increases to thirty-three for the five-year period from 1980 to 1984; and to sixty-two for 1985–89. Clearly the 1980s has seen a spectacular burst in research (including seventeen US Ph.D. theses), although the actual volume of publication is still small compared to what may be considered the significance of the topic.

The neglect of grandparents by researchers in child development, prior to the 1980s, was commented on by Tinsley and Parke (1984). They suggested four reasons. One was the demographic changes occurring in the twentieth century which have resulted in substantial increases in life expectancy; as a result, more people are becoming grandparents, for longer fractions of their lifespan. This has been a relatively new phenomenon (Mancini and Blieszner 1989). Second has been the prevailing tendency (until recently) to view the family as a nuclear one, composed of parents and children. Indeed, it took psychologists a while to take much interest in relationships other than that of mother and child; and while fathers and siblings are now getting more like their due share of attention, it is only even more recently that this 'wider social network' has started to extend to grandparents. It is as if there has been some time lag between the impact of demographic changes, and the corresponding shift of research interest and effort. (It should be noted, however, that for some time family systems researchers and therapists have taken note of grandparents in the extended family; for example, Minuchin 1974, Haley 1976).

Tinsley and Parke identified two other factors possibly responsible for this delay. Consideration of grandparent–grandchild relationships more or less forces investigators to think in a lifespan framework, and consider processes of intergenerational influence (this is brought out especially in this book by the chapters by Vermulst, Brock and van Zutphen, and by Ruoppila). Yet, the lifespan perspective in developmental and child psychology has only become influential in the last decade. Before that, developmental psychology was often subsumed under child development, in practice if not in theory; and this narrowed vision of developmental processes more or less ceasing at adulthood or 'maturity' would not encourage thinking about grandparents.

Also, they pointed to certain methodological difficulties associated with working with grandparents. Older subjects may be ill or in some ways less suitable research subjects; and theoretical and statistical models need to be more complex to cope with the often triadic or polyadic relationships, and patterns of direct and indirect influence, likely to be encountered in analysing grandparent–grandchild influence and interaction.

Besides these influences discussed by Tinsley and Parke, there may also be a cohort effect in the pool of researchers likely to work on the topic. In many Western universities, the expansion that took place in the 1960s and early 1970s (which then ceased and was followed by some retrenchment) has resulted in a pronounced age constriction in teaching and research staff, a large proportion of whom are now in their forties or fifties – that is, soon to be (if not already) grandparents. It may well be a contributing factor that such persons were not especially interested in the topic in their twenties and thirties, but have more recently become so.

Grandparents as negative or positive influences; a shift of opinion?

By and large, the recent research on grandparenthood, including that in this book, reports on it in a predominantly, if not quite uniformly, positive light. Grandparents are seen as having quite frequent contacts of a positive nature with their grandchildren, and acting as important support agents in certain circumstances (see, for example, the chapters by Werner, and by Radin, Oyserman and Benn). This positive view is *not* the case in earlier research. This can be illustrated by the opening paragraph from an article by Staples and Smith (1954: 91):

A review of the literature on adult–child relationships reveals that little consideration has been given to the grandmother as a member of the immediate family group. References to grandparents are for the most part general in nature and based on clinical evidence. Gesell and Ilg (1946) call attention to the numerous hazards of grandparent interference with parental control. Vollmer (1937) observes that grandmothers possess unbending and didactic opinions concerning child care and an unwillingness to recognise the process of maturation. According to Thompson (1952) grandparents and parents frequently have sufficiently differing views on what constitutes desirable child behavior to create conflicts for the children.

Vollmer's (1937) article is entitled 'The grandmother: a problem in child rearing'! This is a title almost unthinkable today. According to Vollmer:

Every pediatrician . . . will have made this discovery: grandmothers exert an extraordinarily pernicious influence on their grandchildren.

(1937: 378)

The practical conclusion is that the grandmother is not a suitable custodian of the care and rearing of her grandchild: She is a disturbing factor against which we are obligated to protect the child according to the best of our ability.

(1937: 382)

In somewhat similar vein are some clinical and psychoanalytical articles, such as Strauss (1943): 'Grandma made Johnny delinquent', Borden (1946): 'The role of grandparents in children's behaviour problems', and LaBarre et al. (1960): 'The significance of grandmothers in the psychopathology of children'. In marked contrast are recent articles such as Tinsley and Parke (1987): 'Grandparents as interactive and social support agents for families with young infants', and Tomlin and Passman (1989): 'Grandmothers' responsibility in raising two-year-olds facilitates their grandchildren's adaptive behavior'; and attempts to enhance grandparent–grandchild interaction, even on a surrogate basis as in foster-grandparent programmes (Saltz, 1971; Robertson, Tice and Loeb, 1985; Werner, this volume).

What has brought about this shift in emphasis? It could be due both to changes in stereotypes, and changes in actual grandparental roles and relationships. The few earlier studies are based mainly on impressions and case studies and may be influenced by a then prevailing (and still influential) set of stereotypes. Grandparents were seen as older people who were likely to be frail and cantankerous (as a function of their age), and likely to interfere in the raising of grandchildren, being inflexible, and variously either too lenient and indulgent, or too strict and old-fashioned in their views. For example, Vollmer's article relies on one personal experience, followed by a series of stereotypical judgements. There are no references cited; Vollmer has not thought about documenting stereotypes, but they are vividly documented for us in his own thoughts.

One independent source of information on stereotypes and changes in them is the depiction of grandparents in children's books. The stereotype of the grandparent as old and frail has been prevalent over this period. Janelli (1988) surveyed forty-two North American children's books, published between 1961 and 1983;

she found that 55 per cent of grandmothers had white or grey hair, 31 per cent wore glasses and 31 per cent had aprons; 39 per cent of grandfathers had bald heads and 36 per cent had both white hair and glasses. This stereotype is increasingly out of step with the reality of grandparents in their forties, fifties and sixties, as pointed out by Hagestad (1985: 35–6):

> The rapidity and scope of recent demographic changes have caught us off guard. We still tend to associate grandparenthood with old age only; we still have trouble thinking of 40-year-old grandparents. The image of grandma commonly found in TV commercials is not in step with current demographic realities. Often, the grandmother presented on the screen should be a great-grandmother. The woman who has small, golden-haired grandchildren is not likely to have silver hair in a bun, serve lemonade on the porch, or worry about slipping dentures and 'irregularity'. She would more realistically be portrayed dressed in a jogging suit on her way to aerobic dancing, or in a suit coming home from work.

This image of aged grandparenthood still persists, as for example in a current (1989/90) advertisement for Help the Aged which portrays an elderly woman probably in her late sixties with a caption 'Adopt a Granny: Help the Aged'. A survey of children's literature in the UK reveals that here too such images continue (Figure 1.1); however, many of the books from the later 1980s have caught up with demographic realities (Figure 1.2) and present a more balanced picture. It is of course true that some grannies will have silver hair! However, since many of these books feature 2- to 8-year-old children, the mean grandparent age should be about mid- to late-fifties to correspond with reality. Until recently, most appear to be in their mid-sixties to seventies, eighties or nineties.

Stereotypes may be shifting, if belatedly, but are there other factors to explain the shift in research emphasis? There is some evidence that grandmothers in the 1950s were indeed stricter than mothers. Staples and Smith (1954) interviewed eighty-seven grandmother–mother pairs, and found the grandmothers to have stricter and more authoritarian views than the mothers did, on every sub-scale. Views of grandmothers (and of mothers) were particularly strict when both lived in the same three-generation household (48 per cent of her sample), and when they had had fewer years of formal education. These gaps between the views of grandparents and parents might have been especially large in the 1950s, as a function of rapidly changing opinions on child-rearing over the previous decades. It might be expected that such differences in views would have lessened by the 1970s. Today's grandparents, at least the younger ones, will have had a much fuller education; also probably fewer live directly with the grandchild. In addition, there is evidence of a general shift in permissiveness of attitudes to child-rearing (Johnson 1985).

Recent evidence does not strongly support the notion of very strict grandparents. For example, Stevens (1984: 1017) interviewed a sample of 101 low-income, black grandmother–teenage mother pairs; he reported that the grandmothers,

Figure 1.1 Cover from Victor J. Ambrus (1982) *Grandma, Felix, and Mustapha Biscuit*, Oxford: Oxford University Press

Figure 1.2 Cover from Mary Hoffman and Joanna Burroughes (1988) *My Grandma Has Black Hair*, London: Methuen

besides having more parenting knowledge, 'also exhibited a more responsive and less punitive interactive style than did their daughters'. Blackwelder and Passman (1986: 80) found that in a sample of twenty-four US grandmother–mother pairs, 'grandmothers' and mothers' disciplining was more similar than different; however, despite the preponderance of similarities, the differences that were found tended to favour the stereotype that grandmothers are more giving, less punitive, and more forgiving than are mothers'. Here the contrary stereotype of the spoiling grandmother is almost being invoked.

The image of the spoiling or too lenient grandparent also has a long history to it. In an interview study of older people in the UK, 155 of whom had grand-children, Townsend (1957: 106) reported that 'the grandparents were notably le-nient towards grandchildren'. At the time, this did not seem to be a function of the grandparents having permissive attitudes, but rather that they did not see their grandparental role as being one of discipline. As one informant put it, 'I used to slosh my children. But I don't like to see my grandchildren walloped'; while another said, 'The grandmother can be free and easy. She [her daughter] has to be fairly strict with them' (Townsend 1957: 106–7).

Perhaps a significant clue to grandparental relations lies in this aspect of the role of the grandparent as someone who might try to influence parental rearing practices. Even by the 1950s and 1960s it appears that only a small minority of grandparents saw their role in this way, as studies such as Albrecht (1954) and Neugarten and Weinstein (1964) indicate. If indeed grandparents before the 1950s did attempt a more authoritarian and didactic role, it would seem that this stereotype was poorly justified by the 1950s and even less so subsequently.

In a cross-cultural analysis of grandparenthood, Apple (1956: 662) found support for the hypothesis that

> formality between grandparents and grandchildren is related to association of grandparents with family authority, while the indulgent, close, and warm rela-tionship is fostered by dissociation of grandparents from family authority.

If, as seems likely, this dissociation has become more prominent or recognized, it could explain why a more positive attitude to grandparents has resulted. To this extent, the shift in emphasis from the problems to the positive potentials of grandparenthood, noted in the research literature, is a well-justified one. Never-theless, a balanced view will keep a place for the negative elements to be found in any kind of relationship. Conflict, as well as helping, between grandparents and grandchildren, is a continuing theme in psychoanalytic writings (Battistelli and Farneti, this volume); and is an important one in the sociobiological perspective (Leek and Smith, this volume).

Research frameworks

The research carried out in the last decade or so, although mainly confined to North America, has laid out some guidelines or frameworks for research which are going to be useful and important for any understanding of grandparenthood (see, for example, Denham and Smith 1989). Among other topics, these include types of grandparents; the impact of divorce and step-grandparents; on-time and off-time grandparenthood; and indirect and direct patterns of grandparent–grandchild influence.

Types of grandparents

The four standard types of grandparent are maternal grandmother (MGM), maternal grandfather (MGF), paternal grandmother (PGM), and paternal grandfather (PGF). Both the sex of grandparent and the lineage (sex of parent) can be important factors. Many studies find that the maternal grandmother is the most involved and has the most frequent contact with grandchildren, with the others in generally decreasing order. For example, Hoffman (1979) found MGMs to be perceived as closest and seen most often by US grandchildren, followed by MGFs and then the PGPs. Eisenberg (1988) reported very similar results, as do Kahana and Kahana (1970) (who, however, found most contact with MGFs if their Table 2 is correct), and Shea (1987) (who also pointed out interactions with sex of grandchild). Several contributors in this volume (Battistelli and Farneti in Italy; M.S. Smith in Canada; Tyszkowa in Poland) report a similar pattern. There are exceptions; Nahemow (1984) reports that in the Iteso tribe of Africa, schoolchildren feel closest to the paternal grandfather. The general trend of MGM>MGF>PGM>or = PGF could be influenced by societal expectations and lineage structure, age of grandparent (generally MGMs will be the youngest of the four grandparents), and perhaps in a more distal causal sense by certainty of relatedness as indicated by considerations from evolutionary biology (M.S. Smith, this volume).

Despite the clear importance of lineage shown in these studies, sex of grandparent has been a more salient feature in much research. The majority of studies, if they have not looked at grandparents generally, have specifically examined grandmothers (for example, Blackwelder and Passman 1986; Johnson 1983; Myers, Jarvis and Creasey 1987; Staples and Smith 1954; Stevens 1984). A smaller number of studies have focused on grandfathers (for example, Kivett 1985; and the work of Radin and her colleagues, as in this volume).

Great-grandparents have had very little specific attention, although numerically they are not a negligible group. By extrapolation, many people will be great-grandparents by their late seventies; some of course much earlier. Burton and Bengtson (1985), in their study of young grandmothers, interviewed a number of great-grandmothers aged 46 to 73 and regarded those aged 42–57 as 'early' in the role; they also interviewed seven great-great-grandmothers and one great-great-great-grandmother. Wentowski (1985) has written on the role as perceived by great-grandmothers. In this volume, Ruoppila includes data on contact with (great-)grandchildren by great-grandparents as well as by grandparents.

7

The impact of divorce and step-grandparenthood

Several studies have suggested that grandparents may have a particularly import-ant role to play when parents divorce. At a time of considerable uncertainty and distress for their grandchildren, a grandparent can be a source of con-tinuity and support for them and for the parent(s) (Johnson, 1985). Sometimes, the paternal grandmother (for example) can maintain contacts with grandchildren when the father finds it difficult to do so. Johnson and Barer (1987) point out the complexity of three-generation family relationships which can ensue after divorce.

A recent issue has been that of custody and the rights of grandparents of a non-custodial parent to have access to their grandchildren. A considerable legal literature on this topic in the USA is reviewed by Thompson *et al.* (1989). In recent years, statutes granting grandparents legal standing to petition for legally enforceable visitation with their grandchildren, even over parental objections, have been passed in all fifty states of the USA.

A grandchild could have three types of step-grandparent, superimposed on the four sex/lineage types mentioned previously. A step-grandparent could result from a grandparent remarrying, a parent remarrying, or even from the parent of a step-parent remarrying! Of these, the situation of a parent remarrying and hence introducing new step-grandparents will be the most common. It was specifically investigated by Sanders and Trygstad (1989) in a US study. They found that grandparent–grandchild relationships were closer, in terms of more frequent contact, greater emotional involvement and role expectations, than step-grandparent–grandchild relations. Nevertheless, about half their grandchild sample still saw the step-grandparent relationship as an important one. The differences appeared to be partly, but not completely, a product of the length of time for which they had known the (step-)grandparent.

On-time and off-time grandparents

The impact of grandparenthood varies considerably depending on when in the lifespan the transition to grandparenthood occurs. This has been vividly illustrated by Burton and Bengtson (1985) in their interview study of black US grandmothers. They described those who experienced the transition between 42 and 57 years of age as being 'on-time', that is, within the normal range of variation at which this occurs. Those who experienced the transition 'late' – for example, in their seventies – were likely to be disappointed that they would have relatively little time left to enjoy their grandchildren, and would be less likely to be sufficiently well and physically active to make the most of the grandparental role. However, some women who became grandmothers between the ages of 25 and 37 years, 'early', were also discontented, though for very different reasons. Being a grand-mother placed obligations on them for which they were not ready. In addition, their new role jarred with what they, quite accurately, perceived to be a stereotype of grandparents as much older and having characteristics with which they might not wish to identify. As one 28-year-old grandmother put it, 'I could break my daughter's neck for having this baby. I just got a new boyfriend. Now he will think I'm too old. It was bad enough being a mother so young – now a grandmother too!' And a 31-year-old grandmother: 'You may think I'm a terrible person for feeling this way but I can't help it. I am just too young to be a grandmother. That's something for old folks, not for me' (Burton and Bengtson 1985: 61, 68).

Although grandparenthood may be felt by these 'early' grandmothers to put unreasonable obligations and constraints upon them, in fact many 'on-time' grandparents may repudiate these obligations too. After all, many are working in responsible and demanding jobs and cannot devote a great deal of time to surrogate care (see, for example, Sticker, this volume). Nevertheless, for those grandparents who can do so, the evidence is that they can play a very valuable role (for instance, Tomlin and Passman 1989; Radin, Oyserman and Benn, this volume).

Indirect and direct patterns of grandparent–grandchild influence

Grandparents can influence their grandchildren's behaviour both directly and indirectly (Tinsley and Parke 1984). Indirect influence is mediated by some other person or agency, without necessitating any direct interaction. For example, the parent–child interaction will be influenced by the way the parent has been brought up and the experiences of child-rearing which the parent has had modelled by his or her parent; that is, the grandparent. Such influences can of course be positive or negative. Huesmann, Lefkowitz, Eron and Walder (1984) found that the severity of discipline received from parents when their subjects were 8 years old, predicted both their subjects' levels of aggression at 30, and their children's aggression at 8 years; that is, grandparents' disciplinary practices twenty-two years earlier predicted the aggression of their grandchildren. This intergenerational transmission of child-rearing practices and values is the theme of several chapters in this volume, notably those by Vermulst, Brock and van Zutphen, and by Ruoppila.

Grandparents can also continue to provide emotional and financial support for parents. We have ample evidence that the quality of parent–child interaction is affected by such factors as social support and economic circumstances (for example, Brown and Harris 1978), so that grandparents can have a powerful indirect influence in such a fashion. As already indicated, times of marital disruption provide an example when such indirect (as well as direct) influence may be strongly operative.

The most obvious forms of grandparental influence are nevertheless direct ones, and have been documented by a number of researchers from Neugarten and Weinstein (1964) onwards. In this volume, the chapters by Hurme, Sticker, Tyszkowa and Werner particularly develop this theme. Perhaps the strongest case of direct influence is acting as a surrogate parent when the child is young (for example, in a single parent family, or teenage pregnancy, or as a caregiver while both parents work). Such a situation is described by Radin, Oyserman and Benn (this volume), who provide considerable evidence that grandfathers can have a positive direct influence in the context of young grandchildren of teen mothers.

Even if not acting as a surrogate parent, a grandparent who has contact with a grandchild can act as a companion and be an important part of the child's social network. Many grandparents enjoy conversations with grandchildren, asking them to run errands, giving them small gifts (see, for instance, Tyszkowa, this volume). They can also be a source of emotional support, acting as a 'buffer' in cases where a grandchild is in conflict with the parents, for example, or where the parents are in conflict with each other. Just 'being there' can be important.

Grandparents can of course pass on information and values directly to grandchildren, and act directly as role models; though nowadays many seem to refrain from doing so if these values differ greatly from those of the parents. A particularly interesting role which grandparents can fill to a much greater extent than parents is that of 'family historian'. Grandparents can typically remember much further back into the family's origins, perhaps recalling what *their* grandparents told them; in this way many generations can potentially be covered, as illustrated in the following example:

> When I was a teenager I talked a lot about family memories with my grandmother, my mother's mother who was in her late eighties (she was born in 1886 and died in 1975). She remembered talking to *her* grandmother (who was born in 1821 and died in 1899) about *her* grandmother who had been an emigrée from the French Revolution. My grandmother's grandmother's grandmother remembered *her* grandmother who had been a very old lady in the 1770s and had been to Versailles either in the last years of Louis XIV or the early years of the regency of Louis XV!
>
> (Alison Gill, personal communication 1990)

Methods of studying grandparenthood

The predominant method of studying grandparenthood has been the interview, or else the questionnaire (or often a semi-structured questionnaire taking the form of an interview). Such a method is also characterized in this volume in the chapters by Hurme; Sticker; Vermulst, Brock and van Zutphen; Ruoppila; Battistelli and Farneti; M.S. Smith; and Smith and Leek. It is clearly a straightforward way of getting someone's *perceptions* of a role or relationship, and sometimes this may be all that is required. However, three generations are involved in considerations of grandparents and grandchildren, and the *differing* perceptions of the three generations may be important information.

Some studies have examined the views of grandparents; for example, Neugarten and Weinstein (1964), Schmidt and Padilla (1983), Cherlin and Furstenberg

(1985), Kivett (1985), Thomas (1986) and Johnson and Barer (1987); perhaps even more have taken the perspective of the grandchild; for example, Kahana and Kahana (1970), Robertson (1976), Hoffman (1979), Schultz (1980), Hartshorne and Manaster (1982), Eisenberg (1988), Creasey, Myers, Epperson and Taylor (1989), Ponzetti and Folkrod (1989), and Sanders and Trygstad (1989). The possibility that perceptions by each generation may differ is ill-explored; for example, as regards degree of contact, quality of relationship and so forth. Hurme (1988), in a study in Finland, found (for instance) that 38 per cent of grandmothers rated their relationship with the grandchild as 'very important', whereas only 27 per cent of mothers rated the grandmother–grandchild relationship this way. Ruoppila, and Sticker (both in this volume) compare perceptions of grandparents, and of their children. Differing perceptions of the three generations deserve more attention in future, both for their theoretical interest and possible practical benefits that might ensue if misunderstandings can be avoided.

Although informants are no doubt usually truthful, and information can be cross-checked or compared, it is perhaps a pity that so many studies have relied on interviews; a situation that certainly contrasts markedly with the methodology of studies of parent–child relationships, which have relied very much more on observation, especially in the last two decades. A few observational studies have been made of grandparental relationships. For example, Myers, Jarvis and Creasey (1987) extended Ainsworth's 'strange situation' procedure to thirteen episodes to include an observational assessment of grandmother–infant as well as mother–infant attachment. Similarly, Tomlin and Passman (1989) observed the behaviour of 2-year-olds in a novel environment, with either their mother or grandmother present. So far as observing in more natural settings is concerned, Tinsley and Parke (1987) observed grandparents and parents interacting with 7-month-old infants in the home. Radin, Oyserman and Benn (this volume) videofilmed grandparent behaviour with infants in the home (as well as obtaining interview data). More naturalistic home observations of grandparent–grandchild interaction would surely be worthwhile.

Some studies have used projective tests, or test situations of a kind which can, perhaps indirectly, elicit views of or feelings towards grandparents. The most direct form is to ask grandchildren to write essays about their grandparents, as done by Ponzetti and Folkrod (1989), and Tyszkowa (this volume). Marcoen (1979) analysed drawings which grandchildren drew of grandfathers and grandmothers. Methods such as free association and dream analysis are mentioned by Battistelli and Farneti (this volume).

It is also possible to look at grandparent–grandchild interaction in quite constrained experimental situations, as done by Blackwelder and Passman (1986) in a study of disciplining young (grand)children at a laboratory learning task.

Theoretical perspectives

Not all the studies of grandparenthood have had a particularly explicit theoretical

11

perspective, but the predominant one (often implicit) would seem to be that of lifespan development. This is natural, since consideration of grandparent–grandchild relationships and the transmission of information and values across generations leads naturally to a lifespan perspective. Many studies of grandparenthood have, however, either been concerned with basic data gathering (for example, how much contact there is with grandparents), the correlates of basic variables (such as age or sex of grandparent or grandchild), or specific problem areas (for instance, whether parental divorce leads to greater grandparent–grandchild contact), none of which have needed a very explicit commitment to any particular set of lifespan concepts, such as that of Baltes, Reese and Lipsitt (1980).

Another related perspective is that of ageing and gerontology. As has been pointed out, not all grandparents are 'aged' in the conventional sense; but this area clearly has an important contribution to understanding relationships where grandparents (or great-grandparents) are indeed aged, or perhaps suffer from particular infirmities of age such as senile dementia (see, for example, Creasey et al. 1989). In a more positive sense, ideas of ageing can be integrated in the lifespan perspective; for example, by considering age-related changes in such concepts as morality or wisdom (see, for instance, Clayton and Birren 1980). This could indicate areas where grandparents could make particularly specific contributions to grandchildren's development.

Another theoretical perspective is that of psychoanalysis. Strongly represented in the few works of the 1940s and 1950s (as it was in several other areas of psychology), the influence of psychoanalysis has waned as other developmental models have come forward. Psychoanalytic ideas have of course continued to be influential and to be developed amongst its own practitioners; however, some psychoanalytic ideas have also had a modest revival in mainstream psychology, in areas such as attachment theory, perhaps because of the failure of the cognitive-developmental paradigm adequately to address the more psychodynamic issues involved in relationships. In this volume, Battistelli and Farneti examine some psychoanalytic ideas in relation to grandparent–grandchild relations (see also Gorlitz 1982).

Evolutionary biology provides a perspective which is potentially very compre-hensive but also seemingly remote from particular aspects of grandparenthood. However, applications of sociobiology to human behaviour do suggest particular sets of hypotheses in areas such as parent–offspring, and hence also grandparent–offspring, helping and conflict. Briefly considered by Fagen (1976) (see also Partridge and Nunney 1977), theoretical applications to three-generation relation-ships need further working out, but some basic predictions can be made. In this volume Leek and Smith consider several such predictions in broad terms, while M.S. Smith considers one particular set of predictions, relating to paternity certainty, in greater depth. Applications of sociobiological ideas to human behaviour remain controversial, of course; and anyway most sociobiologists would look to see an integration of such ideas with those dealing with more immediate causal factors.

Summary

The psychological study of grandparenthood, and of grandparent–grandchild relationships, is experiencing an increase in interest probably fuelled in the main by demographic changes in modern societies. Emphasis has come to be placed on the positive benefits of grandparental involvement with grandchildren, in contrast to the cautions of a few decades ago. However, some stereotypical images of grandparents do still persist.

Future research can usefully give more consideration to the differing perspectives of the three generations, and broaden research methodology further beyond interviews and questionnaires. A variety of theoretical perspectives can be employed to organize and interpret findings. There is continuing scope to extend the descriptive base of our knowledge of the grandparental role, especially in societies outside the USA where most research so far has taken place. In these respects, especially the broadening of our cross-cultural knowledge of grandparenthood, the present volume aims to make its own contribution.

Notes

1   The search was carried out in the *International Bibliography of Research in Marriage and the Family 1900–64*; *Family Resources 1970–89*; *Psychological Abstracts 1927–89*; *Child Development Abstracts 1953–89*; *Dissertation Abstracts 1938–89*; *Index to Theses 1950–89* and *Sociological Abstracts 1963–89* and was supplemented by cross-referencing. The totals quoted include books (but not individual book chapters), and indexed theses, as well as journal articles. I am very grateful to Wendy Aprilchild who carried out the searches.

References

Albrecht, R. (1954) 'The parental responsibilities of grandparents', *Marriage and Family Living* 16: 201–4.

Apple, D. (1956) 'The social structure of grandparenthood', *American Anthropologist* 58: 56–63.

Baltes, P.B., Reese, H.W. and Lipsitt, L.P. (1980) 'Life-span developmental psychology', *Annual Review of Psychology* 31: 65–110.

Blackwelder, D.E. and Passman, R.H. (1986) 'Grandmothers' and mothers' disciplining in three-generational families: the role of social responsibility in rewarding and punishing children', *Journal of Personality and Social Psychology* 50: 80–6.

Borden, B. (1946) 'The role of grandparents in children's behavior problems', *Smith College Studies in Social Work* 17: 115–16.

Brown, G.W. and Harris, T. (1978) *Social Origins of Depression*, London: Tavistock.

Burton, L.M. and Bengtson, V.L. (1985) 'Black grandmothers: issues of timing and continuity of roles', in V.L. Bengtson and J.F. Robertson (eds), *Grandparenthood*, Beverly Hills: Sage.

Cherlin, A. and Furstenberg, F.F. (1985) 'Styles and strategies of grandparenting', in V.L. Bengtson and J.F. Robertson, *Grandparenthood*, Beverly Hills: Sage.

Clayton, V. and Birren, J.E. (1980) 'Age and wisdom across the life span: theoretical perspectives', in P.B. Baltes and O.G. Brim, Jr. (eds), *Life-span Development and Behavior*, vol. 3. New York: Academic Press.

Creasey, G.L., Myers, B.J., Epperson, M.J. and Taylor, J. (1989) 'Grandchildren of grandparents with Alzheimer's disease: perceptions of grandparent, family environment, and the elderly', *Merrill-Palmer Quarterly* 35: 227–37.

Denham, T.E. and Smith, C.W. (1989) 'The influence of grandparents on grandchildren: a review of the literature and resources', *Family Relations* 38: 345–50.

Eisenberg, A.R. (1988) 'Grandchildren's perspectives on relationships with grandparents: the influence of gender across generations', *Sex Roles* 19: 205–17.

Fagen, R.M. (1976) 'Three-generation family conflict', *Animal Behaviour* 24: 874–79.

Gesell, A. and Ilg, F.L. (1946) *The Child from Five to Ten*, New York: Harper & Row.

Gorlitz, P.M. (1982) 'The intrapsychic experiences accompanying the transition into grandparenthood', Doctoral thesis, Northwestern University (abstract in *Dissertation Abstracts International* 43, 1979–B, 1982).

Hagestad, G.O. (1985) 'Continuity and connectedness', in V.L. Bengtson and J.F. Robertson (eds), *Grandparenthood*, Beverly Hills: Sage.

Haley, J. (1976) *Problem Solving Therapy*, San Francisco: Jossey-Bass.

Hartshorne, T.S. and Manaster, G.J. (1982) 'The relationship with grandparents: contact, importance, role conception', *International Journal of Aging and Human Development* 15: 233–45.

Hoffman, E. (1979) 'Young adults' relations with their grandparents: an exploratory study', *International Journal of Aging and Human Development* 10: 299–310.

Huesmann, L.R., Eron, L.D., Lefkowitz, M.M. and Walder, L.O. (1984) 'Stability of aggression over time and generations', *Developmental Psychology* 20: 1120–34.

Hurme, H. (1988) *Child, Mother and Grandmother: Intergenerational Interaction in Finnish Families*, Jyväskylä: University of Jyväskylä Press.

Janelli, L.M. (1988) 'Depictions of grandparents in children's literature', *Educational Gerontology* 14: 193–202.

Johnson, C.L. (1983) 'A cultural analysis of the grandmother', *Research on Aging* 5: 547–67.

Johnson, C.L. (1985) 'Grandparenting options in divorcing families: an anthropological perspective', in V.L. Bengtson and J.F. Robertson (eds), *Grandparenthood*, Beverly Hills: Sage.

Johnson, C.L. and Barer, B.M. (1987) 'Marital instability and the changing kinship networks of grandparents', *The Gerontologist* 27: 330–35.

Kahana, B. and Kahana, E. (1970) 'Grandparenthood from the perspective of the developing grandchild', *Developmental Psychology* 3: 98–105.

Kivett, V.R. (1985) 'Grandfathers and grandchildren: patterns of association, helping, and psychological closeness', *Family Relations* 34: 565–71.

LaBarre, M.B., Jessner, L. and Ussery, L. (1960) 'The significance of grandmothers in the psychopathology of children', *American Journal of Orthopsychiatry* 30: 175–85.

Mancini, J.A. and Blieszner, R. (1989) 'Aging parents and adult children: research themes in intergenerational relations', *Journal of Marriage and the Family* 51: 275–90.

Marcoen, A. (1979) 'Children's perception of aged persons and grandparents', *International Journal of Behavioral Development* 2: 87–105.

Minuchin, S. (1974) *Families and Family Therapy*, Cambridge, MA: Harvard University Press.

Myers, B.J., Jarvis, P.A. and Creasey, G.L. (1987) 'Infants' behavior with their mothers and grandmothers', *Infant Behavior and Development* 10: 245–59.

Nahemow, N.R. (1984) 'Grandparenthood in transition', in K.A. McCluskey and H.W. Reese (eds) *Life-span Developmental Psychology: Historical and Generational Effects*, New York: Academic Press.

Neugarten, B.L. and Weinstein, K.J. (1964) 'The changing American grandparent', *Journal of Marriage and the Family* 26: 199–204.

Partridge, L. and Nunney, L. (1977) 'Three-generation family conflict', *Animal Behaviour* 25: 785–86.

Ponzetti, J.J., Jr., and Folkrod, A.W. (1989) 'Grandchildren's perceptions of their relationships with their grandparents', *Child Study Journal* 19: 41–50.

Robertson, J.F. (1976) 'Significance of grandparents: perceptions of young adult grandchildren', *The Gerontologist* 16: 137–40.

Robertson, J.F., Tice, C.H. and Loeb, L.L. (1985) 'Grandparenthood: from knowledge to programs to policy', in V.L. Bengtson and J.F. Robertson (eds), *Grandparenthood*, Beverly Hills: Sage.

Saltz, R. (1971) 'Aging persons as child-care workers in a foster-grandparent program: psychosocial effects and work performance', *Aging and Human Development* 2: 314–40.

Sanders, G.F. and Trygstad, D.W. (1989) 'Stepgrandparents and grandparents: the view from young adults', *Family Relations* 38: 71–5.

Schultz, N.W. (1980) 'A cognitive-developmental study of the grandchild-grandparent bond', *Child Study Journal* 10: 7–26.

Schmidt, A. and Padilla, A.M. (1983) 'Grandparent–grandchild interaction in a Mexican American group', *Hispanic Journal of Behavioral Sciences* 5: 181–98.

Shea, L.P. (1987) 'Grandparent–adolescent relationships as mediated by lineage and gender', Doctoral thesis, Virginia Polytechnic Institute and State University (abstract in *Dissertation Abstracts International* 49, 351–A, 1988).

Staples, R. and Smith, J.W. (1954) 'Attitudes of grandmothers and mothers toward child rearing practices', *Child Development* 25: 91–7.

Stevens, J.H., Jr. (1984) 'Black grandmothers' and black adolescent mothers' knowledge about parenting', *Developmental Psychology* 20: 1017–25.

Strauss, C.A. (1943) 'Grandma made Johnny delinquent', *American Journal of Orthopsychiatry* 13: 343–47.

Thomas, J.L. (1986) 'Age and sex differences in perceptions of grandparenting', *Journal of Gerontology* 41: 417–23.

Thompson, G.G. (1952) *Child Psychology*, Boston: Houghton-Mifflin.

Thompson, R.A., Tinsley, B.R., Scalora, M.J. and Parke, R.D. (1989) 'Grandparents' visitation rights: legalizing the ties that bind', *American Psychologist* 44: 1217–22.

Tinsley, B.J. and Parke, R.D. (1984) 'Grandparents as support and socialization agents', in M. Lewis (ed.), *Beyond the Dyad*, New York: Plenum.

Tinsley, B.J. and Parke, R.D. (1987) 'Grandparents as interactive and social support agents for families with young infants', *International Journal of Aging and Human Development* 25: 259–77.

Tomlin, A.M. and Passman, R.H. (1989) 'Grandmothers' responsibility in raising two-year-olds facilitates their grandchildren's adaptive behavior: a preliminary intrafamilial investigation of mothers' and maternal grandmothers' effects', *Psychology and Aging* 4: 119–21.

Townsend, P. (1957) *The Family Life of Old People*, London: Routledge & Kegan Paul.

Vollmer, H. (1937) 'The grandmother: a problem in child rearing', *American*

Journal of Orthopsychiatry 7: 378–82.
Wentowski, G.J. (1985) 'Older women's perceptions of great-grandmotherhood: a research note', *Gerontologist* 25: 593–96.

Part one

Grandparental roles

Chapter two

Dimensions of the grandparent role in Finland

Helena Hurme

I have chosen the title 'Dimensions of the grandparent role' for this chapter. My intention is to abolish the myth of a monolithic conception of grandparenthood and instead show that it is a multidimensional role. It is a role which, more than most family roles, has a history, and one of the longest histories of family roles in that the individual who occupies this role has had time to become accustomed to it; but, at the same time, it has perhaps the most old-fashioned models for this role.

The grandparent role has even been termed a 'roleless role' (Clavan 1978). By this, Clavan means that the role is not governed by rights and obligations to the same extent as is the parent role (cf. Strom and Strom 1983). Despite this contention, several studies have focused on the dimensions of the grandparent role.

Grandparenthood clearly has many sides to it. An attempt is made in Table 2.1 to depict the various components of the concept. On the *attitudinal* level, grandparenthood is concerned with the norms which govern the rights and obligations of grandparents; on the *behavioural* level, with the activities that grandparents undertake both with and for their grandchildren. The *affective*, or emotional, level is concerned with the satisfaction with the role, and the *symbolic* level is concerned with the different meanings of grandparenthood to the grandparents.

These aspects of the role vary according to different factors. The single grandchild, the larger family system, cultural factors (such as the country of residence and the degree of urbanization of the place of residence), the individual features of the grandparent (especially their age and type of work, but also personality factors), and, finally, historical time – all these factors influence what has been termed 'dimensions of grandparenthood'.

When speaking of the grandparent role below, reference is made to those studies which have derived different types of grandparenthood – such as 'the distant grandparent', 'the fun-seeker', 'the formal grandparent', often by using factor analysis. Contrary to older studies (for example, Neugarten and Weinstein 1964), where the idea was that each grandparent represented only one type, I am proposing that the different dimensions represent the above aspects of grandparenthood – for instance, the behavioural or affective aspect – to a different extent, and that the individual grandparent stresses one or more dimensions, perhaps in a different combination during different phases of grandparenthood and with different grandchildren. Thus it is more a question of dimensions than of types.

Table 2.1 Factors affecting dimensions of the grandparent role

Factors affecting the role	Aspects of the role	Dimensions of the role	Types of grandparenthood
The individual grandchild age sex personality	*The attitudinal level* conceptions of the rights and obligations of grandparents	Conveying traditions Normative grandparenthood	
The larger family system relations with the child relations with his/her spouse	*The behavioural level* financial help time activities	Participation Substitute grandparenthood	e.g. 'Distant' 'Fun-seeker' 'Formal'
Cultural factors ethnicity local sub-culture (rural/urban, etc.)	*The emotional level* satisfaction derived from the role affects towards grandchild	Satisfaction	
The individuality of *the grandparent* age sex personality type of work, etc.	*The symbolic level* the symbolic meanings of grandparenthood		
Historical time			

Aspects of the grandparent role

At least the following features have been considered in connection with grandparenthood.

Emotional satisfaction

Emotional satisfaction is the one dimension which is perhaps most frequently discussed in connection with grandparenthood, although slightly different names for the concept are used in different studies. It was mentioned in Neugarten and Weinstein's (1964) seminal study. Robertson (1977) called it 'individualized grandparenthood'. This term was based on Robertson's classification of grandparenthood on the one hand on the basis of its social features, and on the other on its individual features. When the grandparent acts according to their own conception of the role and the satisfaction derived from it, and not according to external, normative factors, grandparenthood is individualized. Kivnick (1982a, b), again, defines one of the meanings of grandmotherhood as 'centrality'. By this she refers to the importance of grandmotherhood to the individual. It is generally assumed (for example, Benedek 1970) that the emotional side of the grandparent role is accentuated as the grandparents no longer have the same type of responsibilities towards their grandchildren as they had towards their own children.

Kahana and Kahana (1971) have made the observation that descriptions made by grandparents concerning their role often lack spontaneity. They say that grandparents describe what the grandchildren *do* and what they do together with them, but more seldom what they *mean* to each other. One possible reason for this is that not even a semi-structured interview situation is safe enough to elicit the innermost feelings of the grandparents and therefore no study has yet been able to measure this dimension satisfactorily.

There is some evidence from earlier studies that the emotional side is not only important *per se*, but also that it has some bearing on the general well-being of the grandmother. Markides and Krause (1985) found in a three-generational study with Mexicans that positive affect from the grandchildren predicted psychological well-being in the grandmother.

The dimension 'emotional satisfaction' took a very special form in the study by Neugarten and Weinstein (1964). They found that about 30 per cent of American grandparents could be classified as 'fun-seekers', that is, the grandparents saw themselves mainly as the grandchild's playmates. However, in a study by McCready (1985), using similar methodology, this type was uncommon, and it is probable that it emerges mostly in studies concerning very young grandchildren.

Biological renewal and continuity

A feature which is often mentioned in studies of grandparenthood is the wish to survive through the offspring (for example, Benedek 1970). This dimension represents the formal aspect of grandparenthood. About 30 per cent of the grandparents in Neugarten and Weinstein's (1964) study were of this type. This dimension becomes central, especially in persons who have to wait a long time before becoming grandparents or in those persons who never get grandchildren at all.

Social continuity

This dimension resembles that of biological renewal, but represents a somewhat more 'socialized' continuity. Neugarten and Weinstein (1964) had a type, 'Grandparents as a reservoir of family wisdom', which was represented by only 1 per cent of the grandparents. This dimension also comes close to what Bengtson (1985) has called the most important symbolic task of grandparents – that is, the social construction of biography (clearly paraphrasing Berger and Luckman 1966). This consists of constructing the past of the grandchild and giving it meaning. In this sense it is also a question of constructing continuity. This function of the

21

grandparents has also been called 'the family historian' (Tinsley and Parke 1984).

Being a resource person

Neugarten and Weinstein's study (1964) contained the type 'Surrogate parent'. Of the grandparents in their study 14 per cent were of this type, and it was especially common among mothers whose daughters worked full-time. Tinsley and Parke (1984) stress the fact that being a surrogate parent is especially important in times of crises and especially if a teenage daughter gets pregnant. They remark, however, that grandparenthood is *not* a continuation of the parent role. The grandparents help, but only when asked. It is also only natural that grandparents who live with their children help them more than grandparents who live apart from them (Wilson 1984). Albrecht again, in one of the first articles on grandparenthood (1954) says that there are *different* reasons for grandparents taking over responsibility for bringing up the grandchild. It may happen either because the grandparents derive personal satisfaction from it or because they want to feel that they have power. The reason may also simply be that they want something to do. These are all bad reasons for bringing up the grandchild, according to Albrecht.

Bengtson (1985) says that one of the symbolic features of grandparenthood is to act as an arbitrator and the second is 'to be there'. It would seem that at least the first meaning is not only symbolic, but that it also represents precisely the dimension in question; that is, being a resource person. It may be added that when it comes to the authority of the grandmother *vis-à-vis* the grandchild, there is and has been none. This was found in Updegraff's (1968) study on retrospective reminiscences concerning one's own grandmother in three generations of women.

Haavio-Mannila (1983), in a Finnish study, touches upon the surrogate parent function of the grandparents. She finds that the role of the grandparents in giving care to grandchildren is limited mostly to temporary baby-sitting. In her survey, 76 per cent of the grandmothers and 61 per cent of the grandfathers reported having done this. Fourteen per cent of the grandmothers and 5 per cent of the grandfathers had taken care of the grandchildren in their own home, but only 2 per cent of the grandmothers had done so regularly. Some grandmothers (6 per cent) and grandfathers (4 per cent) had taken care of the grandchild for longer periods.

Acting as a model for the grandchild

Being a role model for the grandchild is a dimension which did not emerge in early studies on grandparenthood. It is stressed, however, by Tinsley and Parke (1984). The dimension is concerned with grandparents wanting to teach the grandchildren how to live, wanting to give them advice and wisdom and showing them how older people think and function.

Detached grandparenthood

In Neugarten and Weinstein's (1964) study, 19 per cent of the grandparents represented what they called 'the distant figure' – a grandparent who is hardly involved at all in the lives of their grandchildren. According to Robertson (1977), both individual and social forces towards grandparenthood are weak in such situations. Robertson argues that such persons do not get satisfaction *even* from being a grandparent. In her study, grandmothers of this type were often widowed or unemployed.

Factors affecting grandparenthood

One of the clearest findings of earlier studies on grandparenthood is that it is *not* a uniform phenomenon, but varies according to several factors. The most important of these will be considered below.

The age of the grandparents is a central factor modifying grandparenthood, as Bengtson (1985) observes. Several authors (Troll 1983, Wood and Robertson 1976, Fischer 1983) have contended that the grandparent role is primarily a role of middle age. Troll (1983), for instance, warns against viewing grandparents as old people. She mentions that the modal age of becoming a grandparent in American society is 49–51 years for women and 51–53 years for men.

This aspect is related to the question whether or not he or she becomes a grandparent 'on time'. Problems can be created if one is late becoming a grandparent or when one's children do not have children. This situation is connected with a fear that the family will die out, but it can also be connected with a fear that if grandchildren are born, the grandparent will be so old and weak as not to enjoy the grandchildren any more and follow their development.

At the other extreme is the situation where one becomes a grandparent while still very young and involved in a career. Such persons would perhaps want to help their children and they would especially like to enjoy their grandchildren while these are still small, but their own commitments prevent them from this. Some grandparents may still be in the reproductive age, as Benedek (1970) observes. In such cases the grandparent's own children often occupy a more central position than the grandchildren.

Clear differences between grandparent types according to their age have indeed been found in earlier studies. Neugarten and Weinstein (1964) found that grandparents younger than 65 years were mostly 'fun-seekers' or of the 'distant' type. Cherlin and Furstenberg (1985) found that older grandparents were more often of the 'distant' or the 'passive' type. Robertson's (1977) study confirmed the fact that the 'symbolic' grandmother – to whom normativity, but not individual satisfaction, was central – more often was young than old, and, probably, more often was involved in a career. Thomas (1986) found no differences in satisfaction with grandparenting in different age groups of grandparents, but the younger grandparents expressed greater responsibility for their grandchildren's discipline, for their grandchildren's care and for offering child-rearing advice.

23

The grandmother and the grandfather role differ. According to Hagestad (1985), this difference resembles Parsons' and Bales' division between instrumental and emotional-expressive leaders so that grandfathers represent the former dimension, and grandmothers the latter. It should perhaps be added that according to Bengtson (1985) most studies show that sex differences among grandparents are smaller now than some decades ago – perhaps in the same way as sex differences in general have become smaller.

Grandfathers have hardly been separately considered at all in studies of grandparenthood. One reason, suggested by Clavan (1978) is that middle-aged men have their working role and the grandfather role is not functionally central so it is not considered. As it is much more common in Finland for women to be employed, the same reason might explain the fact that not even grandmotherhood has been studied here. Grandfatherhood would in any case require more thorough study to be able to say in detail how it differs from grandmotherhood.

There may also be an interaction between the sex of the grandparents and the sex of the child, or even with the sex of the parent of the middle generation, as our own preliminary comparative results show (Hurme and Tyszkowa 1989). On the whole, girls had more joint activities with their grandmothers than their grandfathers, both in Finland and Poland; whereas especially in Poland, boys had most joint activities with their paternal grandfather. The tone of description by the grandchildren was the warmest for maternal grandmothers. In the Finnish sample, a comparison was made between descriptions of grandmothers and grandfathers. The tone of description in essays concerning grandmothers was very significantly ($p<.0001$) more positive than in descriptions concerning grandfathers. Kahana and Kahana (1971) found that maternal grandmothers and paternal grandfathers also showed especially warm feelings towards their grandchildren.

Social class modifies grandparenthood. Clavan especially (1978) has investigated this subject. According to him, it is particularly difficult to define grandparenthood in the middle class, as it is more 'ideological' than real in this class. By 'ideological' he means that there is a position of grandparenthood in the family system, but it is not connected with any normative rights or obligations and thus grandparenthood is a roleless role. This leads to the fact that many grandparents experience a role handicap and they have to create a role.

Clavan tries to show that at least in the USA the grandparent role in the lower social classes is different. In these families the grandmother especially is important, and she has a very central position in the family. Help is often given in the form of services; for example, babysitting, cleaning the house, shopping. This result closely resembles some Polish ones (Kotlarska-Michalska 1984), according to which elderly parents in the intelligentsia mostly helped their children financially, whereas grandparents in the working class mostly gave services.

Urbanization is a factor which might influence grandparenthood, as Kahana and Kahana (1971) have observed. On the one hand, generations often live closer to each other in the countryside than in the city (at least in Finland); on the other hand, there are different norms in cities as compared with the countryside. It would also seem important to take into account differences between stable living districts in old parts of the city and new housing estates.

National differences also influence grandparenthood. There are few comparative studies, but on the basis of general information concerning different cultures it is also possible to draw conclusions concerning grandparenthood. McCready's (1985) study is one of the few comparative works in this area. He found, for instance, that among different nationalities living in the USA, people of Scandinavian origin most often were of the 'formal-distant' types (cf. Neugarten and Weinstein 1964), whereas Polish grandmothers were less often 'distant' than the other groups (English, German, Irish or Italian). The Scandinavian grandparents were also, after Polish and German grandfathers, most often of the 'surrogate' type.

Geographical distance between the grandparents and the grandchildren is also a central modifying factor. Fischer (1983) compared grandmothers who lived very close to their daughter with grandmothers who lived further away. She found that about half of the grandmothers in the latter group wanted more contacts with her grandchild whereas only 14 per cent of the close grandmothers did. Of the geographically distant grandmothers 71 per cent said that their life had not changed when they became grandmothers, whereas 29 per cent of the geographically close gave this answer.

An institutional environment is a factor which has hardly been considered at all in connection with grandparenthood. Only Kahana and Coe (1969) have studied this phenomenon. They found that grandparents living at home have much more frequent contacts with their grandchildren than grandparents in an institution. Of the grandparents living at home 63 per cent had met at least one grandchild during the preceding week, whereas none of the institutionalized grandparents had. Of the institutionalized grandparents 61 per cent compared to 26 per cent of the grandparents living at home said that a visit lasted less than an hour. About half of the institutionalized grandparents and a quarter of those living at home said that their grandchildren do not have time for them.

Biological grandparenthood versus social grandparenthood has become an increasingly important topic with the rising divorce rate. It is more and more common to have not only four grandparents but perhaps eight or even twelve 'grandparents'. The dimensions of grandparenthood for non-biological grandparents are most probably to a large extent identical with the ones mentioned above, but this question still remains to be studied empirically.

The personality and individuality of the grandparent influences grandparenthood as well, as Benedek (1970: 201) observes. She says that 'the emotional content of grandparenthood cannot remain the same for all times and for all persons'. Therefore, longitudinal studies would be needed in the area of grandparenthood.

Grandmotherhood in a Finnish sample

Results are presented below from a Finnish study (Hurme 1988a) which concerned triads of 11–12-year-old children, their mothers and maternal grandmothers. The study aimed at giving a picture of different aspects of intergenerational relations in Finnish families; 453 children wrote essays concerning their grandmothers. Of these children sixty-nine were interviewed concerning their view of their grandmother. The mothers and maternal grandmothers of these sixty-nine children were interviewed as well concerning their mutual relationship and the grandmother–grandchild relation, using a semi-structured interview method. Of the grandmothers and their daughters from the original sample of families (n=453), 121 filled in questionnaires based on these interviews concerning intergenerational relations.

Table 2.2 contains statements from the questionnaire concerning the grandmother role and the 121 grandmothers' reactions to these statements. There were four response alternatives.

Table 2.2 shows the percentages and the mean for each variable taking the alternative responses on a four-point scale from 1 (fully disagree) to 4 (fully agree). The means give a picture of which statements the grandmothers agree with most. They agree that the grandchildren imply company for them, that they don't spoil the grandchildren, that the children continue the family traditions, and that their lives were fulfilled only when they became grandmothers, whereas few if any agree with the statements that the grandchildren have caused big disappointments, that the grandchildren meet them out of duty, or that the grandchildren require too much of their time. (As a comparison, it may be interesting to note that Kornhaber and Woodward (1985) found in a US sample that about 5 per cent of the grandparents were totally disconnected from their grandchildren.) It may be noted that quite a number fully agree with the statement that 'It is only natural that a 45-year-old working grandmother does not have time for her grandchildren'. This clearly shows that the picture of the grandmother role has changed from a grandmother who knits socks and mittens to a more active one.

In order to extract possibly more general underlying dimensions of the grandmother role, factor analysis was performed with these statements as well as with a few questions concerning activities with the grandchild. The full results have been presented elsewhere (Hurme 1988b), and the analysis closely resembles the one in Hurme (1988a), with the exception that here variables pertaining to activities with and for the grandchild were incorporated in the analysis. Besides the variables in Table 2.2, the following variables from the questionnaire were included in the factor analysis. Some of the variables were answered on a yes–no basis, others on 3- to 5-point scales: 27, importance of the grandchild; 28, giving presents; 29, child-minding; 30, surprise visits; 31, telling about the past; 32, giving money; 33, teaching old skills; 34, helps in emergencies; 35, going on holidays; 36, knows favourite dish; 37, knows grandchild's friends; 38, grandchild had been overnight recently; 39, going to church; 40, shopping together; 41, talking about religion.

Table 2.2 Agreement with statements concerning grandmotherhood (percentages)

	%	1	2	3	4	Mean
1.	Part of being a grandmother consists of being able to brag about what my grand-children have done (n=113)	26.5	46.9	23.9	2.7	2.03
2.	My life was fulfilled only when I became a grand-mother (n=115)	15.7	40.0	33.9	10.4	2.39
3.	My grandchildren require too much of my time (n=115)	94.8	2.6	1.7	0.9	1.09
4.	My grandchildren are important especially because they continue the traditions of our family (n=113)	19.5	38.9	32.7	8.8	2.31
5.	I have a feeling that my grandchildren belong to me and not only to their parents (n=115)	33.0	53.0	11.3	2.6	1.84
6.	My daughter spoils her children much too much (n=114)	71.1	22.8	5.3	0.9	1.36
7.	I'd rather meet my grand-children *tête-à-tête* (n=113)	76.1	16.8	7.1	0.0	1.21
8.	I consider it my duty to contribute to the upbringing of my grandchildren finan-cially according to my means (n=114)	62.3	32.5	2.6	2.6	1.46
9.	My grandchildren are closer to me than my own children (n=118)	39.0	37.3	17.8	5.9	1.91
10.	My most important task as a grandparent is to convey knowledge about the past to my grandchildren (n=112)	12.5	62.5	23.2	1.8	2.14
11.	Becoming a grandparent implied growing closer to my own children (n=114)	15.8	46.5	34.2	3.2	2.25
12.	I am ready to give almost all my time to my grand-children (n=110)	28.2	42.7	24.5	4.5	2.06
13.	I consider it the duty of my grandchildren to visit me once a week (n=111)	80.2	15.3	2.7	1.8	1.26

Table 2.2 (Continued)

	%	1	2	3	4	Mean
14. I am too old-fashioned to be useful to my grandchildren (n=113)		60.2	27.4	10.6	1.8	1.54
15. I don't think I spoil my grand-children too much (n=113)		15.0	31.9	38.1	15.0	2.53
16. I have a feeling that my grandchildren meet me only out of duty (n=110)		90.0	6.4	2.7	0.9	1.16
17. Being a grandparent is not the most important thing in my life (n=113)		35.4	36.3	23.0	5.3	1.98
18. I get the greatest satisfaction in life from my grandchildren (n=115)		13.9	44.3	29.6	12.2	2.40
19. I have a feeling that I don't have anything to teach my grandchildren (n=113)		70.8	25.7	1.8	1.8	1.35
20. I consider it my most important task to convey the traditions of our family to my grandchildren (n=112)		24.1	45.5	24.1	6.3	2.13
21. My grandchildren have caused me even big disappointments (n=115)		96.5	3.5	0.0	0.0	1.04
22. Most of all, my grandchildren mean company to me (n=116)		14.7	31.0	37.9	16.4	2.56
23. It is only natural that a 45-year-old working grandmother does not have time for her grandchildren (f=108)		19.4	39.8	25.0	15.7	2.37
24. In my opinion, grandparents should have the same rights as the parents to intervene in the upbringing of the grand-children (f=108)		52.8	26.9	12.0	8.3	1.76
25. The task of the grandparents of both sexes is to be respon-sible for their family (n=106)		44.3	23.6	22.6	9.4	1.97
26. If the grandmother is young and employed, she should leave her work when the grandchild is born to take care of him (n=109)		81.7	12.8	2.8	2.8	1.27

A five-factor varimax rotation gave the clearest picture. The first factor was named *Participation*. Almost all variables implying activities with the child's family – except child-minding and surprise visits – load on this factor (and in this respect the result differs from that of Hurme 1988a). One might even say that this factor is a grandchild-centred factor, because the activities are with the grandchild, not only with the family; for example, the variable 'Most of all, my grandchildren mean company to me'. It is also the one factor which most clearly differentiates this factor analysis from one based only on attitudinal statements concerning the role (Hurme 1988a) as well as from many other studies.

The second factor was named *Satisfaction*. It corresponds to the individualized grandmotherhood mentioned by Robertson (1977). Variables 1, 2, 9, 12, 13, 18 and 39 loaded high on this factor.

The third factor was named *Conveying traditions*. It contains variables related to the family history (cf. Tinsley and Parke (1984); for instance, 'My grandchildren are important especially because they continue the traditions of our family', or 'My most important task as a grandparent is to convey knowledge about past times to my grandchildren', and comes close to the grandparent type 'grandparents as reservoirs of family wisdom', found by Neugarten and Weinstein (1964). Bengtson (1985) has pointed out that one of the most important tasks of a grandparent is the social construction of biography; that is, constructing the past of the grandchild and giving it meaning. Variables 4, 10, 11, 20, 27 and 39 loaded highest on this factor.

Variables 2, 5 ('I have a feeling that my grandchildren belong to me and not only to their parents'), 15, 29 and 30 loaded highest on the fourth factor, which might be termed *Being a substitute parent*. The fifth factor consisted of high loadings on three variables, 24, 25, and 26, and it might be called *Normative grandmotherhood*.

The above factors may be considered central dimensions of the grandmother. The *types* of grandparents mentioned earlier would, then, consist of persons in which such dimensions combine. In order to find out possible types in this study, the factor scores were used in a cluster analysis with those fifty-eight of the cases for whom there were complete data sets on all variables. Because of the small number of cases and a possible bias in their selection, the results are only indicative. Seven clusters gave the clearest result. The clusters represent *types* of grandmothers in this sample.

Two contrasting types of grandmothers emerged most clearly from the cluster analysis. One represented the active grandmother who participates in the life of the child's family and in the upbringing of the grandchild but who does not stress traditions and continuity very much. About 15 per cent of the grandmothers in the cluster analysis were of this type. The other type is the opposite, whose participation is low but who stresses the normative side of grandmotherhood. Again, about 15 per cent were clear examples of this type. It would be interesting to look for these main types in a larger sample as well as to relate it to other factors, such as the age of the grandmother.

In all, this analysis shows that the grandmother role, as experienced by Finnish grandmothers, indeed consists of many aspects. When comparing the results with

29

the point of departure of this analysis – that is, with the four different aspects of grandmotherhood – one can see that three of these are represented in the factor and cluster analyses: the attitudinal level, the behavioural level and the affective level. The fourth, the symbolic level, is more difficult to catch using this type of measurement. It appears more clearly, however, in the qualitative analysis of the results (see Hurme 1988a). This concerns, for instance, the dimension 'Acting as a model for the child', mentioned by Tinsley and Parke (1984); that is, the wish to teach the grandchild how to live or to teach wisdom. One must admit, however, that this symbolic dimension may be more a construct of the researchers than of the grandmothers.

What would be interesting in the future is to follow up changes in the grandmother role over a longer period of time and also to analyse aspects of the role in sub-groups of different ages, in cities and in the countryside, or in different professional groups, as well as compare these empirical results with those concerning grandfathers. A partial answer will be provided by a Finnish–Polish comparative study, the results of which will be published in a few years. This study concerns age groups from 4 to 18 years, and parents as well as grandparents of both sexes are involved in the study.

References

Albrecht, R. (1954) 'Parental responsibilities of grandparents', *Marriage and Family Living* 16: 201–4.

Benedek, T. (1970) 'Parenthood during the lifecycle', in E.J. Anthony and T. Benedek (eds), *Parenthood: Its Psychology and Psychopathology*, Boston: Little Brown.

Bengtson, V. (1985) 'Diversity and symbolism in the grandparental role', in V. Bengtson and J.F. Robertson (eds), *Grandparenthood*, Beverly Hills: Sage.

Berger, P. and Luckman, T. (1966) *The Social Construction of Reality*, Harmondsworth: Penguin.

Cherlin, A. and Furstenberg, F.F. (1985) 'Styles and strategies of grandparenting', in V.L. Bengtson and J.F. Robertson (eds), *Grandparenthood*, Beverly Hills: Sage.

Clavan, S. (1978) 'The impact of social class and social trends on the role of the grandparent', *The Family Coordinator* Oct.: 351–57.

Fischer, L.R. (1983) 'Transition to grandmotherhood', *International Journal of Aging and Human Development* 16: 67–78.

Haavio-Mannila, E. (1983) 'Caregiving in the welfare state', *Acta Sociologica* 26: 61–82.

Hagestad, G. (1985) 'Continuity and connectedness', in V. Bengtson and J.F. Robertson (eds), *Grandparenthood*, Beverly Hills: Sage.

Hurme, H. (1988a) *Child, Mother and Grandmother. Intergenerational Interaction in Finnish families*, Jyväskylä Studies in Education, Psychology and Social Research, 64, Jyväskylä: University of Jyväskylä.

Hurme, H. (1988b) 'Dimensions of the grandmother role', Paper presented at the symposium 'Family life cycle and development of the individual: Problems of intergenerational relations and influence', 2nd European Conference on Developmental Psychology, Budapest, June 1988.

Hurme, H. and Tyszkowa, M. (1989) 'Ecological determinants of children's conceptions of grandparents: Finland and Poland', Poster presented at 10th Meeting of ISSBD, Jyväskylä, July 1989.

Kahana, E. and Coe, R.M. (1969) 'Perceptions of grandparenthood by community and institutionalized aged', Proceedings of the 77th Annual Convention of the American Psychological Association 4: 735-36.

Kahana, E. and Kahana, B. (1971) 'Theoretical and research perspectives on grandparenthood' Aging and Human Development 2: 261-68.

Kivnick, H.Q. (1982a) The Meaning of Grandparenthood, Ann Arbor, MI: UMI Research Press.

Kivnick, H.Q. (1982b) 'Grandparenthood: an overview of meaning and mental health', The Gerontologist 22: 59-66.

Kornhaber, A.M. and Woodward, K.L. (1985) Grandparent/grandchild: the Vital Connection, Oxford: Transaction Books.

Kotlarska-Michalska, A. (1984) 'Wiec rodzinna malzenstw w starszym wieku', in Z. Tyszka (ed.), Wybrane Kategorie Wspolczesnych Rodzin Polskich, Poznan: Wydawnictwo naukowe UAM.

McCready, W.C. (1985) 'Styles of grandparenting among white ethnics', in V. Bengtson and J.F. Robertson (eds), Grandparenthood, Beverly Hills: Sage.

Markides, K. and Krause, N. (1985) 'Intergenerational solidarity and psychological well-being among older Mexican Americans: a three-generational study', Journal of Gerontology 40: 390-92.

Neugarten, B.L. and Weinstein, K.J. (1964) 'The changing American grandparent', Journal of Marriage and the Family 6: 199-204.

Robertson, J. (1977) 'Grandmotherhood: a study of role conceptions', Journal of Marriage and the Family 39: 165-74.

Strom, R. and Strom, S. (1983) 'Redefining the grandparent role', Cambridge Journal of Education 13: 25-8.

Thomas, J.L. (1986) 'Age and sex differences in perceptions of grandparenting', Journal of Gerontology 41: 417-23.

Tinsley, B. and Parke, R. (1984) 'Grandparents as support and socialization agents', in M. Lewis (ed.), Beyond the Dyad, New York: Plenum.

Troll, L.E. (1983) 'Grandparents: the family watchdogs', in T.H. Brubaker (ed.), Family Relations in Later Life, Beverly Hills: Sage.

Updegraff, S.G. (1968) 'Changing role of the grandmother', Journal of Home Economics 60: 177-80.

Wilson, M.N. (1984) 'Mothers' and grandmothers' perceptions of parental behavior in three-generational black families', Child Development 55: 1333-39.

Wood, V. and Robertson, J. (1976) 'The significance of grandparenthood', in J.F. Gubrium (ed.), Time, Roles and Self in Old Age, New York: Human Sciences Press.

Chapter three

The importance of grandparenthood during the life cycle in Germany
Elisabeth J. Sticker

Changes in life cycle and expectation of life have resulted in a larger number of old people and therefore of potential grandparents. Today 21 per cent of our German population are over 60 years old; this rate is still increasing, so that in forty years' time there will be 37 per cent over 60 years old (Bundesministerium für Jugend, Familie, Frauen und Gesundheit 1986). This change in population structure forces us, amongst other things, to come to a better understanding of the grandparental role.

In recent times grandparent–grandchild relationships have been a topic of greater scientific interest than before. This is, for example, demonstrated in the American book *Grandparenthood*, edited by Bengtson and Robertson in 1985. But until now only sparse research evidence has existed regarding relationships of grandparents with grandchildren in Germany. I will briefly review some German publications.

Tews and Schwägler (1973) discuss grandparenthood as a neglected topic of gerontology and sociology of the family; they state that grandparents are best integrated in their families when the relations between the generations are characterized by lack of constraints and by independence.

Loddenkemper and Schäfer (1982) carried out a study on grandparents as agents of socialization for grandchildren; they report that 57 per cent of their sample of 1,127 grandparents were caretakers for their grandchildren because the mothers were working. Schmidt-Denter (1984) studied the social environment of 1,033 children; by contrast, he found that only 9 per cent of the grandparents cared for their grandchildren during the mother's absence at work. The contradiction between these two results may be due to regional differences between the sample: a small town (Koblenz) in the former compared with a big city (Düsseldorf) in the latter study.

Apostel (1989) interviewed eighty-four adults, divided into three age cohorts (20 to 34, 35 to 44, 45 to 80 years), regarding their experiences with grandparents, and their expectations of grandparenthood over the life cycle. Each group was equally distributed into men and women and into country- and city-dwellers. Only seven of the adults were already grandparents; they all lived far away from their grandchildren ($\geq$ 100 km) and saw their grandchildren mostly once or twice monthly.

One of the results in this study was that the experiences with grandparents concentrated on different aspects during the life cycle; namely, on concrete events in childhood, on common activities and grandparental personality in youth, and merely on grandparental personality in adulthood. However, there were few significant differences between the three cohorts regarding the relationship to their grandparents. The differences concerned the evaluation of one's own ageing processes and of one's own grandparents; compared to the older age cohorts, the younger age cohorts, for example, described their own grandparents as more social. The quality of the grandparent–grandchild relationship was independent of grandchildren's age, sex of both generations, living area of the subjects, as well as socio-economic status. The relationship with the mother's mother was somewhat closer than that with the father's mother, which might be due to their longer availability because of their lower average age. For 42 per cent of all grand-children the grandparents had no reported influence on their life; for many others the grandparents played a supportive role (38 per cent); only a few perceived their relationship as neutral or partially conflicting and/or partially supportive (20 per cent). The image of their own grandparents had not changed for two-thirds of the subjects; if changes were perceived, the subjects' evaluations mostly became more positive. Apostel (1989) arrives at the conclusion that, in all phases of life, many grandchildren regard their grandparents as important.

Kaiser (1989) carried out analyses of genealogical trees with seventy professional helpers (physicians, psychologists, social workers) on a family therapy course. He published the results recently under the title 'Family memories – towards a psychology of the multi-generation family'. He found that the subjects were often not aware of the importance of their grandparents as a 'socializing system of the parents and therefore as a highly relevant system of reference for their own development'; however, they did often report that the grandmothers were substitute mothers and in certain cases, where the subjects had a less good relationship with their own mothers because of occupational or familial reasons, they were even a place of refuge for the grandchildren. The grandfathers had a special modelling function for male offspring, but the 'brave, kind grandpa' was the exception rather than the rule, perhaps because the grandfathers were less often present or, when present, less noticeable in the families.

Other information on grandparent–grandchild relationships, though of a predominantly pathological kind, comes from clinical psychology, where the multi-generation family therapy has been developed in recent years (Boszormenyi-Nagy and Spark 1981; Sperling *et al*. 1982); this therapy is based on the assumption that conflicts in childhood result from unconscious conflicts between parents and grandparents, and that these conflicts are recapitulated within the family.

Two publications from Belgium seem to be worth mentioning: Van der Straeten (1971) and Marcoen (1979) both studied the significance of grandchildren's age for the relationship with grandparents. They found that the distinctiveness and evaluation of grandparents varies with the age and cognitive development of the grandchildren. This is in line with American studies (Kahana and Kahana 1970;

Schultz 1980), where age trends in the perception and evaluation of grandparents by grandchildren of different cognitive developmental status were found.

I myself tried to get more information about newer and ongoing studies in Germany by means of publishing some requests in scientific journals and in the public press. The only result was that many interested readers (colleagues, social workers, involved older people) wanted information from me.

Because of this very scarce research evidence on grandparent–grandchild relationships in Germany I carried out some studies on this topic, which will be described. As a theoretical basis for our studies we took the lifespan developmental model; it assumes that development lasts throughout life and so is applicable to generations of all age groups; that is, to grandparents, parents and grandchildren. This is similar to the basis of an extensive study, conducted by Kivnick (1981, 1982) in California; she investigated experiences with grandparents against their whole biographical background; that is, from being a grandchild to becoming parents up to becoming grandparents.

Methods

Since 1985, eight studies on different aspects of grandparent–grandchild relationships have been carried out as masters' theses under my supervision. Table 3.1 gives an overview of sample characteristics and main aspects of the eight studies. The whole sample consisted of 398 subjects. The largest proportion, 175, were grandparents (44 to 91 years old). In addition, there were 101 parents (20 to 50 years old) and 122 grandchildren (up to 28 years old). The first five studies in Table 3.1 each include a separate age group of grandchildren, namely:

infants and toddlers: 0–2 years;
preschool children: 4–5 years;
elementary schoolchildren: 6–10 years;
adolescents: 13–14 years;
young adults: 18–28 years.

In our sample we had 100 grandparent–grandchild dyads from the same families so that pair comparisons were possible.

The subjects were mostly contacted by means of a snowball system, starting with friends and neighbours. By means of this technique we gathered a selected group of subjects, predominantly of middle-class origin, who were probably more interested than the average in their familial relationships. Drawing a representative sample was not possible, since we had no financial resources to pay the subjects for their participation, and our regulations regarding data protection did not allow us to obtain addresses from public authorities.

All subjects were interviewed extensively, on average 1¼ hours, by means of semi-structured explorations regarding several aspects of the grandparent-

Table 3.1 Methods and main aspects of eight German studies on grandparent–grandchild relationships

Author	Year	N	Age	Sample Characteristics	Main aspects
Hören	1985	25	> 45	GP: 21 GM, 4 GF	Comparison between
		25	20–34	Parents:	experienced and
				20 mothers,	inexperienced GP
				5 fathers of infants	
				from *0 to 2 years*	
Flecken	1985	24	44–81	Favourite GP:	GP contact and
				16 GM, 8 GF	functions
		26	*4–5*	Grandchildren:	
				14 girls, 12 boys	
Schulte	1987	20	47–71	GP: 12 GM, 8 GF	Forms of interaction
		20	*6–10*	Grandchildren:	and their perception
				11 girls, 9 boys	
Holdmann	1985	15	54–79	GM with much GD	Meaning of contact
				contact (GM2)	frequency and age
		30	*13–14*	15 GD1[1] 15 GD2[2]	
Laskaridis	1985	41	70–83	GP: 29 GM, 12 GF	Forms of interaction
		46	*18–28*	Grandchildren:	and their perception
				25 women, 21 men	
Murawski	1985	50	70–91	Older people:	Perception and
				31 women, 19 men	meaning of *own GP*
				with *grandchildren of*	
				all age groups	
Buhr	1988	36	22–45	Mothers	Relationships with
				with one child	GP from the view
				up to 12 years	of the mothers
Noll	1987	40	23–50	Parents:	Relationships with
				20 mothers,	GP from the view of
				20 fathers	the parent generation
				with 2–3 children	
				up to 16 years	

Notes:
[1] GD1: Granddaughters with little GM contact (once monthly or less)
[2] GD2: Granddaughters with much GM contact (twice monthly or more)

Italics have been used to indicate the data sources in Tables 3.2–3.8.
Abbreviations:
GP	Grandparents
GM	Grandmothers
GF	Grandfathers
MGP	Maternal Grandparents
PGP	Paternal Grandparents
GCH	Grandchildren
GD	Granddaughters

grandchild relationship. Most subjects referred to their favourite grandchild or grandparent. The exploration method allows for wide questioning and tries to encompass all possible important topics. By this means the subjective reality of the interviewed persons is represented more adequately than by the use of questionnaires. This is also the opinion of the Bonn school, where thousands of such interviews were carried out in the Bonn Longitudinal Study on Ageing (BOLSA) (Thomae 1976).

Because the authors of our studies were largely free to choose their interview questions, the number of included variables differs considerably and the data for some variables are not complete. Each category system was constructed by the author him- or herself, but given considerable overlap between the systems of the different studies the methodology is similar enough so that direct comparisons can be made.

On average 125 categories were included, with a minimum of 40 and a maximum of 223. Most of the categories were rating scales with five points (for example, 'very low', 'low', 'average', 'high', 'very high'). Reliability testing of the codings is not usual in our master's theses, but partial random testing has shown satisfactory coder agreements of at least 80 to 90 per cent.

We used frequency analyses and various non-parametrical inferential tests (such as Chi-Square-tests, Mann-Whitney U-tests and Kendall's tau correlation coefficients). However, given the scarcity of empirical data about grandparent–grandchild relationships, the emphasis of this report will be on the description of important variables. In order to facilitate comparability the tables show percentages instead of numbers despite the small sample size in some sub-groups. A list of abbreviations is given at the foot of Table 3.1. For further information on our studies see also Sticker (1987), Sticker and Flecken (1986), as well as Sticker and Holdmann (1988).

Before reporting the results it should be pointed out that the studies are not longitudinal, but cross-sectional. So we cannot make statements about truly developmental aspects; we can only speculate cautiously.

Results

Frequency of contacts

The frequency of contacts shows considerable variation in our samples with grandchildren of different age groups (see Table 3.2). A high contact frequency is more common for younger grandchildren, whereas a low contact frequency occurs more often for older grandchildren. The frequency of contacts seems to diminish with grandchildren's age.

We examined correlations of contact frequency with important qualitative variables of grandparent–grandchild relationships; for example, closeness of the relationship, amount of fun-seeking in the grandparent's style, and emotional satisfaction with the grandparental role. Interestingly, we found higher correlations with the frequency of contacts when grandparent and grandchild were alone together compared with the contact frequency in general. This holds for all age groups of grandchildren and for the judgements of the grandparents as well as those of the grandchildren. Most grandchildren and grandparents, especially

Table 3.2 Frequency of contacts with grandparents for grandchildren of different age groups (percentages)

Age group of grandchildren[1]	Less than once monthly	Frequency of contacts Once weekly to once monthly	More than once weekly
0–2 years	4	32	64
4–5 years	0	48	52
6–10 years	0	55	45
13–14 years	40	27	33
18–28 years	76	22	2

[1]The data source of the tables can be found by reference to the italicized phrases in Table 3.1.

those with preschool grandchildren, preferred to be alone together rather than having the whole family round.

In our studies we found no significant sex differences regarding contact frequency. In the Noll and the Buhr studies (see Table 3.1), there was an insignificant tendency towards more contacts with maternal compared to paternal grandparents. In general, however, the contact frequency seems to depend more on geographical distance and accessibility than on sex and lineage of the grandparents.

Emotional closeness

Our information on emotional closeness assesses the amount of exchanged confidences and intimacy in the grandparent–grandchild relationship. Grandparents and grandchildren generally felt close emotionally. About three-quarters of the dyads (60–85 per cent) were characterized by 'high' or 'very high' emotional closeness (see Table 3.3). The only exception is the past relationship of grandparents to their own grandparents, which is judged as less intimate, perhaps because fifty years ago emotions were not expressed so freely as today (Murawski study, see Table 3.1).

For less than one-fifth of the dyads the intimacy of the relationship is rated as 'moderate'. A 'very low' emotional closeness did not occur at all for grandchildren up to five years; in the other samples only a few relationships were rated as showing a 'very low' intimacy (2 to 10 per cent).

An example of a 'very high' emotional closeness is given by a 55-year-old grandmother and her 8-year-old granddaughter:

> On principle we talk about everything, obviously also about confidences which concern our family as a whole. We wouldn't consider doing this differently. Susan is very much attached to me and she misses me, if I haven't been with her for a long time. I love her so much, too.

> If I don't like anything, I may say it, whatever it is. . . . I'm not afraid. . . . Sometimes I also tell Grandma a secret.

37

Table 3.3 Emotional closeness of the grandparent–grandchild relationship (percentages)

Age group of grandchildren	Rater	Very low	Low	Moderate	High	Very high
0–2 years	grandparents	0	4	16	28	52
4–5 years	interviewer[1]	0	4	9	8	79
6–10 years	grandparents	5	15	20	35	25
	grandchildren	10	15	15	30	30
0–12 years	mothers → MGP	0	6	9	37	48
	mothers → PGP	6	9	11	43	31
0–16 years	parents → MGP	5	5	13	40	37
	parents → PGP	3	14	17	41	25
all age groups	GP → GCH	2	16	10	46	26
	GP → own GP	6	12	36	24	22

[1]Global rating of the interviewer, based on *nonverbal* communication of the grandparents.
→ Reference persons (e.g., mothers → MGP: emotional closeness between 0- to 12-year-old grandchildren and their maternal grandparents, rated by their mothers).
Abbreviations: See Table 3.1

We found no linear trend of emotional closeness in relation to the age of the grandchildren. However, intimacy was lowest for schoolchildren and their grandparents. There was only an insignificant tendency for the maternal lineage to score higher on emotional closeness than the paternal lineage. Sex differences could not be detected. Again, geographical distance seems to be the more important variable.

Other information about the closeness of the relationship can be inferred from a drawing test, which was performed with the preschool grandchildren (Flecken 1985; see Table 3.1). The children were asked to draw their own family as animals (Familie-in-Tieren-Test by Brem-Gräser, 1980). More than one-third of the children spontaneously drew their grandparents with the other family members. Another third did this only after the additional question: 'How about your grandma and grandpa? Would you like to draw them as animals too?' The other children did not draw their grandparents at all.

In the drawing test the grandparents were represented as predominantly tame and not wild animals: hare, ladybird, hedgehog, whale, snake, cat, little dog, fly, fish pig. One little girl drew her grandfather as a laughing Christmas tree, which undoubtedly indicates a very intimate relationship.

Reciprocal meaning

From our interview data we also obtained some information on the meaning of grandparents and grandchildren for each other.

For about three-quarters of the grandparents (72 to 87 per cent) the grandchildren had a 'high' or 'very high' meaning in their life, and for about one-quarter the grandchildren were of only 'moderate' or 'low' meaning (see

Table 3.4 Meaning of the grandchildren in the life of the grandparents (percentages)

Age group of grandchildren	Rater	Meaning of grandchildren				
		Very low	Low	Mode-rate	High	Very high
0-2 years	grandparents	0	8	20	40	32
4-5 years	grandparents	0	0	13	17	70
13-14	GD1	13	27	13	13	34
	GD2	0	13	7	27	53
	GM2	0	0	13	27	60

GD1 granddaughters with little grandmother contact
(once monthly or less)
GD2 granddaughters with much grandmother contact
(more than once monthly)
GM2 grandmothers of the GD2 group

Table 3.4). The only exceptions to this are adolescent granddaughters with small grandmother contact (GD1); here more than half considered their own meaning for the grandparents as, at most, moderate.

The following example gives the statement of a grandmother, who attributed a 'very high' meaning to her preschool grandson:

Yes, he is the most important thing in my life, because I have nothing else at the moment. They all say I spoil him. I don't know. Mama is a little bit strict, and so I always am careful not to spoil him too much. And it is actually Carsten this and Carsten that: he means so much to me. Since I am a pensioner, I have time for him.

A 'high' and 'very high' meaning of the grandparents in the life of the grand-children is even more common than the reverse, as is seen in Table 3.5 (86 to 100 per cent when excluding the GD1 group again).

Table 3.5 Meaning of the grandparents in the life of the grandchildren (percentages)

Age group of grandchildren	Rater	Meaning of grandparents				
		Very low	Low	Mode-rate	High	Very high
0-2 years	parents	0	0	8	44	48
4-5 years	grandparents	0	0	5	45	50
13-14 years	GD1	0	15	21	21	43
	GD2	0	0	14	36	50
	GM2	0	0	0	30	70

GD1 granddaughters with little grandmother contact
(once monthly or less)
GD2 granddaughters with much grandmother contact
(more than once monthly)
GM2 grandmothers of the GD2 group

The following example demonstrates the high meaning attributed to grandparents by a grandmother of a preschool girl:

Table 3.6 Functions of the grandparents for the grandchildren (percentages)

Age group of grandchildren	0–2 years	4–5 years		0–12 years	13–14 years[1]			All age groups	
Rater / Functions	GP	GP	GCH	Mothers	GD1	GD2	GM2	GP → GCH	GP → own GP
Educating	16	74		10				72	68
Babysitting	32	96	9	32				72	44
Caring	25	96	78	17	53	53	53	38	22
Playing	44			56	40	40	53		
Emotional support									
by talking		35	4	60	64	93	80	84	50
by cuddling	64	21	87		27	40	60	38	36
Transmitting knowledge	25	13	0	28					

1 GD1 = granddaughters with little grandmother contact (once monthly or less)
  GD2 = granddaughters with much grandmother contact (more than once monthly)
  GM2 = grandmothers of the GD2
  GCH = grandchildren
  → Reference person (e.g., GP → own GP; emotional closeness between grandparents and their own grandparents, rated retrospectively)

'Yes, children need grandparents. Also Andrea. Surely the parents are more important. But grandparents – as I am – have time for a child.'

To summarize, grandparents and grandchildren clearly mean a lot to each other, with a slight tendency to rate the grandparents' importance for grandchildren as even higher than the reverse. Adolescent girls with much contact with their grandparents (GD2) showed an insignificant trend towards a higher reciprocal meaning than those with little grandmother contact (GD1).

Functions of grandparents

In most of our studies, several functions of grandparents for grandchildren were rated (see Table 3.6).

For grandparents with grandchildren of all age groups (Murawski study, see Table 3.1) the function as conversation partner dominates (84 per cent). Educational tasks and babysitting also play an important role (both 72 per cent); the rates of these and of all other functions are higher when compared with the past relationship to their own grandparents.

There are noticeable age differences, revealed by the other studies (see Table 3.6). For infants and toddlers the grandparents serve predominantly as cuddling and playing partners (64 per cent and 44 per cent). Nearly all grandparents of pre-school grandchildren have caring (96 per cent) and playing (96 per cent) functions; and many of them help with babysitting (74 per cent). Interestingly, most preschool grandchildren themselves emphasize the cuddling function of their grandparents much more than do their grandparents (87 per cent compared with 21 per cent). Mothers with one child up to 12 years predominantly indicated emotional support and play as functions of the grandparents (60 per cent and 56 per cent).

For adolescent girls, especially for those with much grandmother contact (GD2) the grandmothers function mostly as conversational partners. The grandmothers more often than the granddaughters mention the cuddling and the playing function. In this study the frequency of contacts was an important variable for the emotional support function: talking as well as cuddling were more important for granddaughters with much grandmother contact (GD2) than for those with little grandmother contact (GD1).

Grandparental style

Our data were rated according to the styles of grandparenting described by Neugarten and Weinstein (1964). Table 3.7 gives an overview of the findings in four previous studies and five of our studies.

The fun-seeking style dominates for grandparents with infants and toddlers (72 per cent) and elementary schoolchildren (33 per cent for grandmothers, 50 per cent for grandfathers) as well as for grandparents of children up to the age of 12 years (68 per cent for the maternal and 74 per cent for the paternal lineage, rated by the mothers).

Table 3.7 Grandparental styles (selected previous research and own studies) (percentages)

Previous research	Age of GCH	Subjects	Fun-seekers	Parent surrogate	Grandparents as Reservoir of family wisdom	Formal	Distant
Neugarten & Weinstein 1964[1]	not given	66 GM 64 GF	30 27	15 0	2 6	33 36	20 31
Crawford 1981	9 months	53 GM 54 GF	46 54	28 28	12 12	8 6	6 0
Matthews & Sprey 1984[2]	not given	37 GM 37 GF	55 65	24 11	24 57	./. ./.	./. ./.
Apostel 1989	not given	81 seniors	17	./.	24	38	2
Own studies:							
Hören 1985[3]	0–2 years	25 GP	72	28	4	12	0
Schulte 1987	6–10 years	12 GM 8 GF	33 50	25 0	17 25	25 25	0 0
Buhr 1987[3]	0–12 years	36 mothers → MGP → PGP	68 74	26 6	22 29	20 23	11 8
Laskaridis 1985	18–28 years	25 GM 12 GF	20 30	12 0	4 10	52 40	12 20
Murawski 1985	all ages	50 GP → GP → own GP	20 16	6 10	10 16	42 28	22 30

1 Recalculated percentages after elimination of missing values
2 More than one assignment possible
3 Score 4 + 5 of 5-point scales
./. Percentages not given
→ Reference persons (e.g., mothers → MGP: emotional closeness between 0- to 12-year-old grandchildren and their maternal grandparents. rated by their mothers)
Abbreviations: See Table 3.1.

Most grandparents of young adults had a formal style (52 per cent of the grand-mothers and 40 per cent of the grandfathers), but here also 20 per cent of grand-mothers and 30 per cent of grandfathers were fun-seekers. Grandparents as parent surrogate – all females – were common for infants and toddlers (28 per cent) and for elementary schoolchildren (25 per cent). Grandparents as a reservoir of family wisdom appeared relatively often for elementary schoolchildren (17 per cent for grandmothers, 25 per cent for grandfathers) and for grandchildren up to the age of 12 years (22 per cent for maternal, 29 per cent for paternal grand-parents, rated by the mothers).

We found no distant grandparents in dyads with infants and toddlers and with elementary schoolchildren; in our other sub-samples distant grandparents occurred infrequently (8–22 per cent). However, in the Murawski study (see Table 3.1) the grandparents attributed to their own grandparents a distant style in 30 per cent, compared with 22 per cent for their own style. So a small cohort trend towards more distant grandparents in older cohorts becomes obvious. Further-more, an age trend towards an increase of the distant style with increasing age of the grandchildren can be seen. Both trends were nonsignificant.

Modelling function of own grandparents

In order to reflect upon the biographic perspective too, we enquired about the role of the older people's own grandparents for their behaviour towards the grandchildren.

In the Murawski study (Table 3.1), which focused especially on the modelling function of the grandparents' own grandparents, 64 per cent of the subjects took their own grandparents as an orientation for their behaviour towards the grand-children (26 per cent as positive, 24 per cent as negative and 14 per cent as both positive and negative orientation).

The grandparents' orientation towards their own grandparents might vary with the age of the grandchildren because each developmental phase implies different characteristics of the grandchildren and therefore requires different educational measures. This is also underlined by Matthews and Sprey (1985); in their study 61 per cent considered age of the grandchildren as important for their behaviour as grandparents. So we also looked for this variable in our different age groups of grandchildren.

The proportion of grandparents who take their own grandparents as a model varies considerably for dyads with grandchildren of different age groups:

44 per cent for infants and toddlers;
22 per cent for preschool children;
85 per cent for elementary school children (30 per cent as positive, 15 per cent as negative, 40 per cent as both positive and negative model);
53 per cent for adolescent girls (33 per cent as positive model).
  No clear linear age trend can be detected in these data.

An example of a high positive and of a negative modelling function of own grandparents is given by two grandmothers of adolescent girls:

> I thought it right, . . . I wished that this would be similar for me. . . . She [grandmother] has influenced me so much.

> I have always said: I won't be this sort of grandma in later life.

Meaning of the parent generation

We also asked for perceptions of the extent to which the parents, as the intermediate generation, influenced or mediated the grandparent–grandchild relationship. Such mediating behaviour includes facilitating contacts between grandparents and younger grandchildren, informing the grandparents about favourite toys or activities of the child or making up quarrels between both generations. The results are shown in Table 3.8.

Table 3.8 Amount of parental influence on the grandparent–grandchild relationship (summarized from 5-point scales: 1+2, 3, 4+5, respectively or for → as dichotomous data: no/yes) (percentages)

Age group of grandchildren	Rater	Amount of parental influence			
		Low		Moderate	High
6–10 years	grandparents	25		40	35
	grandchildren	35		45	20
13–14 years	GD1	→	43	←	57
	GD2	→	14	←	86
	GM2	→	43	←	57
18–28 years	grandparents	41		26	33
	grandchildren	36		33	31
0–12 years	mothers → MGP	43		37	20
	mothers → PGP	57		26	17
all age groups	grandparents	→	60	←	40

GD1 granddaughters with little grandmother contact (once monthly or less)
GD2 granddaughters with much grandmother contact (more than once monthly)
GM2 grandmothers of the GD2 group
→   Reference persons (e.g. mothers → MGP: emotional closeness between 0- to 12-year-old grandchildren and their maternal grandparents, rated by their mothers)

Abbreviations: See Table 3.1.

Generally, the ratings are fairly evenly distributed between 'low', 'moderate' and 'high'. The lowest perception of parental mediation occurs for adolescent granddaughters, especially for those who see the grandmother twice monthly or more (GD2, see Table 3.1) and for grandparents of the paternal lineage (rated by the mothers; Buhr study, see Table 3.1).

A high amount of parental influence was attributed to the parent generation by 35 per cent of the grandparents of elementary schoolchildren, but only by 20 per cent of the respective grandchildren. So the grandchildren, compared to the grandparents, tended to underestimate the parental influence on their relationship with the grandparents.

There are no systematic differences in the amount of parental mediation between dyads with grandchildren of different age groups, between maternal and paternal lineages or between the perspectives of different generations.

In the following, two examples are given of no influence and of a distinct influence of the parent generation. The data stem from a grandfather, and a grandmother of young adult grandchildren (Laskaridis 1985):

No, they don't interfere at all . . . . If Bernhard [grandchild] is in our region, then he mostly visits us first, and then he goes to his parents, because they live in the next village.

I have at least the impression, that my daughter talks with Peter [grandchild] about us. He also came to our golden wedding, . . . which he might have come to know only from his mother, because I hadn't seen him for a long time.

In one study, we additionally evaluated the perceived quality of the mediation and in another study the meaning which is attributed to parental mediation independent of its amount and quality. The quality of mediation was evaluated predominantly as positive by grandparents with preschool children (64 per cent). This is demonstrated by the following example:

I always think that Margot and Jens [parents of the grandchildren] have a very positive attitude towards our relationship to the grandchildren; well, they influence the children by their positive talking about us.

Most parents of grandchildren up to 16 years rated the meaning of their own influence on the grandparent–grandchild relationship as low (80 per cent for the maternal and 75 per cent for the paternal lineage).

Discussion

Altogether the frequency of contacts between grandparents and grandchildren in our studies is high when compared with other research data. In the sibling study of Dunn and Kendrick (1982), for example, only 50 per cent of the infants and toddlers met their grandparents at least once weekly. In our study, 64 per cent of the infants and toddlers contacted their grandparents more than once weekly. Kahana and Kahana (1970) found that 25 per cent of the preschool children and 36 per cent of the schoolchildren saw their maternal grandfather only every few months or less; their percentages for this low contact frequency were even higher regarding the other grandparents (up to 87 per cent for preschool children and their paternal grandfather). Such a low contact frequency did not occur for our German preschool and schoolchildren.

The trend towards decreasing contact frequency with increasing age of the grandchildren is corroborated by Apostel (1989) in biographical interviews with adults of different age groups, recalling how their relationship with their grand-parents changed as they grew up.

The amount of contact when alone together seems to be a better indicator of the quality of the grandparent–grandchild relationship than is the frequency of contacts in general. Grandparents who are often alone together with their grand-children have more intimate and more gratifying relationships. The reasons for this may be that in dyadic contacts both interaction partners can concentrate and focus better on each other. Furthermore, it seems that confidences are more readily exchanged when others – even close family members – are not present.

We found the emotional closeness between grandparents and grandchildren of all age groups to be generally high. This is in line with Loddenkemper and Schäfer (1982), who found that 84 per cent of the grandparents indicated attach-ment and love as the motivation for their caretaking functions regarding the grandchildren.

In our studies the reciprocal meaning of grandparents and grandchildren of all age groups is very high. Hartshorne and Manaster (1982) found even higher percentages of reciprocal meaning, rated by young adult grandchildren: 95 per cent for the grandparents' meaning them to, and 98 per cent for their own mean-ing to their grandparents. However, contrary to their result, in our studies the importance of the grandparents for the grandchildren is judged as even higher than the other way round. A reason for this may be that many of our grandparents considered intrafamilial contacts compared to extrafamilial as more important.

The functions of the grandparents vary considerably with the age of the grand-children and with the subjects' perspective. For example, preschool grandchildren emphasize the cuddling function more than their grandparents, whereas the contrary is true for adolescent girls. But for adolescent girls the function as con-versation partner is perceived as more important by the granddaughters with much grandmother contact (GD2) than by their own grandmothers. We see that sometimes the grandparents underestimate the importance of some of their own functions for the grandchildren.

In our studies the percentages of grandparents, who function as regular or casual caretakers for the grandchildren, vary considerably (17 to 53 per cent, when excluding the study with preschool children because of distinct non-uniformity within the dyads) as is the case in previous studies, too: 9 per cent according to Schmidt-Denter (1984) and 57 per cent according to Loddenkemper and Schäfer (1982).

The older people in our studies have developed their grandparental style in very different manners. Compared with the results of Neugarten and Weinstein (1964), the fun-seeking style is more common, whereas the distant and the formal style are less common. In the study of Apostel (1989), who interviewed some grandparents (n=7) as well as adults who anticipated becoming grandparents (n=77), very few subjects preferred the distant style for their own present or future grandparental behaviour. They predominantly chose the formal style (38 per cent) or the reservoir of family wisdom (24 per cent), whereas only 17 per cent decided to be fun-seekers. This may be due to the fact that the anticipation of the subjects was based more on the actual experiences with their own grandparents than on past experiences as grandchildren. Compared to the Crawford study (1981) with 9-months-old grandchildren, our Hören study (1985) with infants and toddlers reveals more fun-seeking grandparents and fewer grandparents as reservoirs of family wisdom (see Table 3.7). The results of Matthews and Sprey (1984), especially the high rate of fun-seekers (55 per cent grandmothers, 65 per cent grandfathers), are more similar to our Buhr study; however, their high amount of grandfathers as reservoirs of family wisdom (57 per cent) is not reproduced in our studies.

Our data on parental mediating functions show that, regardless of grand-children's age, grandparents' lineage and person of the rater, parents are thought to have an influence on the relationship between grandparents and grandchildren. About two-thirds of our subjects rated the amount of parental influence as at least moderate. This is in line with the study of Robertson (1976), where two-thirds of young adult grandchildren considered their parents as 'pacemakers' of the rela-tionship to the grandparents. Nevertheless, in our studies the parents themselves regard their own influence predominantly as moderate or even as low; obviously they often are unaware of the importance of their mediating behaviour.

Conclusions

From our studies we can draw the following conclusions: First, most grandparents and grandchildren are important for each other, and hence their contacts should be encouraged.

Second, it seems to be important for the development of a close relationship that grandparents and grandchildren have enough opportunities to meet alone. These opportunities should be offered first of all by the parent generation, especially when the grandchildren are still young.

Third, grandparents tend to undervalue their meaning for grandchildren in some respects; they should be encouraged to realize their own importance in the life of their grandchildren.

Fourth, parents are often unaware of the extent of their influence on the grandparent–grandchild relationship. They should reflect on their mediating role and realize the potential they possess to facilitate and enhance relationships which are generally positive and meaningful for both the grandparent and the grandchild.

Acknowledgement

This chapter is gratefully dedicated to Professor Ursula Lehr for her 60th birthday.

References

Apostel, U. (1989) 'Grosseltern als Sozialisationsfaktoren. Die Bedeutung der

Grosseltern in biographischer Sicht', Unpublished Ph.D., Bonn.
Bengtson, V.L. and Robertson, J.F. (eds) (1985) *Grandparenthood*, Beverly Hills: Sage Publications.
Boszormenyi-Nagy, I. and Spark, G. (1981) Unsichtbare Bindungen, Stuttgart: KlettCotta.
Brem-Gräser, L. (1980) *Familie in Tieren – Die Familiensituation im Spiegel der Kinderzeichnung*, Munich: Rheinhardt Verlag.
Buhr, M. (1988) 'Die Grosseltern-Enkel-Beziehung im Erleben der Eltern bei Familien mit einem Kind', Unpublished masters' thesis, Bonn University.
Bundesministerium für Jugend, Familie, Frauen und Gesundheit (ed.) (1986) *Vierter Familienbericht: Die Situation der älteren Menschen in der Familie*, Bonn.
Crawford, M. (1981) 'Not disengaged: grandparents in literature and reality, an empirical study in role satisfaction', *Sociological Review* 29: 499–519.
Dunn, J. and Kendrick, C. (1982) *Siblings: Love, Envy, and Understanding*, Cambridge, MA: Harvard University Press.
Flecken, M. (1985) 'Vorschulkinder und ihre Grosseltern. Eine Pilotstudie', Unpublished masters' thesis, Bonn University.
Hartshorne T.S. and Manaster, G. (1982) 'The relationship with grandparents: contact, importance, role conception', *International Journal of Aging and Human Development* 15: 233–45.
Holdmann, K. (1985) 'Die Beziehung zwischen Enkelinnen und Grossmüttern aus der Perspektive von 13– bis 14 jährigen Enkelinnen. Eine Pilotstudie', Unpublished masters' thesis, Bonn University.
Hören, D. (1985), 'Die Beziehung von erfahrenen und unerfahrenen Grosseltern zu Enkelkindern im Kleinkindalter (bis 3 Jahre)', Unpublished masters' thesis, Bonn University.
Kahana, B., Kahana, E. (1970) 'Grandparenthood from the perspective of the developing grandchild', *Developmental Psychology* 3: 98–105.
Kaiser, P. (1989) *Familien-Erinnerungen. Zur Psychologie der Mehrgenerationenfamilie*, Heidelberg: Roland Asanger Verlag.
Kivnick, H.Q. (1981) 'Grandparenthood and the mental health of grandparents', *Ageing and Society* 1: 365–91.
Kivnick, H.Q. (1982) *The Meaning of Grandparenthood*, Ann Arbor: University of Michigan Press.
Laskaridis, A. (1985) 'Formen der Interaktion zwischen jungen Erwachsenen und deren Grosseltern', Unpublished masters' thesis, Bonn University.
Loddenkemper, H. and Schäfer, H. (1982) 'Projekte Grosselternerziehung', *Blätter der Wohlfahrtspflege* 129: 284.
Marcoen, A. (1979) 'Children's perception of aged persons and grandparents', *International Journal of Behavioral Development* 2: 87–105.
Matthews, S.H. and Sprey, J. (1984) 'The impact of divorce on grandparenthood: an exploratory study', *The Gerontologist* 24: 41–7.
Matthews, S.H. and Sprey, J. (1985) 'Adolescents' relationships with grandparents: an empirical contribution to conceptual clarification', *Journal of Gerontology* 40: 621–26.
Murawski, B. (1985) 'Das Erleben der eigenen Eltern und Grosseltern bei alten Menschen', Unpublished masters' thesis, Bonn University.
Neugarten, B.L and Weinstein, K.J. (1964) 'The changing American grandparent', *Journal of Marriage and the Family* 26: 199–204.
Noll, H-J. (1987) 'Die Grosseltern-Enkel-Beziehung im Erleben der Eltern bei Familien mit mehreren kindern', Unpublished masters' thesis, Bonn University.
Robertson, J.F. (1976) 'Significance of grandparents: perceptions of young adult grandchildren', *The Gerontologist* 16: 137–40.

Schmidt-Denter, U. (1984) *Die soziale Umwelt des Kindes*, Heidelberg: Springer.

Schulte, I. (1987) 'Formen der Interaktion zwischen Grundschulkindern und deren Grosseltern – eine Pilotstudie', Unpublished masters' thesis, Bonn University.

Schultz, N.W. (1980) 'A cognitive developmental study of the grandchild-grandparent bond', *Child Study Journal* 10: 7–26.

Sperling, E., Massing, A., Reich, G., Georgi, H. and Wöbbe-Mönks, E. (1982) *Die Mehrgenerationenfamilientherapie*, Göttingen: Vandenhoeck und Ruprecht.

Sticker, E.J. (1987) 'Die Beziehungen zwischen Grosseltern und Enkeln. Aktuelle Befunde von Explorationsstudien in Deutschland', *Zeitschrift für Gerontologie* 20: 169–74.

Sticker, E.J. and Flecken, M. (1986) 'Die Beziehung zwischen Grosseltern und ihren Enkeln im Vorschulalter', *Zeitschrift für Gerontologie* 19: 336–41.

Sticker, E.J. and Holdmann, K. (1988) 'Die Beziehung zwischen 13- bis 14 jährigen Mädchen und ihren Grossmüttern', *Psychologie in Erziehung und Unterricht* 35: 27–33.

Straeten, S. van der (1971) 'De betekenis van de grootourderen vor de kleinkinderen', Unpublished Ph.D., Catholic University, Louvain.

Tews, H.P. and Schwägler, G. (1973) 'Grosseltern – ein vernachlässigtes Problem gerontologischer und familiensoziologischer Forschung', *Zeitschrift für Gerontologie*, 6: 284–95.

Thomae H. (1976) *Patterns of aging: findings from the Bonn Longitudinal Study of Aging*, Basle: Karger.

Chapter four

The role of grandparents in the development of grandchildren as perceived by adolescents and young adults in Poland

Maria Tyszkowa

An important but rarely considered aspect of the social role of grandparents is their influence on the individual development of grandchildren. I shall examine this using retrospective opinions of grandchildren in their adolescence and young adulthood. I shall also analyse how adolescents and young adults perceive the importance and role of grandparents in their life and development.

Individual development as as process of acquiring and structuring experience

A theoretical basis of departure is a concept of individual development as a process of accumulating, elaborating and structuring experience (Tyszkowa 1986a, b). The source of experience as material for development is the individual's own activity, including his interactions with others and assimilation of culture. The individual's overall experience comprises (1) species experience conveyed in the form of organismic structures and connections in the nervous system as well as schemes of inborn functions; (2) individual experience acquired as a result of own actions, life events, contacts and situations; (3) that part of the experience of former generations which the individual takes over by way of interpersonal communication, learning and assimilation of culture.

The experience that the individual gains comprises cognitive, affective and evaluative aspects (Piaget 1967). It must be elaborated in these three aspects and, once elaborated, it is ordered and self-organized. An important role in these processes is played by sign systems, cultural patterns and symbols, as well as communication with other people.

Interpersonal relations and communication requires psychic decentration which makes it easier to elaborate experience in all its three planes, and thus allows for its inclusion into the individual's psychic system. It may be for these reasons that teenagers (as observed by Cziksentmihaly et al. 1977) spend a lot of time talking with their peers and, as we shall see later, are also eager to carry on frequent conversations with their grandparents.

Individual experience is difficult to convey. However, this experience, like biography, has some universal aspects resulting from the similarity of human fate and the fundamental tasks of human life and development (Havighurst 1977).

It is on this that a possibility of communication between representatives of different generations rests.

The family as a developmental context of the individual

The acquisition, accumulation and organization of experience takes place in the course of the individual's activity in his environment. An important part of this environment is the family. This constitutes the basic or primary developmental context of the individual in childhood, and continues to be significant in later years. It is in the family that a person acquires important cognitive, social and emotional experience as well as essential cultural tools for its elaboration and structuring. Interpersonal bonds that usually exist between family members create particularly favourable conditions for the processes of experience elaboration and structuring. This is owing to intensive processes of interpersonal communication of an intimate character; close to self-communication but exteriorized in an interpersonal system.

Until recently, most authors in sociology and psychology treated the family mainly as a nuclear one of two generations (parents and children). The phases of a family life cycle – pre-parental, parental and post-parental – have also been distinguished on the basis of parental roles. Yet, such a theoretical family model does not quite comply with reality since many people live in the larger family network of which a three-generation family (grandparents, parents, children) is a distinct part. In recent years psychologists have been undertaking wider studies of relations and interactions between family members representing different generations.

Among the urban population in Poland, a nuclear family is the prevailing type. Since old parents usually live on their own and not infrequently in places far removed from children and their families, the contacts are limited but the sense of family ties is generally retained. This kind of family circle has been called a scattered and reduced extended family (Tyszka 1979, 1982). In such conditions contacts and relations between grandparents and grandchildren are generally kept and continued.

In my view, grandparents are taken to be a part of a three-generation family. Their position in this arrangement may vary. Together with their personal features, this position determines their mode of existence in the world of grandchildren and the place they have in it. There are also various ways in which grandparents participate in grandchildren's development. As biological ancestors they hand down to their grandchildren a proportion of their genes. They can influence the formation of grandchildren's experience in its kind and scope. If they participate in grandchildren's life and activity they may not only have impact on the shaping of the individual experience of the latter but may also enrich them with some experiences of their own life, thus extending backwards the psychological time of the young generation. Finally, they may, and often do, transmit to grandchildren a part of the symbolic culture of a society, which they have earlier assimilated

51

themselves (Cassirer 1977; Kmita 1985), as well as their own attitudes, opinions and values. Grandparents may also transmit to grandchildren the knowledge of that fragment of the nation's history and civilization in which they themselves took an active part.

Grandparents are generally in that period of life and development when people reflect on their youth and childhood, recapitulating past events and balancing life accomplishments. Grandchildren, on the other hand, go through a period of many new experiences and problems involving processes of puberty and processes of acquiring self-identity. When mutual contacts exist, grandparents and grandchildren may be attractive for each other and their mutual relations may provide support in stressful situations, and help in the individual development of each party.

The above ideas served as a framework within which a programme of empirical investigation was carried out. The aim was to examine different aspects of interaction and relations between grandparents and grandchildren. Starting from the initial concept of individual development I examined the following questions:

Are grandchildren in contact with their grandparents? What is the frequency and character of these contacts?
Do these contacts enrich grandchildren's experience, and if so, to what extent?
Do contacts with grandparents help to elaborate and organize grandchildren's experience, and if so, how?
Do grandparents provide grandchildren with personality patterns?

Method

In order to obtain material to answer these questions I used retrospective and introspective data coming from so-called verbal reports (Ericsson and Simon 1984). I used the occasion of Grandmother's and Grandfather's Day (fairly widely celebrated in Poland) to ask adolescent high-school pupils (group AD) to write compositions at a lesson with their class tutor, and young adult university students (group YA) to do the same at a lecture in educational psychology. High-school pupils were given the title 'Grandparents and I' for their compositions. University students gave their own titles to their works. They were free to choose whether to sign them with their own name, a pseudonym, or not sign at all. Most chose the first option.

Composition as a method for data collection has a long-standing and respectable tradition in developmental psychology. If properly used, it allows rich information to be gathered, particularly if subjects are people with an ability to analyse their life situations and to express themselves well in writing. As a rule, however, the method yields material which is heterogeneous and difficult to compare. I therefore applied careful content analysis to a prepared set of categories allowing basic variables to be separated (these categories were developed in collaboration with Professor Helena Hurme, Abo Akademie, Finland). Only some, which are indispensable for analysing grandparent–grandchildren relations, will be used here. I also distinguished some categories of subjective evaluation of grandparents' role in subjects' development.

The subjects were 75 high-school pupils (31 male, 44 female) aged 15–18, and 67 university students (21 male, 46 female) of pedagogics and psychology aged 21–23 years. (Sex proportions were not balanced since girls form the majority of high-school pupils and young women dominate in the humanities departments of the university.) Two high-school pupils, not having grandparents, wrote about non-relatives, and one treated the subject in a parody manner, leaving seventy-two compositions to be analysed; while one of the university students without grandparents wrote about what he imagined them to be like, leaving sixty-six compositions. Thus 138 compositions in total were analysed.

First, each composition was analysed by means of a set of categories which comprised evaluation of composition level, data concerning grandparents' characteristics, and information about contacts, relations and interactions between grandchildren and grandparents. Second, any subjective evaluation of contacts with grandparents – what these contacts brought into their life, what role grandparents played in their physical, cognitive, social, emotional and moral development, and how they shaped their personality – were categorized. The four categories of grandparent – maternal grandmother (MGM), maternal grandfather (MGF), paternal grandmother (PGM), and paternal grandfather (PGF) – were treated separately.

The role of grandparents in the life and development of grandchildren as illustrated in the compositions

Table 4.1 shows the number of grandparents reported and described in the subjects' compositions. They are those grandparents whom the subjects knew and who played some, more or less significant, role in their life. Each subject described approximately 1.6 grandparent figures in their composition. Considerably more grandmothers than grandfathers were described. Paternal grandfathers were the fewest. Since women are usually younger than their

Table 4.1 Number of grandparents mentioned in 138 compositions

Group of subjects	MGM		MGF		PGM		PGF		
	Alive	Dead	Alive	Dead	Alive	Dead	Alive	Dead	Total
AD (n=72)	32	8	16	9	19	10	13	8	115
YA (n=66)	31	14	14	10	12	14	4	5	104
Total	63	22	30	19	31	24	17	13	219

AD = adolescents; YA = young adults
MGM = maternal grandmother; MGF = maternal grandfather; PGM = paternal grandmother;
  PGF = paternal grandfather

53

husbands, and mothers' parents are usually younger than fathers' parents, it is not surprising that the subjects had more opportunity to know their grandmothers than to know their grandfathers, and to know more maternal grandparents than paternal ones.

Both living and dead grandparents were mentioned in the compositions, and the sex proportions confirm the higher male mortality. The data thus reflect the general picture of the demographic situation in that age group to which grandparents of contemporary Polish adolescents and young adults belong.

The frequency of contacts between grandchildren and grandparents

In order for social and emotional bonds between grandchildren and grandparents to arise and continue, a certain frequency of contacts in the form of visits and perhaps longer periods of staying together is necessary. For the 'frequency of contact' variable, analysis used a 6-point scale: *no visits* mentioned or the fact of no visits stated; *seldom*, one to three times a year; *rather often*, about once a month; *often*, about once a week; *very often*, almost every day; *everyday contact*, living together. The data (for living grandparents only) is shown in Table 4.2.

Table 4.2 Frequency of contacts with 137 living grandparents

Frequency contacts	Categories of grandparents and groups of subjects								
	MGM		MGF		PGM		PGF		
	AD	YA	AD	YA	AD	YA	AD	YA	Total
No visits	6	1	3	0	2	0	1	0	13
Seldom	7	7	1	2	6	4	6	2	35
Rather often	3	5	6	3	3	3	3	1	27
Often	6	4	4	2	2	2	2	0	22
Very often	4	6	1	3	4	1	1	1	21
Everyday contact	4	8	0	3	1	2	0	1	19

AD = adolescents; YA = young adults
MGM = maternal grandmother; MGF = maternal grandfather; PGM = paternal grandmother; PGF = paternal grandfather

Out of 137 living grandfathers and grandmothers for whom the issue was mentioned, adolescent and adult grandchildren kept contact with 124 of them. Only in thirteen cases (9.5 per cent) did subjects not report any contacts with grandparents, which does not mean that no such contacts existed. Only four subjects openly declared an almost complete absence of contact with any grandparent – one with MGM ('Grandma quarrelled with Mummy every time she came to us and now we no longer see her'), one with PGM (due to conflicts between grandmothers and parents), one with MGF (after he remarried and moved away) and one with both MGPs (due to conflicts caused by their joining Jehovah's

Witnesses). Thus having no real contact with living grandparents was rare in our sample and was caused by conflicting relations between the old and the middle-aged generation in the family.

The frequency of contacts between grandchildren and grandparents largely depends on the distance between their places of residence. The most frequent contacts occur when grandparents and grandchildren live close to each other in the same locality. The contacts grow weaker with grandchildren's age; the most frequent occur in childhood. Their intensity decreases in later stages of grand-children's development, especially after they go to secondary school or leave for college. None the less, grandchildren tend to keep in touch with their grandparents. This may be because the emotional bond, formed in childhood, still endures; also adolescents and young adults may visit their grandparents either because the latter represent to them their lost childhood or because the state of their health demands this.

In nineteen (13.9 per cent) cases grandparents lived with the subjects' families. Another seventeen subjects (nine from AD, eight from YA) remembered that they were brought up in grandparents' homes in the first few years of life (up to 5–7, or even 10 years). In all these cases grandparents actually performed the role of parents, and close bonds with grandchildren had lasted up to the time of the study. Grandparents took over complete child-care in these cases, especially when the baby was their daughter's first-born and at the same time their first grandchild.

When the contact of grandchildren with grandparents was fairly frequent (from once a month to almost every day), and the character of the relation positive, the latter often played the role of significant persons, sometimes subjectively more important than parents to the former. However, grandparents, especially grand-mothers, tend to be less attractive to grandchildren when they actually live together with them.

Emotional tone of statements about grandparents

The subjects' statements about grandparents represented different kinds of emotional attitude: from love and admiration through neutral description to signs of aversion and hostility. These seem to express a generalized evaluation of grandchild–grandparent relations in their emotional aspect. This is a well-known condition of effective influence on socialization (Aronson, 1972).

The emotional tone of the utterances concerning a given grandparent were analysed as: *negative* (for example, 'keeps nagging at me', 'she's terrible', 'I don't like my grandmother because she hasn't done anything for us'); *neutral* (neither positive nor negative, statements of a descriptive character); *positive* (such as 'nice', 'good', 'fine', positive characteristics prevailing in the description); or *very positive* (only very positive features or a description of extremely close, positive relations). The frequency of occurrence of each class, for the 194 living or dead grandparents for whom such information was available, is shown in Table 4.3.

Table 4.3 Emotional tone of utterances concerning 194 living and dead grandparents

Emotional tone	Categories of grandparents and groups of subjects								
	MGM		MGF		PGM		PGF		
	AD	YA	AD	YA	AD	YA	AD	YA	Total
Negative	4	2	0	0	1	5	1	0	13
Neutral	13	6	7	7	16	8	9	3	64
Positive	15	18	15	5	8	7	9	4	62
Very positive	8	19	4	12	3	7	2	2	55

X^2 for emotional tone negative/neutral v. positive/very positive
- for MGPs v. PGPs: $X^2(1) = 10.4$; $p < 0.01$
- for MGM v. PGM: $X^2(1) = 20.0$; $p < 0.001$
- for MGM v. MGF: $X^2(1) = 4.3$; $p < 0.05$
- for PGM v. PGF: $X^2(1) = 8.9$; $p < 0.01$
- for MGF v. PGF: $X^2(1) = 11.5$; $p < 0.01$

AD = adolescents; YA = young adults
MGM = maternal grandmother; MGF = maternal grandfather; PGM = paternal grandmother;
PGF = paternal grandfather

Some researchers (such as Cohler and Grunebaum 1980; Hurme 1988) point to a strong relationship of maternal grandmothers with their daughters' families, and commonplace observation indicates that grandmothers much more frequently than grandfathers look after grandchildren. It was therefore expected that the emotional tone of statements about grandmothers, particularly MGMs, will be more positive than the tone of utterances about grandfathers. The results confirm these expectations. The emotional attitude of grandchildren towards grandparents is generally positive and expresses a deep attachment. However, the attitude to MGPs is more often positive and very positive than towards PGPs, and to grandmothers more positive than to grandfathers. Grandmothers are also more frequently presented in an emotionally negative tone, whereas in the case of grandfathers (both MGFs and PGFs) such an attitude is very rare. Grandmothers, especially MGMs, by taking a prominent place in grandchildren's lives, become the object of emotions varying in character and intensity. Grandfathers, on the other hand, contact with whom is more festive, can be the object of mainly positive emotions, though of moderate intensity. This may also be connected with grandchildren's age; adolescents especially rebel against grandmother's authority when she assumes the role of a second (or rather first) mother and the main person in the family. Close contacts in such cases create an occasion for conflict. A closer analysis also reveals that negative attitudes towards grandmothers are more frequently expressed by grandsons than granddaughters.

An unfriendly and negative emotional attitude towards grandparents can also be caused by their personality characteristics or/and social and cultural distance dividing a grandchild and his nuclear family from grandparents.

Thus, for instance, an 18-year-old granddaughter writes about her MGM: 'She's always running about, grumbling, nagging and shouting. She's full of aggression and doesn't understand, doesn't feel a need for any closeness or affection.' Another 18-year-old wrote about her PGM: 'I don't like my grandmother, she's sloppy and disagreeable. I don't know what to talk with her about. I don't like visiting her. When I see her I feel a mixture of contempt, compassion and guilt.' And a 17-year-old granddaughter wrote about her PGF: 'lazy old egoist'.

Conflicting relations between grandparents and parents also have a negative bearing on the grandchild–grandparent relationship. A 22-year-old granddaughter writes about her MGM: 'My relations with grandmother have always been official. Grandma doesn't like my mother because father married Mum against her [grandmother's] will. What should I love her for? She's never lent us a helping hand and she openly discriminates against us, her grandchildren.'

The emotional attitude towards grandparents and the character of the grandchild–grandparent relationship are also in a large measure conditioned by what they are imagined and expected to be. From the content analysis of compositions, adolescents and young adults imagine their grandparents to be helpful, devoted to their children and grandchildren, protective, cheerful and, above all, utterly self-giving without expecting anything in return. According to these expectations, grandparents should give up their own life and take care of grandchildren, or be of help to their adult children or grandchildren whenever they need it. This is the reason why any example of different grandparent behaviour provokes a reaction of surprise, dislike and sometimes hostile resentment. This is clearly expressed in the opinion of a 22-year-old student, negative towards her MGPs, who writes: 'Grandparents took a rather strange position – they thought that children should exclusively be taken care of by parents. And when mother had a hard time raising us, they would go to the cinema, or on holidays, or have fun. Oh yes, they bought us sweets and many necessary things but they would never take care of us.'

Among the many positive features and highly valued behaviour of grandmothers and grandfathers, the fact that they sacrificed their time (and still do so), cared for grandchildren and sometimes provided them with a home in childhood is appreciated most by adolescent and adult grandchildren.

Activities performed together with grandparents

In the compositions, subjects listed a number of activities which they performed together with grandparents. The frequency of these is shown in Figure 4.1. The most frequent activities performed together with grandparents, as spontaneously reported by the subjects, are conversations, walks and games (in childhood, playing together). This shows their subjective importance to adolescents and young adults. It may also be an adequate reflection of reality.

Conversations carried on by adolescent and adult grandchildren with grandparents seem to be of particular significance to them because hard-working parents do not have enough time or patience for conversation with their children, and because the existence of a mutual bond with and, at the same time, a distance from their grandparents allows them to talk about matters which they would not like to reveal to their parents. Many subjects stressed that conversations with

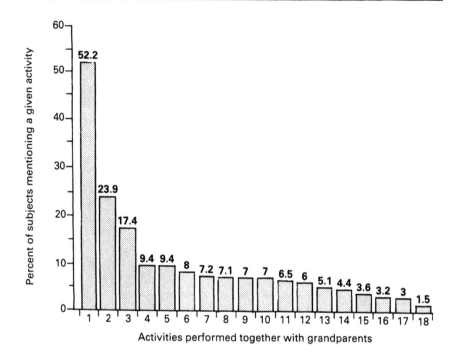

Categories of activities performed together with grandparents

1 Conversations
2 Walks
3 Plays and games
4 Cooking
5 Cleaning, housework
6 Gardening, work in the field
7 Shopping
8 Looking all over the family pictures and souvenirs
9 Fancy work, tampering
10 Excursions, travelling
11 Preparing parties and participating in them
12 Playing music, singing
13 Reading
14 Visiting relatives and friends
15 Fishing
16 Discussions and making more important decisions
17 Taking care of pet animals
18 Common prayers

Figure 4.1 Joint activities with grandparents

grandparents are carried out in an atmosphere of peace, understanding and tolerance. Thus, a 17-year-old grandson writes that he likes to talk with his grandmother (PGM) because 'she is patient and understanding. She knows how to advise for and advise against'. That is why adolescent and adult grandchildren talk with grandparents about their problems, and also ask advice in taking more important decisions.

Other activities performed together with grandparents involve recreation, learning practical skills and being introduced into family traditions. All these activities are connected with a pleasant atmosphere and are evaluated as emotionally positive. Mutual contacts, relations and activities performed in common provide grandchildren with various kinds of experience, and create the basis for grandparent influence upon the individual development of grandchildren.

How adolescents and young adults perceive the role of grandparents in their life and development

As we have seen, the subjects in most cases gave a positive evaluation of their grandparents. What did they value most in grandparents and about their contact with them?

The analysis showed that adolescents and young adults value their grandparents first of all as seniors of the family, 'a stem from which the other members of the family grow', or, in the words of a 15-year-old boy: 'Grandparents are important and I love them because if it hadn't been for them there wouldn't be my father, my mother and me.' Grandparents are also valued and emotionally accepted because they hold the family together as a kind of 'axis around which the whole family centres'. It is with them that holidays and family celebrations are spent, they provide the meeting ground for all uncles, aunts and their families – that is, the whole circle of the extended family. Such occasions give a sense of belonging, of community and closeness based on kinship. Grandparents are also loved in response for their own love of grandchildren, for their affection and devotion. Their love can be trusted. It gives a sense of support. As one 17-year-old high-school boy writes: 'I believe and I know that they always want the best for me.'

One decisive influence on grandchildren's attitude to grandparents, their subjective evaluation and (indirectly) the grandparents' role in grandchildren's development, is whether they give them their time freely. This thought appears in most compositions of both age groups. Sacrificing one's time is considered as the greatest gift and is highly appreciated regardless of whether it took place in childhood or later in life. Inherent here is not only a noteworthy intuition (what greater gift can one person offer another than his or her time, that is, a part of his or her life?) but also a premise of mutual interactions. Time spent together creates an opportunity for sharing of experience and the formation of social and emotional ties. Mutual close contacts also allow grandparents and grandchildren to talk and exchange thoughts and experience. ('When we go fishing with Grandpa, we talk. We tell each other about ourselves.' 'With Grandma I can talk about my problems.') Conversations with grandparents not only favour the exchange but also the elaboration of experience. Besides, they undoubtedly perform an important psychotherapeutic role.

The analysis of composition content allows us to distinguish several spheres of the grandparents' influence on and role in the development of grandchildren. The number of subjects who mentioned each of the following categories in their composition is stated.

Participation in providing care and support (fifty subjects)

Some of the subjects (thirty-nine) were brought up in childhood by and in the home of grandparents. Others had grandmothers for babysitters while mother was at work. Many spent vacation at their grandparents', not only in preschool and younger school age but later as well. This was an opportunity to be longer with grandparents living in distance places or in the country. If grandparents lived in wooded areas, or in a landscape grandchildren were unfamiliar with, the holidays had an additional advantage. They were always attractive, a fact which grandchildren in later years associate with grandparents. Referring to holidays spent together with grandparents, some young adults entitled their compositions 'Grandparents are sunny holidays', 'Attractive holidays', and so on.

Both grandparents raising grandchildren and those with whom grandchildren spent holidays provided them with care as well as the best food and living conditions they could afford. They bought them such things as toys, more attractive clothes and so forth. They satisfied many of their biological and psychic needs and provided them with good conditions for physical development and health. This child-care, however, also has a social and psychological dimension. It ensures grandchildren a feeling of security and belonging. Five of the adolescents and twelve of the young adults reported with gratitude and pride: 'It was thanks to them (her) that I never was a child with a key round my neck'; that is, homeless after school before parents' return from work. Several subjects also remembered that from time to time, when they were tired of kindergarten community living, parents took them 'on leave' and sent them to grandparents.

Visits with grandparents are also a good occasion for rest and psychic relaxation after everyday duties and stress at home and in school. A quiet, unhurried and friendly atmosphere and, above all, strongly felt love and acceptance by grandparents allow grandchildren to relax, feel comfortable and express themselves freely. That is also why conversations with grandparents are subjectively important for grandchildren. Not infrequently adolescents and young adults report that they slip away from home to grandparents, especially when they go through some periods of trouble. Their love and wisdom of life is a source of psychic and moral support in moments of stress and frustration quite common in adolescence and young adulthood. The possibility of a gentle conversation or simple immersion in a loving atmosphere and being personally important allows them to regain positive self-evaluation and strengthens resistance to stress.

Participation in the process of socialization (seventy-six subjects)

When grandparents bring grandchildren up they actually perform the social role of parents. However, even if they live apart but their contacts are frequent enough, grandparents perform an important role in grandchildren's socialization. They support parents in the process of children assimilating socially accepted norms of behaviour and rules of conduct. As the child grows older, they also reinforce behaviour proper for his or her sex. 'Grandmother taught me how to be a woman,' writes a 22-year-old student remembering her contacts with grandmother in her puberty. Through their own behaviour grandparents provide models of performing social roles, thus strengthening the impact of parents' models and, to some extent, rendering them relative. This helps children to acquire a certain flexibility in the manner of behaviour.

Grandparents teach grandchildren a number of practical skills, especially those connected with housekeeping and gardening. These roles are performed both by grandmothers (more often towards granddaughters) and grandfathers (more often towards grandsons). Grandparent–grandchild contacts are also an occasion to convey information about the world – about nature, society and technology. This includes information connected with grandmother's or grandfather's profession or interests. Thus, for instance, a chemist grandfather gives the child information about drugs and chemistry. But also a worker grandfather, very keen on fishing, gives his grandson much valuable information about fish, their habits and behaviour. Such knowledge, acquired occasionally in conditions of good emotional interaction, can be more deeply assimilated and is felt to be one's own, more natural than school or book knowledge.

Grandparents hand down to grandchildren information about their family, about ancestors, relatives and their own past. This is the first source of the feeling of being rooted in society. In the period of genealogical curiosity (approximately 9–10 years) it provides material for constructing one's own genealogy. For this reason it is very important that the child should have contact with grandparents and information about the families of both parents.

Grandparents also perform a role in introducing grandchildren to the world of symbolic culture, as sensitive 'ushers' (Miller 1981) opening the door to a world of literature and art. Nearly all the subjects remember that a grandfather or a grandmother told them fairy-tales in childhood, sang lullabies and folk-songs or read books to them. Grandparents living in or coming from the country taught them folk couplets and told tales, anecdotes and fables that they themselves had heard in their youth. Later in grandchildren's development this took the form of common reading, watching television films, talking about books, films and music, as well as, in some cases, playing music together. This early contact with art, arranged by grandparents, has a definite influence on the formation of imagination and aesthetic sensibility. This is also helped by common walks and sightseeing, when grandparents point out to the children the beauty of nature, architecture and various details in the surroundings.

Five subjects reported that grandmothers taught them to say their prayers, took them to church and instructed them in principles of religious faith, thus introducing them into that branch of symbolic culture which is religion.

Grandparents can perform an important role in introducing grandchildren into national traditions and history of the country, and patriotic ideals. Almost 20 per cent of the subjects reported that grandparents told them about the country's past: in childhood – legends and historical episodes; later – most often the history of the Second World War. The stories of war and Nazi occupation form grandchildren's first ideas about that period of the history of the country long before they start learning history at school. At the same time, it is lively knowledge, shown through the filter of personal experience and thus most credible. Only grandparents who survived concentration camps are unwilling to tell grandchildren about their experience.

Grandparents as personality models (twenty-two subjects)

Adolescents and young adults frequently emphasize that grandparents (or one grandparent) provided them with models of personality and life patterns, complementing or (occasionally) supplanting parents. The varied evaluation of grandparents obtained suggests that the statements are reasonably true and do not just reflect a general stereotype.

Grandchildren admire first of all hard work, honesty and patriotism of their grandparents. They also show respect for their energy, activity and intellect. The role of models in patriotism is played by those grandparents who were killed in the war or died long ago but live on in family tradition. To see the photographs of a grandfather who, a little over twenty, went to war and died before her mother was born makes one of the subjects, a girl student, reflect upon both his sacrifice and the senselessness of war. Grandchildren may also take over from grandparents attitudes towards life, work, other people and values. The subjects are surprised to discover their similarity to grandparents in certain respects. They find it impressive that grandparents are 'proud and worthy people', 'reliable and respected', 'professionals in their jobs'.

Adolescents and young adults may take a critical and severe view of their grandparents' lives, and their judgement is generally just. At the same time, however, they can appreciate their real achievements in life: that they raised their children to be honest, wise and good people, that they enjoy the respect of their community and, above all, their resourcefulness and the ability they showed to overcome adversities of life. Hence admiration for grandmothers who, having early lost their husbands, managed by themselves to raise their children; for grandfathers who, not having any education themselves, managed to ensure education for their children; admiration finally for those who, for many years in marriage, had love and respect for each other and created a warm and serene home for their children and grandchildren.

Grandchildren find many of these features worthy of imitation, and in some cases grandparents are for them personality patterns. Analysing their grandparents' lives leads them to the conclusion that, as one of the subjects expressed it, theirs is 'a pattern of life that can be lived actively and not just gone through'. Another subject sums up grandparents' influence on his development with these words: 'It is to them that I owe who I am.'

The course of life and death of grandparents as a source of ideas about and reflection upon human life (thirty-two subjects)

Experiences connected with grandparents as well as observation of grandparents and parents and the knowledge of their life leads grandchildren to realize that there are different stages of life and, in particular, different stages of adulthood and old age. Photographs of grandparents in their youth or even childhood are material to form ideas about the course of human life and the stages a person goes through. Although young people cannot imagine their old age, the experience of contact with grandparents helps them to form and develop biographical consciousness.

Contact with grandparents, especially in adolescence and later, leads grandchildren to understand that the old-fashioned views of the former, their different tastes and habits and their ignorance of some skills and habits (such as working modern video equipment) come from the fact that their life was lived in a different epoch, in different social and cultural conditions. 'Grandma doesn't like pop music', writes a 17-year-old grandson, 'because in her youth they used to play waltzes, polkas and other such old-fashioned pieces.' Contact with grandparents thus provides an opportunity to understand that different qualities of people from different age cohorts are created by different conditions of living. It also leads to a certain relativization of one's convictions and values. This requires grandchildren to learn decentration, so important for psychic development, and tolerance for that which is different.

Grandparents' lives, and also their deaths, help adolescents and young adults reflect upon strategy and style of human life in general. More reflexive individuals are also led to ponder over their own life. If grandparents' life-styles are highly regarded they are given due respect 'for how they lived' and 'because they knew how to live their lives with dignity'.

A serious illness and especially death of grandparents is a powerful experience for grandchildren. Eight subjects wrote about their grandmother's or grandfather's serious sclerosis and the changes caused by the illness. Adolescents are made aware, sometimes painfully, of the relation between the organic state on the one hand and behaviour and and psychic functions on the other. Even grandsons who have earlier been in sharp conflict with their grandmothers put themselves at their disposal in such cases, run to the chemist's for medicines and help parents in caring for the sick grandma.

A grandfather's or a grandmother's death, if it happened after the grandchild's ninth to tenth year (cf. Hurlock 1978), causes an experience which the subjects define as a shock. The subjects, both adolescents and young adults, describe this as a sudden realization that death is irreversible and that everything has to pass. They experience probably the first irreversible loss of someone well-known and loved. They become aware that not every illness can be helped, that the past cannot come back and, finally, that every human being (they too) will die one day. (This last realization brings sometimes a passing hypochondriac attitude.)

Emotionally, the experience is presented as sadness and grief mixed with helplessness and remorse for having neglected grandparents, for not having shown enough attachment and for having annoyed them. Generally speaking, a certain number of the subjects state that the death of (the first) grandfather or grandmother meant for them 'the end of childhood'. The experience stays in grandchildren's memory for many years after their grandparents' death.

Critical remarks concerning grandparents: their negative impact (fifteen subjects)

Adolescents and young adults also point to some negative sides of grandparents' influence on the development of grandchildren. The attitude most often defined as unfavourable is over-protectiveness. Comforting in childhood, it later begins to disturb grandchildren as they subjectively perceive it. This is because over-protectiveness cramps their self-dependence and subjectivity, in a way 'incapacitating' them. Moreover, it makes them look ridiculous in the eyes of their peers, a fact which grandparents (usually grandmothers) seldom realize.

According to some subjects, grandparents are too liberal – 'They let us do anything, even against parents' orders.' This may not only cause family conflicts but also confuse the child and make him or her feel guilty towards the parents (a kind of double loyalty). Therefore, grandchildren criticize grandparents for their 'love with no bounds and no demands'.

Grandparents (especially grandmothers living together with grandchildren) may be seen as meddlesome and trying to interfere excessively in grandchildren's life and affairs. These features are especially manifest in grandchildren's adolescence. They cause conflicts and weaken emotional relations.

Parent–grandparent conflicts are felt to be annoying, and the blame is usually put on grandparents. However, grandchildren feel that any dislike or even hostility they may feel towards grandparents is a sign of abnormal relations in the family.

Other grandparents' characteristics, such as old-fashioned views, rigidity, hypocrisy in relations with people, and so on are also treated by grandchildren as vagaries and obstacles in mutual contact. By making communication and acceptance difficult, these features can seriously restrict grandparents' possible educational influence. Only those grandparents who themselves, as individuals, develop will have a strong influence on grandchild development.

If a grandmother's or grandfather's attitude towards them is cool and distant, grandchildren may feel bitter and resentful, as if they were deprived of something that by nature is their due. In these cases they sharply criticize grandparents for their alleged egoism or inability to sacrifice.

Not to have grandparents or any contact with them, at least in childhood, is regarded as a factor responsible for 'the impoverishment of life'.

Summary and discussion

This research dealt with the role of grandparents in the life and development of grandchildren, as perceived by the latter. A broader study would consider the perspectives of different family generations and carry out a scientific evaluation of the results of grandparents' influence on grandchildren. Our investigation was only an attempt at exploring this issue. The conclusions from this study thus reveal only the general outline and only one side of the problem in question.

Any interaction of individuals upon themselves (grandparent–grandchild relations also involving such two-directional feedback interaction) is only possible when there is a flow of information and interpersonal exchange. Direct contact and a certain amount of common experience are favourable to this. Our adolescent and young adult subjects have had and (if their grandparents are still alive) do have relatively frequent contact with grandparents. In a dominant number of cases (117 versus 77), they feel bound by strong positive emotional ties.

The way grandparents are perceived by adolescents and young adults is influenced by the frequency and character of contacts with them, by certain social and individual characteristics of grandparents (as well as grandchildren), and by the ideas that representatives of the young generation have of what their grandparents should be like.

Intergenerational contacts and ties in Polish families generally remain close and strong despite the fact that representatives of different generations often live far from one another and may differ considerably in the level of education or in life-style. This is also largely true of grandchild–grandparent relations. Occasionally, however, great cultural differences make closer ties difficult and eliminate possible mutual interaction. This may be thought of as a particular cost of the rapid development of the country in the post-war period, particularly of industrialization and urbanization.

The relation of grandparents – that is, people in late and mid-adulthood – to grandchildren is characterized by love, observable by even those grandchildren who are critical towards their grandparents, and not infrequently by sacrifice. Manifest here is not only generativity, characteristic of people in this stage of life (Erikson 1968, 1980), but also a conviction, frequent in the older generation of Poles, that children and grandchildren must be provided with a bountiful and happy childhood even at the cost of one's own greatest deprivations. These attitudes may originate in Polish grandparents' tendency to compensate for their own childhood privations and tragic experiences. They may in turn produce in grandchildren some inordinate expectations concerning grandparents. These expectations most certainly have a bearing upon the way adolescents and young adults perceive and evaluate their grandparents.

Adolescents and young adults first of all associate grandparents with their own

65

childhood. In later years contacts between grandparents and grandchildren become less intense but the sense of ties lasts.

The analysis of the subjects' compositions confirmed hypotheses concerning grandparents' influence upon grandchildren's development. As grandchildren perceive it, grandparents in most cases influence their individual development. In childhood and adolescence (and perhaps later), grandchildren learn much from them. This involves not only a number of practical skills but also general knowledge, and attitudes to the world and to other people. Grandparents may acquaint grandchildren with the knowledge of their family and ancestors. They often lead them – especially in childhood – into different domains of symbolic culture, representing other segments of national culture than those presented by parents and school. Grandparents living in or coming from the country transmit to city-born grandchildren some elements of folk culture. This confirms results of research by ethnographers (Jasiewicz 1989). From grandparents' accounts of events in their life as well as their childhood and youth experience, grandchildren gain information about the nation's most recent history. This is a living intergenerational transmission of experience. Grandchildren and grandparents belong to different cohorts not simply as regards age but also as regards historical time (Schaie 1984), defining their different experience of life and different educational training in childhood and youth. In regard to their lifespan, grandparents have lived through several periods of the life cycle longer than grandchildren. They possess a great wealth of experience which they are generally (except in some extremely tragic instances) eager to share with grandchildren. The acquaintance with grandparents' life stories provides grandchildren with material for reflection upon general laws governing the course of human life and a basis for the formation of biographic imagination.

Close contacts, interactions and especially conversations with grandparents play an important role in the elaboration, ordering and evaluation of grandchildren's individual experience, helping also in its structuring. This is of great significance for grandchildren's individual development. Grandparents may also occasionally play the role of personal models important for the formation of grandchildren's personality. However, it is only frequent and close contacts, and especially longer periods of staying together and performing activities in common with grandparents, which allow attachment and create a basis for transmission of experience, talks important to both parties and grandparents' influence as behaviour and personality models.

References

Aronson, E. (1972) *The Social Animal*, San Francisco and London: W.H. Freeman.
Cassirer, E. (1977) *Esej o czlowieku* (The Essay on Man), Warsaw: Czytelnik.
Cohler, B.J. and Grunebaum, H.U. (1980) *Mothers, Grandmothers and Daughters: Personality and Child-care in Three-generation Families*, New York: John Wiley & Sons.
Czikszentmihaly, M., Larson, R. and Prescott, S. (1977) 'The ecology of adolescent

activity and experience', *Journal of Youth and Adolescence* 6: 281–94.

Ericsson, K.A. and Simon, H.A. (1984) *Protocol Analysis: Verbal Reports as Data*, Cambridge, MA: MIT Press.

Erikson, E.H. (1968) *Identity: Youth and Crisis*, New York: Norton.

Erikson, E.H. (1980) *Identity and the Life Cycle*, New York: Norton.

Havighurst, R. (1977) *Developmental Tasks and Education*, New York: Longmans Green.

Hurlock, E.B. (1978) *Child Development*, New York: McGraw-Hill.

Hurme, H. (1988) *Child, Mother and Grandmother*, Jyväskylä, University of Jyväskylä.

Jasiewicz, Z. (1989) 'Opowiadanie i spiewanie dzieciom w rodzinie' (Telling stories and singing to children in a family), in M. Tyszkowa and B. Zurakowski (eds), *Obszary sptokan dziecka i doroslego w sztuce* (The areas of child-adult encounters in art), Poznan: Panstwowe Wydawnictwo Naukowe.

Kmita, J. (1985) *Kultura a poznanie* (Culture and Cognition), Warsaw: Panstwowe Wydawnictwo Naukowe.

Miller, R. (1981) *Socjalizacja, wychowanie, psychoterapie* (Socialization, education and psychotherapy), Warsaw: Panstwowe Wydawnictwo Naukowe.

Piaget, J. (1967) *La psychologie de l'intelligence*, Paris: Armand Colin.

Schaie, K.W. (1984) 'Historical time and cohort effects', in K.A. McCloskey and H.W. Reese (eds), *Life-Span Developmental Psychology: Historical and Generational Effects*, New York: Academic Press.

Tyszka, Z. (1979) *Socjologia rodziny* (Sociology of the family), Warsaw: Panstwowe Wydawnictwo Naukowe.

Tyszka, Z. (1982) *Rodziny wspolczesne w Polsce* (Contemporary Polish families), Poznan: UAM.

Tyszkowa, M. (1986a), 'Psychic development of the individual: a process of structuring and restructuring experience', in P. van Geert (ed.), *Theory Building in Developmental Psychology*, Amsterdam: North Holland Publishers.

Tyszkowa, M. (1986b) 'Cykl zycia rodziny a rozwoj indywidualny' (The family life cycle and the development of the individual), in M. Ziemska (ed.), *Spoleczne konsekwencje integracji i dezintegracji rodziny*, vol. 2, Warsaw: TWWP.

Chapter five

Grandparent–grandchild relationships amongst US ethnic groups

Emmy E. Werner

Everyone needs to have access both to grandparents and grandchildren in order to be a full human being.

Margaret Mead, *Blackberry Winter: My Earlier Years*

After decades of benign neglect, grandparents have been 'rediscovered'. In 1978, the US Congress passed legislation setting the first Sunday after Labor Day (in September) as Grandparents Day. American grandchildren and their parents now purchase millions of Grandparents Day cards each year. However, the political and commercial attention paid to grandparents is not quite matched by our scientific knowledge about their roles and the nature of their interactions with their children and grandchildren. This chapter will review what we do know about grandparent-grandchild relations among the different ethnic groups in the USA.

Our knowledge is based on clinical impressions, survey data and a few longitudinal studies which have been conducted in the past decade. With few exceptions (Cherlin and Furstenberg 1986; and Kornhaber and Woodward 1981), the empirical evidence is based on relatively small samples of grandparents and/or grandchildren, and the interpretation of these data reflect, to some extent, the biases of the different professions which are concerned with grandparents: anthropologists, psychologists, psychiatrists, social workers and sociologists.

Research on grandparents and grandparent–grandchild relations tends to be descriptive; what conceptual underpinnings one may detect come mostly from social role theory. Lately, developmental psychologists have introduced attachment theory into the study of elder–child relationships, and a few investigators have found it helpful to view grandparent–grandchild relationships from an evolutionary perspective.

Kahana and Kahana (1971) have provided a perspective on grandparenthood that gives some organization to the knowledge we have so far. They suggest that grandparenthood can be viewed as a *social role*, involving ascribed status and expectations of role performance, *vis-à-vis* the family or the society at large. Cherlin and Furstenberg's (1986) book, *The New American Grandparent: a Place in the Family, a Life Apart*, followed this approach, as have many other studies conducted by sociologists. At the opposite end, grandparenthood can be viewed as an *emotional state* or *intrapsychic* experience, part of an individual's development. This view emerges predominantly in studies by psychiatrists – for example, in the 1981 book by Kornhaber and Woodward, *Grandparents/Grandchildren: the Vital Connection.*

Grandparenthood can be considered a *transaction* between grandchild and grandparent, involving reciprocity. Three recent reviews by developmental psychologists on grandparents as socializing agents and sources of support have emphasized this point of view (Campbell and Buholz 1982; Tinsley and Parke 1984; and Werner 1984).

Grandparenthood can also be viewed within the context of a *group process within the family*, involving relationships and interdependencies between three generations. Cohler's and Gruenebaum's (1981) book, *Mothers, Grandmothers, and Daughters*, takes this approach. Finally, grandparenthood may be considered a *symbol*. It can be a reflection of continuity, potency and usefulness to society. Lillian Troll's (1983) view of grandparents as 'family watchdogs' is such a symbol.

Regardless of our perspective on grandparent–grandchild relations, we can agree on a few important facts: changes in family structure, fertility, mortality, mobility, means of communication, and labour-force participation have transformed American grandparenthood dramatically since the Second World War. More people are living long enough to become grandparents, but there are fewer grandchildren to go around. Modern grandparents can keep in touch more easily with their grandchildren, and they have more time to devote to them. Their grandchildren, in turn, may need them more. Most mothers in the USA now enter the labour force when their children are only infants, or at best, of preschool age; and nearly half of all American children will experience their parents' divorce and will spend an average of five years in a single-parent home. These trends are aggravated if grandchildren are born into a context of poverty, as is every fifth child in the USA today (Children's Defense Fund 1989).

Roles of grandparents in contemporary America

The average age of becoming a grandparent for the first time in the USA is in the mid and late forties. In the future Americans will have their first grandchild probably at an age approximating that of Europeans, since the 'modal' age at which American women marry is advancing, and becoming more consistent with the pattern in other industrialized nations (Giraldo 1980).

In spite of the vast distances of the country and the great mobility of Americans, most grandparents live in close proximity (within a half hour of transportation) to at least one of their children, and have regular contact with them and their grandchildren (Cherlin and Furstenberg 1986; Harris *et al.* 1975). In a large national survey, including some 550 grandparents, the majority (60 per cent) saw their grandchildren at least once or twice a month. Among the grandparents who saw their children less often, *distance* was the major geographical barrier to contact and closer ties (Cherlin and Furstenberg 1986; Timberlake 1980).

The types of services rendered for their grandchildren seem to be similar for grandparents in the United States and Western Europe, and include babysitting, looking after the grandchildren when their parents go to work, and occasionally being a surrogate parent for a grandchild. Grandparents' involvement with and services for their grandchildren tend to reach a peak in their preschool years.

The grandparents' *own* perceptions of their roles have been explored by a number of investigators, from the classic study by Neugarten and Weinstein (1964) to research undertaken by Wood and Robertson (1976), Kivnick (1982), and Cherlin and Furstenberg (1986). Although these studies include different generations of grandparents, living in different regions of the country (from the Eastern seaboard to the Midwest to the Far West), they come to similar conclusions: intergenerational relationships between grandparents and grandchildren seem to vary on a continuum from *remote* relationships (for about 28 per cent) to *companionate* relationships for the majority (some 55 per cent), to very *involved* relationships for a minority. Grandmothers tend to do more of the 'kin-keeping', grandfathers concentrate more on shared tasks and activities with their grandchildren (Cherlin and Furstenberg 1986; Thomas 1986).

Clavan (1978) has suggested that the grandparent role differs by degrees of *functional centrality* in middle and lower socio-economic class families. For the middle class, the role is more *ideological* than real, in the sense that, although there is a kinship position of grandparent, there are no normative rights and obligations attached to this position in the USA. Becoming a valued grandparent is an option open to the grandparent which she or he may not choose to take, and usually involves only *supplementary* parenting. In poor families, on the other hand, the grandparent is more integrated into family life, and performs many valued and needed parenting activities, including serving as a *surrogate* parent. Here the grandparent role becomes more real.

Supplementary parenting by grandparents

In studies of American families in which the third generation is included, the most frequent help extended by grandparents is babysitting. This seems to be true regardless of geographical location, social class or ethnicity. In a classic study of kin contact among Caucasian families in the Midwest, Hill and his associates (1970) found that some 78 per cent of the parents received this help, and that 50 per cent of the grandparents, and 16 per cent of the great-grandparents provided it. The same was true for black families of that generation in the American South. Jackson (1971) reported that 80 per cent of the offspring of black middle-class elders, and 92 per cent of the offspring of black manual workers reported getting help in child-care from gandparents.

Five years later, Kitano and Kikumura (1976) reported that many Japanese-Americans on the West Coast absorb grandparents into the household who assist with child-care, and Huang (1976) found that most Chinese-American children grow up in the midst of adults, including grandparents who act as babysitters.

Seña-Rivera (1979) studied Mexican-American working-class families in the Midwest and reported the same trends. All families mentioned frequent babysitting and assistance with child-care by both maternal and paternal grandmothers.

Since these studies were done, there has been an enormous increase in the proportion of women with young children who are in the labour force (Werner 1984). Among such two wage-earner families, grandparents are the preferred in-home caretaker regardless of whether mother or father work full- or part-time. Among the family day-care providers (equivalents of British 'child minders') interviewed in a national study by the US Department of Health and Human Services (1980) in Los Angeles, Philadelphia and San Antonio, the majority provided care for their grandchildren or (grand) nieces and nephews. This was especially true for black and Hispanic care-givers. Children stayed in their care from infancy or till they entered school, an average of four years.

The reliance of US parents on supplementary care by grandparents has been encouraged by recent changes in the US tax laws. Money paid to a grandparent for child-care qualifies the taxpayer for child-care credit, as long as the grandparent is not a dependent of the parent. The deductible amount allowed for child-care has been increased in the 1981 tax reform legislation.

Surrogate parenting by grandparents

The grandparent role, especially the role of the maternal grandmother, becomes essential for the survival of the family in poor and/or female-headed households. The single-parent family headed by a woman is the fastest-growing household type in the USA, and it also tends to be the poorest – especially among blacks (Reid 1982).

In the mid-1980s, nearly two-thirds of black parents were either separated, divorced, widowed or never married. More than half (55 per cent) of the black births were to unmarried mothers, and 28 per cent of black births were to adolescents (Wilson 1989). The persistent poverty of more than half of black single-parent families is probably the most important factor associated with extended family formation. Many black single mothers reside with their family of origin; such co-residential sharing is a way of reducing the impact of poverty. However, black middle- and working-class families are also more likely to contribute to the support of extended family networks than are other ethnic middle- and working-class fmilies (Martin and Martin 1978; McAdoo 1978). The prevalence and persistence of the extended family in the black community attest to its viability (Hale 1982; Stack 1974; Wilson 1986).

Research conducted in the context of the black extended family has typically focused on the presence of a maternal grandmother. These black grandmothers perceived themselves, and were perceived by their daughters, as being actively involved in child-rearing activities (Wilson 1984). When the maternal grandmother is a homemaker, she tends to be her grandchild's primary care-giver (Field *et al.* 1980; Lindblad-Goldberg and Dukes 1985).

Grandmothers may represent a model for effective care-giving. They tend to be more responsive and less punitive in their interactions with their grandchildren than are their teenaged daughters. They also help the young mother acquire accurate information about her baby's normative development (Stevens 1984).

Several studies have shown that high involvement of the maternal grandmother with child-care also benefited the grandchild indirectly because it allowed their teenage mothers to improve their situation. Adolescent mothers who remained in their mother's household were more likely to complete high school, and were less likely to rely on public assistance than were teenage mothers in separate households (Furstenberg 1980; Furstenberg et al. 1987). They were also more connected to their peers and less isolated socially (Colletta and Lee 1983).

Although black families have the highest rate of female-headed households in the USA, single-parent households are on the increase among Native Americans as well, especially in urban areas. Miller (1979) studied 120 Native American families from a number of different tribes in the Greater San Francisco/Oakland area, and found that one-third of the households were headed by a woman.

The involvement of grandparents in child-care is very high among Native Americans. Grandparents have an important voice in child-rearing, and in the absence of a biological grandparent, children and parents may adopt an unrelated elder into the family to fill the role of mentor and disciplinarian. This attitude transcends tribal lines and geographical boundaries. Bachtold (1982), in a comparative study of Caucasian and Native American preschool children, found a high incidence of child-care by grandparents among the Hupa in northern California. Red Horse et al. (1978) reported that 92 per cent of the elderly in a Native American community in the South-west fulfilled such care-giving roles, on a daily basis, for their children, grandchildren, and great-grandchildren. Unfortunately, social welfare professionals (who tend to be middle-class Caucasians) are still inclined to place Native American children into foster care instead of the care of their grandparents when the parents are absent or incapacitated.

Fosterage or informal adoption by grandparents has also been a long tradition in Polynesian island societies (Carroll 1971). Our research among contemporary Hawaiian families has demonstrated that it is still prevalent today. Grandparents 'hanai' (that is, informally adopt) their grandchildren after their own children have grown up, especially if an unmarried teenage daughter bears a child, or the family unit of their adult children is disrupted by death, desertion or divorce (Werner and Smith 1977, 1982; Werner 1989).

Prospective adopters among Hawaiian-Americans are rarely denied the privilege of adoption because of economic circumstances, old age or ill health. On the other hand, the mother who gives up her child to the grandparents is not stigmatized. There seems to be little effort to sever legal and social relations between a child and his natural parents. Instead, fostering or adoption by grandparents creates an additional parental relationship rather than replacing the bond between parents and children.

Our follow-up in adulthood of the children of Kauai (Werner 1989) has shown that this fostering especially benefits teenage mothers. Three-fourths in this group went on to get additional education, and none had to rely on welfare while they brought up their children jointly with the grandparents. Furstenberg and his associates (1987) reported a similar trend for black teenage mothers.

Divorce, remarriage and related changes in grandparent–grandchild relationships

There is one life event – divorce – that has touched almost every contemporary family in the USA, regardless of ethnicity or social class. It is estimated that between 40 per cent and 50 per cent of American children born in the late 1970s and early 1980s will experience their parents' divorce. Because most divorced mothers and fathers remarry, and the divorce rate in remarriages is higher than that in first marriages, many American children are exposed to a series of marital transitions that modify their lives and their relationships with their grandparents (Hetherington *et al.* 1989).

Poor parents are more likely to divorce than those with stable incomes, but even among middle-class families, divorce is associated with a marked drop in income for households in which mothers retain custody or assume the major role in joint custody (Hernandez 1988). During such family crises, the *latent* support of grandparents turns into *active* support, especially on the maternal side. Retrospective accounts of grandparents, reported by Cherlin and Furstenberg (1986), and findings of longitudinal studies that have documented the role of grandparents during and after the divorce process (Johnson 1988) both suggest that the relationship between grandparents and grandchildren will be maintained or even enhanced if the daughter's marriage breaks up, but relationships between grandparents and grandchildren tend to diminish if the son's marriage ends in divorce.

Following a divorce, often for economic reasons, between 25 per cent and 44 per cent of newly divorced custodial mothers reside with their mothers (Hernandez 1988). Especially during the initial transition period, after the dissolution of the marriage, grandmothers often share child-care responsibilities and household chores with their daughters and provide emotional support for their grandchildren.

More custodial mothers, however, prefer to establish their own households, when they have the economic resources to do so, thus avoiding feelings of dependency and conflicts over child-rearing issues with their parents. Such conflicts tend to occur more often with grandmothers than with grandfathers (Hetherington *et al.* 1989). In turn, most middle-class Caucasian grandmothers become more ambivalent and dissatisfied with their roles if they are forced to perform parenting functions over extended periods of time, since they are more comfortable with the role of friend and companion to their grandchildren than with the role of surrogate parent (Johnson 1988).

Several longitudinal studies have documented changes in intergenerational ties that take place in the years after divorce, and after remarriage (Furstenberg and Spanier 1984; Hetherington *et al*. 1989; Johnson 1988; Wallerstein and Blakeslee 1989). All involve middle-class Caucasian samples from different regions of the United States: California, Pennsylvania and Virginia. All report that grandchildren tend to have more frequent contact with grandparents on the custodial parent's side than with those on the non-custodial parent's side. The fate of grandparent–grandchild relations following divorce is linked to the grandparent–parent relations which have evolved and is also strongly affected by physical proximity.

Some 75 per cent of divorced mothers and 80 per cent of divorced fathers eventually remarry. Information from parents who have remarried and from step-grandparents (Cherlin and Furstenberg 1986; Furstenberg and Spanier 1984) reveals that marriages can result in an expansion of kin for the grandchildren, especially for younger children. Children who had more contact with step-grandparents had no less contact with their biological grandparents. Whether or not a grandparent has a continuing tie to a grandchild after divorce – or whether or not a step-grandparent establishes a strong tie to a step-grandchild after remarriage – depends on the actions of both parents and grandparents.

In response to political pressure by 'Grandparents' Rights' groups, most states of the Union now have passed some form of visitation rights legislation (Wilson and DeShane 1982). The purpose of the visitation rights statutes is to offer grandparents (and, in California, great-grandparents as well) an independent right of action that is not contingent on the rights already given to the child's parents. Grandparents can now utilize state habeas corpus proceedings to ask for an impartial evaluation of their request for visitation privileges with their grandchildren. The decision-making power of determining what is 'in the best interests of the child' is thus shifted from the parents to the courts. There seems to be a growing legal consensus in the USA that, in the majority of cases, a grandchild will profit from continued contact with his biological grandparents, even after the dissolution of his parents' marriage, and that a continued relationship between blood relatives should be encouraged (Borzi 1977).

So far we have little empirical evidence about the effects of the grandparents' visitation rights on all parties concerned – the grandparents, the grandchildren, and the parents. Should 'joint custody' become more common in the future in the USA, paternal and maternal intergenerational ties probably would become more equal, and there might be less need for court intervention. For the time being, however, divorce appears to result in a matrilineal tilt in intergenerational continuity (Cherlin and Furstenberg 1986).

Parental attitudes and grandparent–grandchild relationships

Parental attitudes are important influences on grandparent–grandchild relationships. The middle generation serves as a bridge between grandparent and grandchild, with the women in that generation more prominent in the function of a *gatekeeper* than their husbands (Cherlin and Furstenberg 1986; Hill *et al*. 1970).

When good relationships exist between the adult generations, especially between the adult daughter and her mother, and where attitudes and values are consonant, interactions with grandparents can have a positive and stabilizing effect on the grandchildren's development.

The amount of harmony depends on the balance between autonomy from and dependence on each other that parents and grandparents have achieved. This seems to be especially true for the mother–grandmother relationships. Two studies have explored such tri-generational interdependencies between grandmothers, mothers and grandchildren among Caucasian families in the American Midwest and South; one in an urban working-class setting, the other in the context of rural poverty (Cohler and Gruenebaum 1981; Fu, Hinkle and Hanna 1986). They conclude that such interdependence across generations becomes a source of conflict only when the mother of the child has not resolved her own problem of identity. On the other hand, continued involvement in a multigenerational family also can provide an important source of emotional support which fosters successful coping in adversity. Within the contemporary American society, findings reported from a large national survey of grandparents suggest that the best relationship between generations is that in which the grandparent is willing to provide assistance and emotional support while recognizing the needs of the parent generation for autonomy and independence (Cherlin and Furstenberg 1986).

Grandchildren's perceptions of their grandparents

A handful of cross-sectional studies in the USA have examined the meaning of the grandparents' role from the perspective of the grandchildren. These perspectives vary from early childhood to adulthood, and depend on the age of the grandchildren and degree of involvement with the grandparents.

One of the pioneering studies in this area was conducted by Kahana and Kahana (1970), who examined the views of three groups of children, aged 4–5, 8–9 and 11–12 years. More frequent contact was reported by all three age groups with maternal than paternal grandparents, and the maternal grandmother was the most frequently favoured grandparent. Four- to five-year-olds valued their grandparents for their indulgent qualities – the food, love and presents they shared. Eight- to nine-year-olds focused on mutual interests and shared experiences, and preferred active, fun-loving grandparents. Eleven- to twelve-year-olds focused on interpersonal qualities of their grandparents.

The findings by Kahana and Kahana were replicated and extended by Schultz (1980). The youngest group in his study (mean age 4.6 years) was selected to represent the pre-operational stage of cognitive development; the middle group (mean age 9.3 years) corresponded to the concrete operational stage; the youths in the oldest group (mean age 19.2 years) represented the stage of formal operational thought. The youngest group was found to have the strongest emotional attachment to both sets of grandparents. The two older groups were more discriminating; they used a greater variety of abstract descriptions for the grandparent with whom they interacted the most, and attributed more empathy and greater feelings of attachment to that grandparent.

In one of the largest studies of the grandchild–grandparent bond, Kornhaber and Woodward (1981) interviewed some 300 grandchildren in the age range from 5 to 18 years. They noted distinct developmental changes in children's views of their grandparents: preschool children who came from homes where both parents worked, or where the mother headed the household, perceived their grandparents as *nurturers*; school-age children saw them as *wizards* and *mentors*; and for adolescents, they became *role models* and *family historians*.

Cherlin and Furstenberg (1986), based on interview responses from a national sample of adolescents, conclude that for a sizeable proportion (32 per cent), grandparents become *parentlike* figures when they live close by and provide assistance and emotional or moral support.

Effects of grandparents on their grandchildren's behaviour

Do grandparents make a significant difference in the lives of their grandchildren? The tentative answer is yes – but more so if the grandparents are highly involved, and if the grandchildren are confronted with adversity. In that case, grandparents can become protective buffers that enhance the resiliency of their grandchildren (Werner 1990). Such positive effects have been shown in the lives of American children from a variety of ethnic groups (black, Caucasian, Hispanic, Hawaiian) in different regions of the USA.

Crockenberg (1981) demonstrated that the social support provided by grandparents to Caucasian and Hispanic mothers and babies during the first year of life was an important predictor of secure attachment for infants at age 1. This protective effect was especially potent for mothers with irritable babies. Farber and Egeland (1987) reported that young offspring of abusive mothers managed to grow into securely attached toddlers when they had grandmothers who provided them with emotional support. Musick *et al.* (1987) found that infants and preschoolers who attended a therapeutic nursery for offspring of psychotic mothers were more likely to 'bounce back' from the effects of multiple separations from the ill parent if grandparents joined with the well parent in providing care for the child, and if they cooperated with the nursery-school staff.

Furstenberg (1980) noted that low-income, black teenage mothers, who kept their babies, tended to have preschool children with higher scores on tests of cognitive development if they were cared for by more than one adult – in most cases by the maternal grandmother. Working with poor, black elementary school-children in a Chicago suburb, Kellam *et al.* (1977) discovered that grandmothers made a positive contribution to the school achievement and adaptation of their grandchildren in grades one and three. Mother/grandmother families were nearly as effective as two-parent families in assuring that their offspring had positive relationships with peers and teachers, that they paid attention in the classroom, and that their achievements were commensurate with their abilities. Children from mother/grandmother families also showed fewer symptoms of distress, nervousness and sadness than did children reared by single mothers or in mother/stepfather families. This was especially true for boys.

Bryant (1985) noted that 7- to 10-year-old Caucasian children from large families talked more often intimately with their grandparents than children from smaller families. In such large families, a significant positive relationship was found between children's reports of intimate talks with grandparents and a measure of empathy. For boys, involvement with grandparents was also positively related to social-perspective-taking skills.

Several longitudinal studies have shown that grandparents can have a significant positive effect on the behaviour of their grandchildren if they provide emotional support when the parents divorce. Regardless of age, whether preschooler or adolescent, youngsters, who coped well in school and maintained good relationships with peers and teachers during the parental break-up, tended to have ongoing relationships with grandparents who lived nearby and who were attentive to their needs (Wallerstein and Kelley 1980). Grandfathers can play a particularly important role in skills training and the provision of activities for young grandsons in divorced families. Sons in the custody of mothers showed fewer behaviour problems when they had an involved and supportive grandfather than when no such father figure was available (Hetherington et al. 1985, 1989).

Grandparents turned out to be a major stabilizing factor in the lives of black and Caucasian adolescents from delinquency-prone homes in metropolitan St Louis. In a series of studies of three generations of poor families, Robins and her associates (1975) examined the relationship between the arrest records of grandparents and grandchildren. By age 17, delinquency records were lowest for Caucasian males, when neither grandparent had been in trouble with the law; second lowest for black males and females, when neither grandparent had been arrested. Robins and her colleagues concluded that the extended family in the persons of law-abiding grandparents can be a protective factor, keeping their grandchildren from delinquency, even if one or both parents have a criminal record.

Access to nurturance by and counsel from grandparents also contributed significantly to the resilience of a cohort of 698 Japanese, Hawaiian and Filipino youths who live on the island of Kauai (Werner and Smith 1989). Most of these youngsters were born and reared in chronic poverty by parents who were semi- or unskilled plantation workers. About a third were exposed to perinatal trauma, parental discord and psychopathology. In interviews at age 18, and more recently, at age 30, many of the resilient young people who had successfully overcome these childhood adversities gave credit to their grandparents for the nurturance they had received in childhood, and the structure and guidance they had provided in adolescence. The presence and support of caring grandparents, especially in homes where a parent was absent or incapacitated, was a significant buffer in their lives that tipped the balance from vulnerability to resiliency. Now in their early thirties, many of these adult men and women still consider their grandparents 'valued elders' who are their mentors and role models. Young adults who have recently lost grandparents still mourn their death. The women, especially, miss the presence of a favourite grandmother in their lives.

Foster grandparents and intergenerational mentor programmes

At the time of writing, the United States has a variety of community programmes that offer men and women of grandparent age an opportunity to get involved in intergenerational activities. Among programmes that can be found in every state of the Union are the Retired Senior Volunteer Program (RSVP), the Foster Grandparents Program, and the Intergenerational Activities Projects sponsored by the American Association of Retired Persons (AARP).

Since 1965, the Foster Grandparent Program has offered elders with low income the opportunity to provide companionship and caring for a variety of high-risk children and youths in return for a tax-exempt stipend. Some foster grandparents work in hospitals and residential institutions for children who are physically, mentally or emotionally handicapped. Others work in day-care programmes for children who come from single-parent, low-income homes, or in shelters for homeless or immigrant children; still others serve as parent aides in the homes of families in crisis. After initial orientation and training, foster grandparents work some twenty hours a week with their child or family, and usually develop close relationships with their small charges (Reagan 1982).

Several evaluation studies have documented positive effects on both the children and the elders involved in this programme. For example, Saltz (1971) assessed the changes brought about in the behaviour of children who were placed in a residential home because of parental abuse, neglect, alcoholism or mental illness. Infants (aged 1 to 7 weeks) with foster grandparents vocalized more and cried less than did infants without foster grandparents. Older infants and toddlers (aged 4 months to 2 years) showed significant improvement in motor and social development after six months of interaction with such elders. Preschool children (aged 2 to 6 years) with supplementary foster grandparent care made significant gains in cognitive development and in social competence. The gains were greatest for those children who received such part-time mothering by elderly aides for a period of up to four years. For the foster grandparents, in turn, the experience with the children in their care was associated with improved life satisfaction, health and vigour.

Intergenerational mentoring programmes for older children and youths in the USA involve volunteers from the Foster Grandparents Program, from RSVP and retirees from labour unions. They aid potential high-school drop-outs who are failing in school, gaol-bound juvenile offenders and teenage mothers. Evaluation studies have shown that these programmes are characterized by two kinds of relationships: *primary* relationships, which are attachments approximating *kin* relations; and *secondary* relationships, where the elders act more like 'friendly neighbours', and focus on the teaching skills and on positive reinforcement, while maintaining a greater emotional distance from the youngsters.

Benefits from exposure to elder mentors were reported by all youths who participated in such intergenerational programmes. Youths in secondary relationships acquired important functional skills (such as reading and maths), but youths in primary relationships gained in self-esteem as well. Perhaps one of the most striking findings was that the most effective elders were individuals who had endured strained family relations, struggled in low-paying jobs, and had battled and overcome personal problems, such as alcoholism. Partly as a result of surmounting such difficulties, these older mentors seemed to form a compassionate bond with the troubled youth, and were able to draw on their own experiences to help their young partners (Freedman 1989).

Summary

American grandparents in all ethnic groups tend to play the role of 'family watchdog' (Troll 1983), a latent source of support, ready to provide assistance if a family crisis occurs. While the majority prefer companionate relationships with their grandchildren, an increasing number of grandparents are significantly involved in the lives of their grandchildren. Positive effects of grandparents on the behaviour of children of divorce, children of teenage mothers, and the offspring of abusive and mentally ill mothers have been demonstrated – especially in the context of poverty. The quantity and quality of grandparent–grandchild relationships differ, however, with the gender and stage of the life cycle of the participants. They also depend on geographical proximity and the attitudes of the parents, especially the mother's relationship with the grandmother.

In the contemporary USA, the participation of grandparents in shared child-care is increasing, as is the recognition of their legal rights. For the growing number of elders in the USA without grandchildren (US Bureau of the Census 1983), the Foster Grandparent Program and mentor programs with high-risk children and young people offer alternative options for valued intergenerational contact. More interdisciplinary research on the role and effects of elders in the domestic and public spheres is needed that has a firm theoretical foundation *and* can be translated into a coherent family policy and just family laws.

References

Bachtold, L.M. (1982) 'Children's social interactions and parental attitudes among Hupa Indians and Anglo-Americans', *Journal of Social Psychology* 116: 9-17.

Borzi, P.C. (1977) 'Statutory visiting rights of grandparents: one step closer to the best interests of the child', *Catholic University Law Review* 26: 387-401.

Bryant, B.K. (1985) 'The neighborhood walk: sources of support in middle childhood', *Monographs of the Society for Research in Child Development* Serial No. 210.

Campbell, V. and Buholz, M. (1982) 'Parenting by related adults', in M.J. Kostelnik and H.J. Fitzgerald (eds), *Patterns of Supplementary Parenting*, vol. 2, New York: Plenum Press.

Carroll, V. (1971) *Adoption in Eastern Oceania*, Honolulu: University of Hawaii Press.

Cherlin, A.J. and Furstenberg, F.F. (1986) *The New American Grandparent: a Place in the Family, a Life Apart*, New York: Basic Books.

Children's Defense Fund (1989) *A Vision for America's Future: an Agenda for the 1990s: a Children's Defense Budget*, Washington, DC: Children's Defense Fund.

Clavan, S. (1978) 'The impact of social class and social trends on the role of grandparents', *Family Coordinator* 27: 351-58.

Cohler, B.J. and Gruenebaum, H.U. (1981) *Mothers, Grandmothers, and Daughters: Personality and Child Care in Three Generations*, New York: Wiley.

Colletta, N.D. and Lee, D. (1983) 'The impact of support for black adolescent mothers', *Journal of Family Issues* 4: 127-41.

Crockenberg, S.B. (1981) 'Infant irritability, mother responsiveness, and social support influences on the security of infant–mother attachment', *Child Development* 52: 857-65.

Farber, E.A. and Egeland, B. (1987) 'Invulnerability among abused and neglected children', in E.J. Anthony and B. Cohler (eds), *The Invulnerable Child*, New York: Guildford Press.

Field, T.M., Widmayer, S.M., Stringer, S. and Ignatoff, E. (1980) 'Teenage, lower class black mothers and their preterm infants: an intervention and developmental follow-up', *Child Development* 51: 426-36.

Freedman, M. (1989) 'Fostering intergenerational relationships for at-risk youth', *Children Today* (March–April): 10-15.

Fu, V., Hinkle, D., and Hanna, M. (1986) 'A three-generational study of the development of individual dependency and family interdependence', *Genetic, Social and General Psychology Monographs* 112: 153-71.

Furstenberg, F.F. (1980) 'Burdens and benefits: the impact of early childbearing on the family', *Journal of Social Issues* 36: 64-87.

Furstenberg, F.F. (1988) 'Child care after divorce and remarriage', in E.M. Hetherington and J.D. Arasteh (eds), *Impact of Divorce, Single Parenting and Stepparenting on Children*, Hillsdale, NJ: Erlbaum.

Furstenberg, F.F. and Spanier, G.B. (1984) *Recycling the Family: Remarriage after Divorce*, Beverley Hills, CA: Sage Publications.

Furstenberg, F.F., Brooks-Gunn, J., and Morgan, S.P. (1987) *Adolescent Mothers in Later Life*, Cambridge: Cambridge University Press.

Giraldo, Z.I. (1980) *Public Policy and the Family: Wives and Mothers in the Labor Force*, Lexington, MA: Lexington Books.

Hale, J. (1982) *Black Children: Their Roots, Culture and Learning Styles*, Provo, UT: Brigham Young University Press.

Harris, L. and Associates, Inc. (1975) *The Myth and Reality of Aging in America*, Washington, DC: National Council on Aging.

Hernandez, D.J. (1988) 'Demographic trends and the living arrangements of children', in E.M. Hetherington and J.D. Arasteh (eds), *Impact of Divorce, Single-Parenting and Stepparenting on Children*, Hillsdale, NJ: Erlbaum.

Hetherington, E.M., Cox, M. and Cox, R. (1985) 'Effects of divorce on parents and children', in M. Lamb (ed.), *Non-traditional Families*, Hillsdale, NJ: Erlbaum.

Hetherington, E.M., Stanley-Hagan, M. and Anderson, E.R. (1989) 'Marital transitions: a child's perspective', *American Psychologist* 44: 303-12.

Hill, R., Foote, N., Aldous, J. and MacDonald, B. (1970) *Family Development in Three Generations*, Cambridge, MA: Schenkman Publishing.

Huang, L.J. (1976) 'The Chinese American family', in C. Mindel and R. Haberstein (eds), *Ethnic Families in America*, New York: Elsevier.

Jackson, J.J. (1971) 'Sex and social class variations in black aged parent–adult child relationships', *Aging and Human Development* 2: 96–107.

Johnson, C.L. (1988) 'Active and latent functions of grandparenting in the divorce process', *Gerontologist* 28: 185–91.

Kahana B. and Kahana, E. (1970) 'Grandparenthood from the perspective of the developing grandchild', *Developmental Psychology* 3: 98–105.

Kahana, E. and Kahana B. (1971) 'Theoretical and research perspectives on grandparenthood', *Aging and Human Development* 2: 261–68.

Kellam, S.G., Ensminger, M.E. and Turner, R.J. (1977) 'Family structure and the mental health of children', *Archives of General Psychiatry* 34: 1012–22.

Kitano, H.H. and Kikumura, A. (1976) 'The Japanese American family', in C. Mindel and R. Haberstein (eds), *Ethnic Families in America*, New York: Elsevier.

Kivnick, H.Q. (1982) 'Grandparenthood: an overview of meaning and mental health', *The Gerontologist* 22: 59–66.

Kornhaber, A. and Woodward, K. (1981) *Grandparents/Grandchildren: the Vital Connection*, New York: Doubleday/Anchor Press.

Lindblad-Goldberg, M. and Dukes, J.L. (1985) 'Social support in black low-income, single-parent families', *American Journal of Orthopsychiatry* 55: 42–58.

McAdoo, H.P. (1978) 'Factors related to stability in upwardly mobile black families', *Journal of Marriage and the Family* 40: 761–76.

Martin, E.P. and Martin, J.M. (1978) *The Black Extended Family*, Chicago: University of Chicago Press.

Mead, M. (1972) *Blackberry Winter: My Earlier Years*, New York: William Morrow.

Miller, D. (1979) 'The Native American family: the urban way', in E. Corfman (ed.), *Families Today*, vol. 1, Washington, DC: US Government Printing Office.

Musick, J.S., Stott, F.M., Spencer, C.K., Goldman, J. and Cohler, B.J. (1987) 'Maternal factors related to vulnerability and resiliency in young children at risk', in E.J. Anthony and B.J. Cohler (eds), *The Invulnerable Child*, New York: Guilford Press.

Neugarten, B.L. and Weinstein, K.J. (1964) 'The changing American grandparent', *Journal of Marriage and the Family* 26: 197–205.

Reagan, N. (with Wilke, J.) (1982) *To Love a Child*, Indianapolis: Bobbs-Merrill.

Red Horse, J.G., Lewis, R. and Feit, H. (1978) 'Family behaviour of urban American Indians', *Social Casework* 59: 67–72.

Reid, J. (1982) 'Black America in the 1980s', *Population Bulletin*, 37: 1–37.

Robins, L.N., West, P.A. and Herjanic, R. (1975) 'Arrests and delinquency in two generations: a study of black urban families and their children', *Journal of Child Psychology and Psychiatry* 16: 125–40.

Saltz, R. (1971) 'Aging persons as child-care workers in foster grandparent programs', *Aging and Human Development* 2: 314–40.

Schultz, N.W. (1980) 'A cognitive-developmental study of the grandchild-grandparent bond', *Child Study Journal* 10: 7–26.

Seña-Rivera, J. (1979) 'La familia Chicana', in E. Corfman (ed.), *Families Today*, vol. 1, Washington, DC: US Government Printing Office.

Stack, C.B. (1974) *All Our Kin*, New York: Harper & Row.

Stevens, J.H. (1984) 'Black grandmothers' and black adolescent mothers' knowledge about parenting', *Developmental Psychology* 20: 1017–25.

Thomas, J.L. (1986) 'Age and sex differences in perceptions of grandparenting', *Journal of Gerontology* 41: 417–23.

Timberlake, E.M. (1980) 'The value of grandchildren to grandmothers', *Journal of*

Gerontological Social Work 3: 63–76.

Tinsley, B.R. and Parke, R.D. (1984) 'Grandparents as support and socializing agents', in M. Lewis (ed.), *Beyond the Dyad*, New York: Plenum.

Troll, L.E. (1983) 'Grandparents: the family watchdogs', in T. Brubaker (ed.), *Family Relationships in Later Life*, Beverly Hills, CA: Sage Publications.

US Bureau of the Census (1983) 'Provisional projections of the population of states by age and sex: 1980–2000', *Current Population Reports* ser. P-25, no. 937, Washington, DC: US Government Printing Office.

US Department of Health and Human Services (1980) *Family Day Care in the United States: National Day Care Home Study*, Final Report, vol. 2: Research Report, Washington, DC: US Department of Health and Human Services.

Wallerstein, J.S. and Kelley, J.B. (1980) *Surviving the Break-up: How Children and Parents Cope with Divorce*, New York: Basic Books.

Wallerstein, J.S. and Blakeslee, S. (1989) *Second Chances: Men, Women and Children: a Decade After Divorce*, New York: Ticknor & Fields.

Werner, E.E. (1984) *Child Care: Kith, Kin and Hired Hands*, Baltimore, MD: University Park Press.

Werner, E.E. (1989) 'Children of the Garden Island', *Scientific American* 260: 106–11.

Werner, E.E. (1990) 'Protective factors and individual resilience', in S.J. Meisels and J.P. Shankoff (eds), *Handbook of Early Intervention*, Cambridge: Cambridge University Press.

Werner, E.E. and Smith, R.S. (1977) *Kauai's Children Come of Age*, Honolulu: University of Hawaii Press.

Werner, E.E. and Smith, R.S. (1982) *Vulnerable but Invincible: a Longitudinal Study of Resilient Children and Youth*, New York: McGraw-Hill.

Wilson, K.B. and DeShane, M.R. (1982) 'The legal rights of grandparents: a preliminary discussion', *The Gerontologist* 22: 67–71.

Wilson, M. (1984) 'Mothers' and grandmothers' perceptions of behavior in three-generational black families', *Child Development* 55: 1333–39.

Wilson, M. (1986) 'The black extended family: an analytical review', *Developmental Psychology* 22: 246–58.

Wilson, M.N. (1989) 'Child development in the context of the black extended family', *American Psychologist* 44: 380–85.

Wood, V. and Robertson, J. (1976) 'The significance of grandparenthood', in J. Gubrium (ed.), *Time, Roles and Self in Old Age*, New York: Human Sciences Press.

Part two

The effects of grandparenting

Chapter six

Grandfathers, teen mothers and children under two

Norma Radin, Daphna Oyserman and Rita Benn

The cognitive deficits and nonadaptive social functioning associated with children of teen mothers in the USA have been well-documented (Baldwin and Cain 1980; Furstenberg 1976; Furstenberg, Brooks-Gunn and Morgan 1987; Phipps-Yonas 1980). For example, these children tend to perform more poorly on intelligence and academic tests and to be more impulsive and distractible than peers born to older mothers. The scope of the problems can be expected to increase in the coming decade as data on parenting show that the birthrate of unmarried adolescents 14 to 18 years of age has been rising steadily since 1965, particularly for very young adolescents under 15 and among 15 to 17-year-old whites (Guttmacher Institute 1981; Thornton and Freedman, 1983). Augmenting the difficulty is the increasingly large percentage of unwed young mothers who keep their babies rather than give them up for adoption. In 1981, the figure was 96 per cent (Guttmacher Institute 1981). It has been estimated that there are over half a million babies born each year to adolescent mothers in the United States (Hayes 1987), thus half a million infants who are likely to face difficulties in attaining their optimal development.

The investigation to be described focused on individuals who may help prevent some of those intellectual and adaptive deficits from developing; that is, grandfathers who function as surrogate fathers to the offspring of their adolescent daughters. Several bodies of literature converged to undergird this premise. Demographic data provided evidence that in the vast majority of cases, the biological father of the adolescent mother's baby is not an active participant in caring for the child, and in the United States, a substantial percentage of teen mothers live with both parents. Another body of literature provided theoretical and empirical evidence that paternal involvement with young children has beneficial outcomes for the child. Further, the literature on grandparenthood gave strong support for the view that grandfathers feel positively towards their young grandchildren and are likely to participate in their care, particularly if help is needed. The literature from these three domains will be very briefly reviewed.

As to demographic data, it has been reported that only 29 per cent of the fathers of adolescent mothers' babies are involved with the child (Vecchiolla and Maza 1989), and only 27 per cent of teen mothers in a large-scale study were living with a spouse one year after giving birth (Furstenberg and Crawford 1978). A more recent study reported a further decline as the child became older; when adolescents' infants reached 18 months of age, only 16 per cent of the babies' fathers were found to be married to or living with the teen mothers (Hardy, Duggan, Masnyk and Pearson 1989). Published figures on the number of adolescent mothers living with two parents vary from 25 per cent to 50 per cent. For example, the figure of 50 per cent emerged in a large-scale, longitudinal study of adolescent mothers (Furstenberg and Crawford 1978).

Evidence concerning the influence that fathers exert on their children's cognitive development has been particularly pronounced for sons (Blanchard and Biller 1971; Pedersen, Rubinstein and Yarrow 1979; Radin 1981, 1986). It appears that the more nurturant the father, the greater the stimulation of the boy's cognitive growth; it has also been shown that the more contact with the father, the more the boy's intellectual development flourishes. Detrimental to sons' mental growth, however, is paternal hostility and restrictiveness (Harrington, Block and Block, 1978; Radin 1981). The influence that fathers exert on daughters' cognitive growth is more complex, but it is clear that father presence stimulates the girls' mathematical skills (Goldstein 1982; Rosenberg and Sutton-Smith 1966). In addition, a number of investigations have shown that fathers have a powerful influence on the social competence of children, particularly sons; for example, on their self-direction, persistence at a task and peer relations (Easterbrooks and Goldberg 1984; Hetherington, Cox and Cox 1982; Nietfeldt 1984). However, there is also evidence that women who achieved a high level of success are likely to have had a strong relationship with their fathers who expected their daughters to be competent (Biller 1981).

Concerning grandfathers, it has been found that males become more nurturant as they age (Guttman 1977; Livson 1981), and one way in which men can express these qualities is through taking care of their grandchildren. It has even been proposed that grandparenthood is particularly gratifying for men because it gives them a second chance to succeed in an emotional role that they have avoided, or was denied to them as fathers (Baranowski 1985). It also appears that the baby itself elicits positive feeling on the part of both grandparents. For example, the results of a large study of pregnant adolescents yielded the information that the grandchild was universally esteemed in the family regardless of how the teen's parents felt about her pregnancy (Furstenberg 1980). Grandparents often do become involved as surrogate parents to the offspring of their teenage children (Denham and Smith 1989). This fact is significant because there is evidence suggesting that surrogate father figures – for example, stepfathers and male teachers – enhance the development of young children, especially in the case of boys (Biller 1981; Santrock 1972).

Based on the above theoretical and empirical literature, it was hypothesized that the greater the quantity and the better the quality of the grandfather's involvement with the young child of the teen mother, the higher the level of cognitive development of the child and the more adaptive the socio-emotional functioning of the child at 12 months and 24 months. In addition, the question of whether the sex of the child mediates the influence exerted by the grandfather was explored because of indications that father effects are stronger for sons than daughters. It is possible that the same sex linkage exists between men and their grandchildren.

Method

Subjects

The sample consisted of sixty-six families composed of a teen mother living with her father or a father figure, and her first-born child 1 or 2 years of age who was not low birth-weight. In 61 per cent of the families the male figure was the teen's father, in 36 per cent her stepfather, and in 3 per cent her grandfather. No other adult male was in the home. In all but two families there was also a grandmother present. Seventy-six per cent of the babies were white and 24 per cent minority, primarily black. Seventy per cent of the babies were 1 year of age and 30 per cent 2 years of age. There were thirty-nine white 1 year-olds in the study, seven white 2-year-olds, eleven minority 1-year-olds, and nine minority 2-year-olds. Forty-seven per cent of the babies were female and 53 per cent male.

In Table 6.1 appear demographic data about the total sample. As the table indicates, the subjects were primarily working class; the average social stratum on the Hollingshead Four Factor Index of Social Status (Hollingshead 1975) for the total sample was three, described by Hollingshead as consisting of skilled craftsmen, clerical and sales workers. About a half of the sample received some form of welfare aid. The grandparents' education on the average ended with high school and their average age was in the low to mid-forties. The teen mother's average age was approximately 17½ years and her education was between tenth and eleventh grade.

The sample was obtained primarily from public schools offering special programmes for pregnant and parent teens residing in seven counties in the metropolitan Detroit area. To obtain the sample, the typical scenario involved contacting teachers in such schools, asking for permission to discuss the study with potentially eligible students, identifying students who met the project's criteria, and informing those who agreed to participate that a letter would be sent to their parents explaining the study and requesting their participation.

The teens' parents were subsequently phoned, or contacted in some other way, and if they agreed to take part in the study after being informed of what participation involved, the parents were told that we would contact them within one month of the infant's first or second birthday (depending on the age of the child). The grandparents were interviewed individually at home, and each grandparent was also videotaped playing with the target grandchild for ten minutes. The teen mother was interviewed at home on one occasion, and the child was administered one of the instruments used to assess cognitive development. On

Table 6.1 Demographic data about the sample[1]

Variables	N	Mean or %	SD
Family Hollingshead score[2]	62	32.64	8.31
Family class on Hollingshead scale[3]	62	3.23	0.80
Grandmother's age in years	64	41.52	7.59
Grandmother's highest grade in school[4]	63	4.05	0.97
Grandmother's occupational rating[5]	47	4.60	1.85
Hours grandmother works per week	48	35.75	11.88
Grandfather's age in years	64	45.28	8.49
Grandfather's highest grade in school[4]	66	3.82	1.02
Grandfather's occupational rating[5]	60	3.80	1.62
Hours grandfather works per week	60	48.38	14.56
Teen mother's age in years	66	17.59	1.10
Teen mother's highest grade in school[4]	66	3.33	0.64
% of families with any type of public assistance	66	47.00	

Notes
1. The figures are based on information provided by the teen mother. Her views were employed because there was a teen mother for every family in the study; this was not true for grandmothers and grandfathers.
2. The Hollingshead (1975) score is determined by multiplying the scale value for occupation by 5 and the scale value for education by 3 and then adding those two figures. Computed scores range from a high of 66 to a low of 8. The family score is determined by adding the total score for each employed spouse and dividing by 2. If only one spouse is employed, that individual's total score becomes the family score.
3. According to the Hollingshead (1975) Four Factor Index of Social Status, family scores are placed into 5 social strata with the highest stratum being major business and profession and the lowest, unskilled labourers and menial service workers. Although Hollingshead did not assign numbers to these strata, in an earlier version of the scale (Hollingshead and Redlich 1958), numbers were assigned with 1 representing the highest stratum and 5 the lowest. When total family scores range between 30 and 39, Hollingshead (1975) describes this group as representing skilled craftsmen, clerical, sales workers. This stratum is essentially equivalent to class 3 in his 1957 scale.
4. According to Hollingshead's (1975) 7-point rating scale for education, in which 7 is the highest rating and 1 the lowest, 3 refers to tenth or eleventh grade completed and 4 refers to high school completed.
5. According to Hollingshead's (1975) 9-point rating scale of occupations, where 7 represents the highest rating and 1 the lowest, 3 refers to machine operators and semi-skilled workers and 4 refers to skilled manual workers and craftsmen.

a second occasion, the teen was driven to Merrill-Palmer Institute in Detroit with her infant for an hour-long videotaped laboratory assessment session, which included a ten-minute play episode identical to that conducted with the grandparent and the child, and a Strange Situation assessment. The interview schedules for grandparents and the teen mothers were identical except for appropriate references to the other members of the family. The gender of the interviewer matched the gender of the respondent.

Each parent and teen was paid $10 per session or given a videotape of the play session, and presented with a book for the baby. When one of the grandparents refused to participate, the family could be included in the study so long as the teen, the baby and at least one grandparent took part. In twelve families, the grandfather refused to be interviewed; in one family, the grandmother refused.

Despite diligent efforts to include as many families as possible in the study, there was a 50 per cent refusal rate. The major reason given for the refusals was lack of time as the teen was working and going to school, or the grandmother was too busy working and helping to care for the baby. In some cases, it was evident that either the teen or the grandparents did not wish to discuss the difficult situation, although it was explained to all potential subjects that the focus of the study was on grandparent influence on the young children.

Instruments

There were two independent variables, quantity and quality of grandfather participation in childrearing, and five dependent variables, security of attachment, compliance with teen mother requests, negative affect, mastery motivation and mental development.

Quantity of grandfather involvement was assessed by including in the interview schedule the Paternal Involvement in Childcare Index (PICCI), slightly modified to make the instrument relevant to the grandparents of children 1 or 2 years of age; the index was originally developed for administration to parents of preschoolers. On a number of studies the PICCI has been shown to be valid and have internal reliability (Nietfeldt 1984; Radin 1982; Radin and Goldsmith 1985; Sagi 1982). The Cronbach alpha for the father's score was found to be .62; for the mother's score it was .72. To assess the test–retest reliability of the instrument, in this investigation a shortened version was administered twice, one week apart, to 102 parents of preschool-aged children. The average correlation of the twenty-three items in the two administrations was .72 ($p < .001$).

The PICCI score is comprised of five components: (1) grandfather involvement in the physical care of the child; (2) in the socialization of the child; (3) availability to the child; (4) in decision-making about the child; and (5) overall estimate of his participation in the care of the child. Total scores were obtained for the teen's view and the grandmother's view of the grandfather's involvement, and these were added together to yield a grand total PICCI score. Because twelve of the sixty-six grandfathers who were involved in the investigation refused to be interviewed, it was decided not to rely on the viewpoint of the three family members as initially planned. The PICCI total scores of the grandmother and teen mother were significantly correlated at the .001 level of significance ($r = .49$; $d.f. = 61$). The grandfather's view of his involvement was also significantly associated with the perceptions of the other family members. The correlation between grandfather and grandmother PICCI total scores was .58 ($d.f. = 49$; $p < .001$); the figure was .44 ($d.f. = 50$; $p < .01$) for the association between grandfather and teen mother total PICCI scores.

The quality of grandfather involvement was assessed in fifty-two families (in two families the grandfather refused to be videotaped) through the play session with the child which consisted of two five-minute segments. In the first, the grandparent was told to permit the child to lead the play with the age-appropriate toys brought by the interviewer, and in the second five-minute segment, the adult was asked to lead the play and try to have the baby follow. The entire videotaped session was subsequently coded, using a coding scheme which integrated one developed by Radin and colleagues (Epstein and Radin 1975; Kamii and Radin 1967; Radin 1972) and found to be valid in prior studies, and the Eyberg and Robinson Dyadic Parent–Child Interaction Coding System (Eyberg and Matarazzo 1980). The validity and reliability of the latter instrument are well established (Eyberg and Matarazzo 1980; Robinson and Eyberg 1981).

Twenty-six adult behaviour categories were coded for the frequency of their occurrence during the ten-minute period. Most were verbal behaviours but some were nonverbal. Intercoder reliability was assessed using Cartwright's (1956) alpha which yields the percentage of agreement between two coders. The alpha value was 89 per cent for the project's two coders who independently scored nine videotapes. The twenty-six categories were collapsed into three major categories: nurturance, restrictiveness and neutral behaviours (neither nurturant nor restrictive). The nurturance cluster was composed of three sub-clusters which, on theoretical grounds, were felt to be aspects of parental nurturance: reinforcement of the child, sensitivity to the child and consultation with the child (Kamii and Radin 1967). Restrictiveness included items such as giving orders with no explanation and threatening the child. In the neutral category were behaviours neither nurturant nor restrictive, such as physically stopping an undesired behaviour. In addition, to control for the sheer activity or verbal fluency of the adult, the total number of nurturant and restrictive behaviours were divided by the total number of coded adult behaviours, yielding scores for the relative nurturance and relative restrictiveness of the adult's observed behaviour. Because relative nurturance and relative restrictiveness were very highly negatively correlated ($r = -.99; p < .001$), only relative nurturance was used as the measure of quality of grandfather behaviour.

For the dependent variables, both socio-emotional and cognitive child outcomes were employed. In the former category were security of attachment to the teen mother, compliance with the teen mother's requests, and negative affect. Security of attachment was assessed in the Strange Situation (Ainsworth et al. 1978; Main and Solomon 1986), which was coded using the A, B, C, D classification scheme. Compliance was assessed in two contexts using codes adapted from Matas, Arend and Sroufe (1978), during a clean-up situation and during the five-minute period of the play session when the teen mother was attempting to get the baby to follow her lead. In addition, the number of toys the infant or toddler put away during the clean-up episode was calculated and used as another measure of compliance. For data-reduction purposes, these three scores for compliance were combined into a single measure by averaging the Z scores for each of the assessments. Only two of the three scores were significantly associated, but the mean was used nevertheless because the measures were conceptually identical.

Negative affect was assessed in three contexts: negative affect displayed in the Strange Situation prior to the first mother–child reunion during which there is only moderate stress; negative affect shown in the play situation with the teen mother, and fear displayed during the administration of the Bayley Scales. For the first two situations, negative affect – that is, fear, anger and distress – was assessed using an established observation rating scale (Gaensbauer and Harmon 1981). For the third measure, the score for fear was a factor score derived from the Infant Behaviour Record completed after the administration of the Bayley. Again, for data reduction purposes, a single score was used: namely, the average of the three Z scores computed for each of the three assessments of negative affect. In this case, the three scores were not significantly associated with one another but again the mean Z score was used as the components were conceptually alike.

In the cognitive category were intellective status as measured by the Mental Development Index (MDI) on the Bayley Scales of Mental Development (Bayley 1969); and mastery motivation. Mastery motivation was assessed by an adaptation of the procedure developed for 1-year-olds (Yarrow *et al.* 1983), and through tasks developmentally appropriate for 2-year-old children (Matas *et al.* 1978). The measure used was a Z score for the length of time the child persisted working on the tasks (for example, trying to find a way to get toy animals out of a little barn). The Z score was computed for 1- and 2-year old children separately because of the discrepancy in their scores.

For all child observation codes (attachment, mastery motivation, affect and compliance), raters had to achieve a .90 reliability rating prior to coding the subject videotapes.

Results

Independent variables

The mean for the quantity of grandfather involvement, 34.8 (SD = 8.5), was approximately two-thirds that obtained for father involvement using a slightly modified version of the Paternal Index of Childcare (PICCI) in a study of working-class families with a preschool-aged child (Radin and Harold-Goldsmith 1989). As the score is composed of a total of several sub-scores reflective of various aspects of child-care, there is no specific behaviour to which it can be related. However, one of the items of which it is composed, the percentage of time the grandfather was the primary care-giver when the child was awake and not out of the home, is readily interpretable. The mean percentage was 11.1 per cent (SD = 7.7) from the grandmother's perspective and 10.0 per cent (SD = 6.5) from the teen's perspective. These figures are approximately one-half of the percentage found for middle-class, traditional fathers of preschoolers (Radin 1982).

As to quality of involvement, the mean percentage of observed grandfather behaviours which were nurturant in quality was 76 per cent (SD = 12). This figure is comparable to the percentages obtained in a study of working-class fathers of preschoolers using a similar observational procedure; the figure was 74 per cent for unemployed fathers and 88 per cent for employed fathers (Harold-Goldsmith, Radin and Eccles 1988). Some comments made by grandfathers during the interview provide a flavour of the overall warmth that appeared to permeate their relationship with the child in most families. (The same positive affect was not always expressed about the teen mother.) 'We always wanted more kids but could not have more. He was a godsend. Couldn't have asked for a better baby.' 'We all share in his care and as long as I'm alive and financially able, he'll never go without. I enjoy him.' 'The amount of love the infant gets is unreal.' And this comment was made by a teen's stepfather, 'This is the first time I've had a baby in the house and I enjoy the hell out of it.'

The two independent variables were negatively correlated ($r = -.37; p < .01; d.f. = 48$); this relationship is in keeping with research findings on paternal behaviour in the United States suggesting that fathers who are heavily involved in child-rearing display a 'tougher', more restrictive stance with their offspring than those who are less involved.

Dependent variables

In so far as child outcome measures are concerned, the mean score on the Mental Development Index on the Bayley Scales was 104 (SD = 14.74); the mean on national norms is 100. Thus the children were well within the normal range. This finding is consonant with the literature, which reports that cognitive deficits for the children of adolescent mothers do not generally emerge until the preschool years (Hayes 1987). Based on the Strange Situation, it was found that 68 per cent of the babies were securely attached, a figure comparable with published reports on middle-class families (Ainsworth *et al.* 1978; Benn 1986) and with a comparable population of teen mothers (Benn and Saltz 1989). The three remaining child outcome scores were means of standardized Z scores and therefore cannot be described in terms of child behaviours. The only dependent variables that were significantly intercorrelated were the mastery motivation and MDI ($r = .34; p < .01; d.f. = 64$), a finding in keeping with the literature (Yarrow *et al.* 1983). The dependent variables were correlated with the demographic variables listed in Table 6.1. Only one significant association emerged; the lower the grade in school of the adolescent mother, the more the fear expressed by the child. While this relationship appears to have face validity, it may well be due to chance factors, as sixty-five correlations were computed.

Because the sample consisted of diverse racial groups, *t* tests were performed to determine if there were significant differences between the white and minority sub-groups on the independent, dependent and demographic variables. There were no significant differences in quantity or quality of grandfather involvement or in demographic characteristics, but there were significant differences in four of the five child outcomes. The minority children obtained significantly lower scores on mastery motivation, on the MDI, on security of attachment, and significantly higher scores on negative affect. It should be pointed out that, in the United States, black families experience greater hardships than white families, which are not reflected in the demographic variables listed in Table 6.1; for example, housing discrimination and poorer access to medical facilities.

A comparison was also made of the independent and dependent variables across age and sex of children. On neither the grandfather variables nor the child outcome measures were there any significant differences across age or gender of the child.

Major findings

To test the hypothesis that a high level of quantity and quality of grandfather involvement is associated with more desirable child outcomes for both 1- and 2-year-old children, hierarchical multiple regression equations were computed using the five child outcomes as dependent variables, and race and quantity of grandfather involvement, in that order, as the predictor variables. The analysis was then repeated using quality of grandfather involvement in place of quantity. This procedure was followed because of the significant association obtained between race and child outcomes for four out of the five dependent variables. The regressions were computed for the total sample and for each age sub-group to test the hypothesis and for each gender sub-group to explore the impact of gender of child on grandfather influence.

Table 6.2 Regressions with a significant beta weight for the grandfather variable

Group	Dependent variable	Independent variable	R^2	F	Beta wt	% Var. expl.	Partial r
Total (N=52)	Compliance		.13	3.62^2			
		Race			.11	0	.04
		GF nurturance			$.36^2$	13	$.36^2$
(N=62)	Negative affect		.22	8.34^4			
		Race			$.33^3$	12	$.34^3$
		Amount of GF involvement			$-.32^3$	10	$-.34^3$
1-yr-olds (N=38)	Compliance		.15	3.20^1			
		Race			$-.02$	1	$-.11$
		GF nurturance			$.39^2$	14	$.38^2$
(N=44)	Negative affect		.29	8.37^4			
		Race			$.33^2$	13	$.35^2$
		Amount of GF involvement			$-.41^3$	16	$-.43^3$
2-yr-olds (N=13)	Mental Development Index on Bayley Scales		.68	10.52^4			
		Race			$-.42^2$	31	$-.56^2$
		GF nurturance			$.62^3$	37	$.73^3$
Males (N=32)	Negative affect		.23	4.26^2			
		Race			$.25^2$	7	.26
		Amount of GF involvement			$-.40^2$	16	$-.41^2$

Note: GF refers to grandfather; beta wt refers to the standardized beta weight; % Var. expl. refers to the percentage of variance explained.

[1] $p < .06$.
[2] $p < .05$.
[3] $p < .01$.
[4] $p < .001$.

In Table 6.2 appear data about the regressions with significant beta weights for quantity or quality of grandfather participation in child-rearing, controlling for race of child. As the table indicates, for the total sample, the more nurturant the grandfather, the more compliant the child with the adolescent mother's requests. Table 6.2 also indicates that the greater the amount of grandfather involvement in child-care, the less negative the child's affect in the total group; race was also a significant predictor. When both race and quantity of grandfather involvement were entered into the equation, 22 per cent of the variance in negative affect was explained, 12 per cent by race of child and 10 per cent by amount of grandfather involvement. The least amount of negative affect was found for white children with a large amount of grandfather participation in child-rearing.

The pattern for 1-year-old children mirrored that of the total sample, except that more of the variance in negative affect was explained by amount of grandfather involvement. For 2-year-old children, a completely different pattern of relationships emerged. Here the quality of the grandfather's involvement was predictive of the youngster's mental development. Race also affected the MDI. When both race and quality of grandfather participation were entered into the regression equation, 68 per cent of the variance in the child's MDI score was explained, with race accounting for 31 per cent and grandfather nurturance explaining 37 per cent. The highest MDI scores were obtained for white children whose grandfathers were highly nurturant.

Table 6.2 also reflects the fact that there were no significant associations between quantity or quality of grandfather involvement and child outcomes for girls. For boys, however, the more the grandfather participation, the less negative the grandson's affect, with race also emerging as a significant predictor. Together, race and grandfather involvement accounted for 23 per cent of the variance in grandson's negative affect, with race accounting for about one-half of the amount of variance explained by the quantity of grandfather involvement. Again, the least amount of negative affect was found when the child was white and there was a large amount of participation by the grandfather in the care of the child.

Discussion

A cautionary note is needed before discussing the results. The adolescent mothers in this investigation were almost all involved in educational programmes and may be more competent than teenage mothers who drop out of school. Thus the findings should not be generalized beyond that population. Further, only 50 per cent of the eligible families agreed to participate. Whether families who refused were unique in some way, either more troubled or less troubled, cannot be determined at this point.

Overall, it can be said that grandfathers do appear to exert positive influence on the infants and toddlers of their adolescent daughters living at home; the hypothesis in general was supported. Fifty regression equations were computed, ten for the total group (two for each child outcome) and ten for each of the four sub-groups. At the 5 per cent probability level, two and one-half significant findings would have emerged by chance alone. However, significant grandfather predictors were found in six regression equations and all in the direction predicted. In no case was a high level of quantity or quality of grandfather involvement associated with an undesirable child outcome.

Thus it appears that the positive association found in prior investigations between paternal behaviour and enhanced functioning of young children is replicated in the relationship between grandfather behaviour and the development of his grandchild. For both generations, the more nurturant the male behaviour, the better the child outcomes, and the more involved the male, the more socially competent the child. That the pattern of fathers had a stronger impact on boys than on girls was also replicated with grandfathers.

The finding that cognitive functioning was affected in 2-year-olds but not in 1-year-olds was not anticipated but is understandable. The wider range of domains tapped in the toddler assessment would be more sensitive to the effects of a stimulating environment than would the sensory-motor items comprising the assessment of the 1-year-old infant. The literature on father influence focuses almost entirely on children at the toddler age and older. Thus it is possible that the masculine style of interacting with children – that is, more physical and stimulating behaviour (Lamb 1981) – may elicit more responses from children who are mobile and able to interact actively with the environment. It is therefore possible that the 'exciting' quality of male behaviour with children to which the enhanced functioning of the children's intellect has been attributed (Radin 1986) is operative primarily with youngsters who are capable of seeking aspects of the environment to explore.

The particular power of grandfather nurturance to enhance cognitive development can be understood in terms of the components of the nurturance score; one component was reinforcement and the second was consultation with the child. The use of reinforcement is likely to make the grandfather an attractive figure, and according to social learning theory (Bandura 1977), attractive role models are more likely to be emulated. Thus the nurturant grandfather's verbal behaviours and problem-solving strategies had a greater probability of being modelled. Consultation, reflecting response to the child as a thinking human being, included asking questions of the child. It has been found that asking questions of children who are mildly retarded or of elderly persons enhances their memory (Ratner 1989; Rice and Meyer 1985). These findings suggest that encouraging those with somewhat limited mental ability to retrieve information has a stimulating effect on cognitive functioning. Grandfathers seeking information from the 2-year-old are likely to have a similar enhancing effect.

The third component of nurturance, sensitivity to the child, may help explain why there was greater compliance with the adolescent mother's request when a nurturant grandfather was in the home. Sensitivity was operationalized as responding fully or partially to the explicit and implicit needs of the child. A nurturant grandfather therefore provides a role model for cooperation and compliance with other individuals' needs and requests. The fact that the grand-father is also reinforcing would tend to increase the likelihood that he will be modelled. Hence the grandchildren of sensitive, reinforcing grandfathers are likely to be cooperative and compliant with other adults, including their young mothers.

Because of the strong negative relationship between relative nurturance and relative restrictiveness, the results of this study also suggest that greater restric-tiveness by grandfathers has a detrimental impact on children's compliance with their mothers. This finding is concordant with those obtained by Crockenberg (1987), whose study of the 2-year-old children of teen mothers indicated that maternal punitiveness led to noncompliance by the child. This investigation suggests that punitiveness by any caregiver in the family yields the same out-come. The finding of a negative impact of grandfather restrictiveness on the intellectual development of young children is also concordant with prior research. Restrictive, punitive paternal behaviour has been shown to be associated with lower levels of cognitive functioning in preschoolers (Harrington *et al.* 1978; Radin 1981).

The study's data indicated that larger amounts of grandfather participation in child-care are associated with fewer displays of negative emotions by the child: less fear, less distress and less anger. This finding may be related to the theory espoused by Parsons (Parsons and Bales 1955) that fathers play the major instrumental role which is competence-directed and that it is primarily fathers who encourage their children to acquire competence necessary for adaptation to the task-oriented aspects of their future life (Lamb 1981). Perhaps this male instrumentality, particularly when expressed by highly involved males, helps to foster the child's sense of competence, especially in the case of boys, and enables the children to interact with the environment in a more confident, adaptive, less fearful manner. Modelling of the competence-directed, instrumental male figure may also be involved, resulting in a diminished tendency for the child to be distressed and fearful.

In conclusion, the results of this study suggest that one strategy for fostering the development of the young children of adolescent mothers is the promotion of greater nurturance and involvement by the fathers of the teens in rearing their infants and toddlers. The fact that the young children have not as yet demonstrated any deficits, that their attachment to their mothers appears to be secure and that their cognitive development is within the normal range, suggests that this is an ideal time for preventive intervention. Rather than focusing interventions solely on adolescent mothers, or on adolescent mothers and their mothers, it should be recognized that another potential resource exists within the family system, the teen's father, who warrants the attention of those concerned about promoting the welfare of the baby. At the time of writing there are few, if any, such pro-grammes in existence; however, some interventions focused on teen mothers could readily be modified to make them applicable to grandfathers. For example, there are numerous projects in which local women who were chosen because they are good maternal role models are employed to visit adolescent mothers' homes on a regular basis and assist the teens to adopt a loving, competent parental role. In much the same way, grandfathers from the community who are good role models could be hired to visit other men with young unmarried daughters at home with infants and assist these male neighbours to play a loving grandparent role. The comments of some of the grandfathers who participated in this study suggest that such male role models would not be too difficult to find. Particularly salient were the words of one grandfather, who said: 'The big factor is that we all show our affection and love for him. That's more important than anything.'

Acknowledgements

This investigation was supported in part by Maternal and Child Health Grant 86-2118-J1 awarded to Norma Radin. An earlier version of this chapter was presented at the biennial meeting of the International Society for the Study of Behavioural Development, Jyväskylä, Finland, in July 1989. We would like to express our deep appreciation for the time and effort donated to this study by the participating families and school districts.

References

Ainsworth, M.D.S., Blehar, M.C., Waters, S. and Wall, S. (1978) *Patterns of Attachment*, Hillsdale, NJ: Erlbaum.
Baldwin, W. and Cain, V. (1980) 'The children of teenage parents', *Family Planning Perspective* 12: 34–43.
Bandura, A. (1977) *Social Learning Theory*, Englewood Cliffs, NJ: Prentice Hall.
Baranowski, M.D. (1985) 'Grandfatherhood: new perspectives', *Nurturing News* 7: 11–13.
Bayley, N. (1969) *Bayley Scales of Infant Development*, New York: Psychological Corporation.
Benn, R.K. (1986) 'Factors promoting secure attachment relationships between employed mothers and their sons', *Child Development* 57: 1224–31.
Benn, R. and Saltz, E. (1989) 'The effect of grandmother support on teen parenting and infant attachment patterns within the family', Paper presented at the Biennial Meeting of the Society for Research in Child Development, Kansas City, MO.
Biller, H.B. (1981) 'The father and sex role development', in M.E. Lamb (ed.), *The Role of the Father in Child Development* (2nd edn), New York: John Wiley & Sons.
Blanchard, R.W. and Biller, H.B. (1971) 'Father availability and academic performance among third-grade boys', *Developmental Psychology* 4: 301–5.
Cartwright, D.S. (1956) 'A rapid non-parametric estimate of multi-judge reliability', *Psychometrika* 21: 17–29.
Crockenberg, S. (1987) 'Predictors and correlates of anger toward and punitive control of toddlers by adolescent mothers', *Child Development* 58: 964–75.
Denham, T.E. and Smith, C.W. (1989) 'The influence of grandparents on grandchildren: a review of the literature and resources', *Family Relations* 38: 345–50.
Easterbrooks, M.A. and Goldberg, W.A. (1984) 'Toddler development in the family: impact of father involvement and parenting characteristics', *Child Development* 55: 740–52.

Epstein, A. and Radin, N. (1975) 'Motivational components related to father behavior and cognitive functioning, *Child Development* 46: 831–39.

Eyberg, S.M. and Matarazzo, R.G. (1980) 'Training parents as therapists: a comparison between individual parent–child interaction training and parent group didactic training', *Journal of Clinical Psychology* 36: 492–99.

Furstenberg, F.F., Jr. (1976) *Unplanned parenthood: the social consequences of teenage childbearing*, New York: Free Press.

Furstenberg, F.F., Jr. (1980) 'Burdens and benefits: the impact of early childbearing on the family', *Journal of Social Issues* 36: 64–86.

Furstenberg, F.F., Jr., Brooks-Gunn, J. and Morgan, J. (1987) *Adolescent mothers in later life*, New York: Cambridge University Press.

Furstenberg, F.F. and Crawford, A.G. (1978) 'Family support: helping teenage mothers to cope', *Family Planning Perspectives* 10: 322–33.

Gaensbauer, T.J. and Harmon, R.J. (1981) 'Clinical assessment in infancy utilizing structured playroom situations', *Journal of American Academy of Child Psychiatry* 20: 264–80.

Goldstein, H.S. (1982) 'Fathers' absence and cognitive development of 12- to 17-year-olds', *Psychological Reports* 51: 843–48.

Guttman, D. (1977) 'The cross-cultural perspective: notes toward a comparative psychology of aging', in J.E. Birren and K.W. Schall (eds), *Handbook of the Psychology of Aging*, New York: Van Nostrand & Reinhold Co.

Guttmacher Institute (1981) *Teenage Pregnancy: the Problem that Hasn't Gone Away*, New York: The Alan Guttmacher Institute.

Hardy, J.B., Duggan, A.K., Masnyk, K. and Pearson, C. (1989) 'Fathers of children born to young urban mothers', *Perspectives* 21: 159–63.

Harold-Goldsmith, R., Radin, N. and Eccles, J.S. (1988) 'Objective and subjective reality: the effects of job loss and financial stress on fathering behaviors', *Family Perspective* 22: 309–25.

Harrington, D.M., Block, J.H. and Block, J. (1978) 'Intolerance of ambiguity in preschool children: psychometric considerations, behavioral manifestations, and parental correlates', *Developmental Psychology* 14: 242–56.

Hayes, C.D. (ed.) (1987) *Risking the Future: Adolescent Sexuality, Pregnancy, and Childbearing*, vol. 1, Washington, DC: National Academy Press.

Hetherington, E.M., Cox, M. and Cox, R. (1982) 'Effects of divorce on parents and children', in M.E. Lamb (ed.), *Nontraditional Families: Parenting and Child Development*, Hillsdale, NJ: Erlbaum.

Hollingshead, A.B. (1975) 'Four-factor index of social status', Unpublished MS, available from Department of Sociology, Yale University, New Haven, CT 06520.

Hollingshead, A.B. and Redlich, F.C. (1958) *Social Class and Mental Illness, a Community Study*, New York: John Wiley & Sons.

Kamii, C.K. and Radin, N. (1967) 'Class differences in the socialization practices of Negro mothers', *Journal of Marriage and the Family* 29: 302–10.

Lamb, M.E. (1981) 'Father and child development: an integrative overview', in M.E. Lamb (ed.), *The Role of the Father in Child Development*, New York: John Wiley & Sons, pp. 1–70.

Livson, F.B. (1981) 'Paths to psychological health in the middle years: sex differences', in D.H. Eichorn, N. Hann, J. Clausen, M. Honzik and P. Mussen (eds), *Present and Past in Middle Life*, New York: Academic Press.

Main, M. and Solomon J. (1986) 'Discovery of an insecure, disorganized/disoriented attachment pattern', in T.B. Brazelton and M.W. Yogman (eds), *Affective development in infancy*, Norwood, NJ: Ablex Publishing Corp., pp. 95–124.

Matas, L., Arend, R. and Sroufe, L. (1978) 'Continuity of adaptation in the second year: the relationship between quality of attachment and later competence', *Child Development* 49: 547–56.

Nietfeldt, C.L. (1984) 'Parental and child correlates of preschool boys' social competence', Unpublished dissertation, University of Michigan.

Parsons, T. and Bales, R.G. (1955) *Family Socialization and Interaction Process*, Glencoe, IL: Free Press.

Pedersen, F.A., Rubenstein, O.L. and Yarrow, L.J. (1979) 'Infant development in father-absent families', *Journal of Genetic Psychology* 135: 51–61.

Phipps-Yonas, S. (1980) 'Teenage pregnancy and motherhood: a review of the literature', *American Journal of Orthopsychiatry* 50: 403–31.

Radin, N. (1972) 'Maternal warmth, achievement motivation, and cognitive functioning in lower-class preschool children', *Child Development* 42: 1560–65.

Radin, N. (1981) 'The role of the father in cognitive, academic, and intellectual development', in M.E. Lamb (ed.), *The Role of the Father in Child Development* (2nd edn), New York: John Wiley & Sons.

Radin, N. (1982) 'Primary caregiving and role-sharing fathers', in M.E. Lamb (ed.) *Nontraditional Families: Parenting and Child Development*, Hillsdale, NJ: Erlbaum, pp. 173–204.

Radin, N. (1986) 'The influence of fathers upon sons and daughters and implications for school social work', *Social Work in Education* 8: 77–91.

Radin, N. and Goldsmith, R. (1985) 'Caregiving fathers of preschoolers: four years later', *Merrill-Palmer Quarterly* 31: 375–83.

Radin, N. and Harold-Goldsmith, R. (1989) 'The involvement of selected unemployed and employed men with their children', *Child Development* 60: 454–59.

Ratner, H.H. (1989) 'Improving memory in educable mentally retarded children', Paper presented at the Second Annual Regional Conference on Maternal and Child Health Research, Rockville, MD (Sept.).

Rice, E. and Meyer, B. (1985) 'Reading behavior and prose recall performance of young and older adults with high and average verbal ability', *Educational Gerontology* 11: 57–72.

Robinson, E.A. and Eyberg, S. (1981) 'The dyadic parent–child interaction coding system: standardization and validation', *Journal of Consulting and Clinical Psychology* 49: 245–50.

Rosenberg, B.G. and Sutton-Smith, B. (1966) 'Sibling association, family size and cognitive abilities', *Journal of Genetic Psychology* 107: 271–79.

Sagi, A. (1982) 'Antecedents and consequences of various degrees of paternal involvement in child-rearing: the Israeli project', in M.E. Lamb (ed.), *Nontraditional Families: Parenting and Child Development*, Hillsdale, NJ: Erlbaum, pp. 205–22.

Santrock, J.W. (1972) 'The relations of onset and types of father absence to cognitive development', *Child Development*, 43: 455–69.

Thornton, A. and Freedman, D. (1983) 'The changing American family', *Population Bulletin* 38: 1–43.

Vecchiolla, F.J. and Maza, P.L. (1989) *Pregnant and Parenting Adolescents*, Washington, DC: Child Welfare League of America.

Yarrow, L.J., McQuisten, S., MacTurk, R., McCarthy, M., Klein, R. and Vietze, P. (1983) 'Assessment of mastery motivation during the first year of life: contemporaneous and cross-age relationships', *Developmental Psychology* 19: 159–71.

Chapter seven

Transmission of parenting across generations

A.A. Vermulst, A.J.L.L. de Brock and R.A.H. van Zutphen

Parental behaviour is determined by a multitude of factors. Within this multitude of factors, the parents' experience in childhood of the child-rearing practices of their own parents is assumed to be a very important factor (Belsky 1980).

On the one hand, the parenting attitude of parents may have a specific modelling function for the way in which their children might handle child-rearing practices later. Current parenting then will be especially influenced by the things that they have seen, learned or imitated in the past from their own parents. In this context, Angenent (1985) mentions the concept of a child-rearing tradition in which parental behaviour patterns are passed down from one generation to another. The child-rearing attitude of parents will tend to repeat itself again and again in a similar way to the parent's own upbringing as a child by his or her own parents. Consequently, according to Angenent (1985), intergenerational child-rearing traditions then will be hard to break through.

On the other hand, past experiences of the child-rearing practices of one's own parents may have a more general effect on the way in which one will handle one's own children later on, and on the type and quality of the contact one will have with these children. Within developmental psychology it is often assumed that early interpersonal experiences play a crucial role in the initiation and growth of a mature and harmonious psychosocial development, during the rest of the lifespan. The quality of the relationship between the infant and the mother or mother-substitute will provide the basis for the opportunity in later life to engage adequately in interpersonal relationships. A grown-up who has had an unsatisfactory relationship with the mother as a result of a lack of affection will not only approach other persons with a certain distrust, but also with a lack of ability to share warmth and intimacy (Erikson 1950; Cohler and Grunebaum 1981). When such a person has children of his or her own, such an inadequate interpersonal attitude will have negative effects on the way in which these children will be brought up. To a certain degree these children will also be treated in the same way in which the parent was treated formerly by his or her parents.

From a theoretical point of view, attachment theory can give an additional explanation for the transmission of these characteristics. Recently there has been a growing interest in the influence of the 'attachment biography' of parents on their responsiveness and on the quality of the attachment relationship with their children. It is supposed that parents transmit their own attachment biography to the young child (van IJzendoorn and Lambermon 1988).

From a more sociological point of view, various forces within the family or society can be pointed out which can be distinguished from more interpersonal dyadic mechanisms, and which also contribute to the existence of intergenerational relationships in the field of child-rearing practices. In this connection Bengtson (Bengtson *et al.* 1976; Dunham and Bengtson 1986) introduces the concept of family solidarity as the sum of expectations, activities, feelings and functions that are shared by the different members of the family. According to Bengtson, this solidarity exists not only between family members of one generation, but even more strongly between members of different generations. In this way family solidarity constitutes the foundation for the replication of generations within a process of social and biological duplication. Dimensions of this solidarity aimed at the sharing of meanings, values, beliefs and orientations with regard to parenting play a role in the transmission of parenting attitudes to the next generation.

This transmission, however, is not a rigid process. From a macro-level point of view it is repeatedly stated that generations are not fixed, unchangeable entities. The dynamics of the social-cultural and historical context in which generations follow each other will provide the conditions under which every generation will distinguish itself from former and future generations by a number of specific and characteristic qualities (Cohen 1971; Dunham and Bengtson 1986; Kearl and Hermes 1984). These distinctive characteristics will also have their effects on parenting and its resulting determinants.

Relative and absolute transmission of parenting

The psychological points of view tend to suggest that the transmission of parenting (and its characteristics) might be more or less of an absolute quality, whereas the sociological perspective is inclined to emphasize the uniqueness of each generation and, as a consequence of that, that parenting and its determinants across generations will change. There are many indications in the literature which point to the fact that transmission of parental characteristics is not an absolute, but a relative, transmission. Relative transmission of parental characteristics means that characteristics will be transmitted to some extent within families but that under the influence of social-cultural and historical conditions, overall shifts in the extent of some characteristics will be observed too. This means that correlations will still be observed between parents and children in relation to several parenting characteristics, but at the same time differences between levels of parents' and children's characteristics (for example, in terms of mean values) can exist.

In several studies, differences in parenting characteristics between parents and grandparents have been found that can be interpreted in terms of a relative transmission process (Cohler and Grunebaum 1981; Gallagher 1979; Staples and

Smith 1954). These studies generally tend to conclude that a shift has appeared from a more or less conformist and authoritarian parenting attitude in the older generation, to a more child-centred and permissive attitude in the younger generation of mothers (differences between levels). Furthermore, parents with the least authoritarian and restrictive grandparents appear to have the most egalitarian relationship with their children (correlations). Sometimes it is not always clear whether differences between grandparents and parents can be interpreted in terms of transmission of parenting attitudes in a relative way (a shift of attitudes), or in terms of actual independent differences in attitudes between generations (no transmission).

Another study referred to a process of absolute transmission. Ho and Kang (1984) reported no significant differences between mothers and grandmothers in attitudes and concepts of personality development of children, and conclude that strong similarities exist between both generations. Unfortunately, no correlations between the two generations are shown, and a more thorough inspection of the analyses shows that the authors used t-tests for independent samples where t-tests for dependent samples should have been applied. Re-analyses would probably lead to several significant differences in attitudes and conceptions, and a relative transmission process would then best describe this case too.

In other studies, directed to problematic child-rearing characteristics, a certain degree of transmission has been observed too. There appears to be an intergenerational continuity in the experience of problems in child-rearing (Honzik 1986; Quinton and Rutter 1984). Dysfunctional parenting, such as child abuse, can also continue through generations (Browne and Sagi 1987). In an elaborate longitudinal study, Elder and Caspi (1986) tried to show the existence of an intergenerational cycle of parental problem behaviour in the context of unstable family relationships. They suggest that when parents are confronted, in their childhood, with conflicts and strains between their own parents, and experience hostile child-rearing practices, then this relationship in the older generation between impulsive and uncontrolled parental behaviour and problematic family relations appears to repeat itself to a certain degree in the next generation of parents. McLanahan and Bumpass (1988) found evidence in their study for the assumption that mothers who as a result of a divorce were raised by one parent in their childhood show a higher rate of having their own marriage end in a disruption than do mothers from two-parent families. Here, too, however, there is reason to believe that transmission is not absolute, but is better referred to as a relative process. Problematic child-rearing characteristics will not always be transmitted to the next generation, while present child-rearing problems are not always necessarily the result of problems in the preceding generation.

The preceding notions lead to the conclusion that transmission of child-rearing characteristics can best be characterized in terms of a process of relative transmission. This conclusion corresponds to the present state of affairs in the research of intergenerational relations in the broader area of lifespan psychology (Rosnick and Meck 1987).

Processes of transmission

Even if there is some agreement that relative transmission often takes place, little is known about the process behind intergenerational similarities and relationships (Rosnick and Meck 1987). According to Quinton and Rutter (1984) this is certainly true in the area of parenting; they state that at present practically nothing is known about the mechanisms that mediate the continuity or discontinuity of child-rearing practices from one generation to the next (see also Stevens 1984). Subsequently, Quinton and Rutter mention the possibility that the transmission of parenting problems to the next generation, which they found in their study, might not only be the consequence of the learning and passing on of certain specific techniques of disciplining, but also might be the result of other mechanisms. They suggest that the link between problems in parenting in both generations might be mediated by socio-economic variables (transmission of social and material disadvantages) and personality variables (transmission of inadequate coping skills).

It appears that mothers play a very important role in this transmission. Elder, Downey and Cross (1986) found that continuity between generations was especially maintained by women. The quality of the relationship between mothers and their own mothers was a significant predictor for the quality of the relationship with their children. With fathers no such connection was found. According to Pederson (1969), mothers report a closer relationship with their parents than do fathers. Moreover, mothers play a more active role in maintaining contact with their parents than fathers (Bott 1971). Cohler and Grunebaum (1981) conclude that transmission of values and parenting behaviours is mostly carried out by mothers. For this reason, the present research is restricted to grandmothers and mothers.

Research aims

The research reported here focuses on two central questions. In order to study the amount and nature of the intergenerational transmission of parenting as well as the way in which this process takes place, we employ a process model of parenting (Belsky 1984). This model suggests how different child-rearing characteristics are related to one another.

First, we examine whether Belsky's model can be reproduced separately for grandmothers, and for mothers. The second question pertains to how the transmission of child-rearing characteristics can be mapped by means of an intergenerational model. Here, the two models of maternal and grandmaternal functioning will be related to each other. The combination of both models results in an intergenerational model by which relative transmission can be described and studied. Because our underlying assumption is of a process of relative transmission (correlations between generations as well as mean differences between several parenting variables existing simultaneously), we will first look at characteristics transmitted from grandmother to mother. The extent to which this takes place will also be examined. Subsequently, the extent to which the parental functioning

103

of the mother can be explained by the parental functioning of the grandmother will be examined. Finally, we will investigate the similarities and differences between grandmothers and mothers, and check if findings in the literature – for example, that mothers compared to grandmothers show less restrictive parenting attitudes – will be found in this study too.

Belsky's model of parental functioning

In Belsky's model (1984), three general determinants of parenting can be distinguished: first, the personal functioning of parents as developed (among other things) by the child-rearing experiences in childhood with their own parents. The development of the personality as a result of the history of experiences with their own parents can be regarded as a sub-determinant. The second factor is contextual sources of stress and support in the family and in the primary social environment of the parent. Third is child characteristics, especially those qualities which either make it easy or difficult to handle the child adequately. The model, slightly modified from Belsky's article, is presented in Figure 7.1.

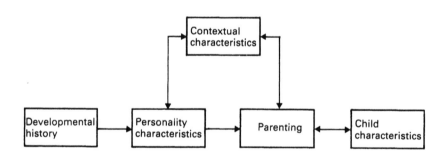

Figure 7.1 A model of parental functioning

Personal characteristics of parents are established through a developmental history. The arrows indicate that contextual characteristics and personality characteristics can influence each other mutually. The same mutual relations exist between contextual characteristics and parenting and between child characteristics and parenting. Personality has a direct influence on parenting. This model is global, which means that the direction of the arrows depends on the choice of the variables that represents the various determinants. The reader should note that parental functioning refers to the combined functioning of all determinants in the model, while parenting refers to only one aspect of it.

This model can be considered as potentially an intergenerational model, in which the sub-determinant 'developmental history' can be used to point out the intergenerational aspect. Belsky, Hertzog and Rovine (1986) do this by presenting to the parents a self-report questionnaire in which important aspects of the developmental history of the personality are measured.

A combined intergenerational model of parental functioning

In our opinion, the intergenerational aspect can be measured more adequately if the sub-determinant 'developmental history' in the model in Figure 7.1 is itself replaced by another complete model of parental functioning, referring to the time in which the present parent was still a child; for convenience we will call the latter a model of grandparental functioning. By combining the parental and the grandparental model, an intergenerational model is developed by which the transmission of parental functioning can be studied.

A second modification to Belsky's original model concerns the variable of social class. Social class is not explicitly mentioned by Belsky (1984), but in the literature a clear relationship between social class and parenting behaviour and attitudes has been demonstrated (Gecas 1979; Gerris *et al.* 1986; Kohn 1963, 1976; Vermulst *et al.* 1986). In the lower social classes, parenting attitudes tend to encourage conformist behaviour of children, and child-rearing practices are focused on the external imposition of rules. In the higher social classes, parents are more inclined to encourage the self-determination of the child, and child-rearing practices are more focused on independence. In our model, the social class variable will be placed preceding personality characteristics, since (in accordance with Gerris *et al.* 1986; Kohn 1963, 1976; Vermulst *et al.* 1986) social class is supposed to influence the personality characteristics of the parent directly. Social class will have an indirect influence on the other determinants of the model.

For the intergenerational model we suppose that four characteristics from the grandparental model – social class, personality characteristics, contextual characteristics and parenting – can exert a direct influence on the corresponding characteristics of the parental model. This starting point is partly based on the notion that parenting attitudes and behaviour may be acquired as the result of imitation of the ways in which one was raised by one's own parents. From the social class of grandparents we also expect a direct influence on the social class of parents. For contextual characteristics this assumption applies to a lesser extent because these characteristics are dependent on personality characteristics and to a lesser extent on parenting behaviour. As a result, contextual characteristics will be transmitted in a more indirect way. Child characteristics of the grandparental model cannot be directly transmitted to child characteristics of the parental model. The child of the present parent does not know how the child of the grandparent behaved and developed himself. Here an indirect effect will appear: the child in the grandparental model is the present mother, and an indirect influence through the personality characteristics of the present mother will be the case.

It is also possible that characteristics of the grandparental model influence other characteristics in the parental model than those just mentioned. However, we assume that such influences are indirect. For instance, a certain kind of parenting behaviour from the grandparents can affect the personality characteristics of the present parent. In that case we assume that the influence goes via the child characteristics of the grandparental model. The complete intergenerational model is presented in Figure 7.2.

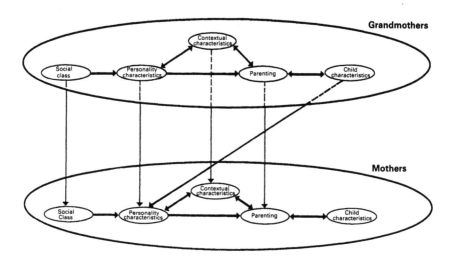

Figure 7.2 An intergenerational model of parental functioning

Operationalizing the determinants of the model

To measure social class we chose the variable *educational level*. According to Gerris *et al.* (1986), Kohn (1963, 1976) and Vermulst *et al.* (1986) it is the education of the parent which determines the nature of parenting orientation. The educational level is a more appropriate indicator for the model than a variable such as socio-economic status or occupational level.

The determinant personality characteristics will be represented by two variables: *psychological well-being* and *conformity*. The choice of these two variables was made following Belsky and Kohn. Belsky (1984) concluded in his review that a high level of psychological well-being in the parent can make a substantial positive contribution to adequate parenting. A disturbance in parental psychological well-being often leads to depression, which in turn results in a disrupted family climate that is hostile or repellent to children. The functioning of the child will be negatively influenced. Belsky also found indications that a low level of psychological well-being (rather than a high level of well-being) is transmitted through generations. Kohn (1963, 1976) regarded the amount of conformity orientation as a key variable in the explanation of differences between low and high social classes with respect to parenting behaviour.

Contextual characteristics that play an important role in parenting, according to Belsky, are those which give support to the parents or which can become a source of stress for the parents. The marital relationship, the social network and work are supposed to be important sources of stress and support here. A general measure embracing diverse aspects of stress and support is the variable *perceived support*. A smaller extent of support has a negative influence on parenting and will result in more restrictive and punishing behaviour. Perceived support also has a direct connection with psychological well-being: parents who do not feel psychologically well perceive a smaller extent of support.

In order to describe parental behaviour, two central dimensions of parenting in the literature will be focused on. These are control or restrictivity, and warmth or affectivity (Janssens 1986; Rollins and Thomas 1979). We employ the two dimensions *restriction* and *affection*.

Child characteristics will be measured by means of the *behavioural style* of the child. Belsky (1984) reported that a difficult temperament in the child can frustrate parenting behaviour. For this reason the behavioural style of the child will be used as an indicator of temperament.

Method

Subjects

Fifty-five grandmother–mother dyads participated in this study. All respondents were from the east of Holland (the area Nijmegen-Arnhem and the Achterhoek). The ages of the grandmothers ranged from 52 to 81 years (mean 66); that of the mothers from 28 to 43 years (mean 36); the mothers were interviewed about specific daughters, whose age ranged from 7 to 13 (mean 10). The grandmothers' average number of children was 4.7 and the mothers was 2.3. The socio-economic background of the participants, in terms of educational level, is approximately the same as the national level.

Procedure

About one-third of the grandmother–mother dyads was approached through primary schools. The teachers were asked to give letters to girls who were between 8 and 12 years of age and whose grandmothers were still alive. By means of this letter the girls' mothers were asked to participate in our project and to motivate their mothers also to participate. In this way twenty grandmother–mother dyads were recruited. The others (thirty-five) responded to an advertisement in the local newspapers.

All the grandmothers lived separately from the mothers, and they were visited separately by interviewers. The interview consisted of two parts. The first part was a demographic questionnaire to gain information about the socio-economic background of the participants, the educational level of the parents, the number of children in the family and their ages, marital status and so on. The second part consisted of several structured questionnaires. The first part was completed with the interviewers. Instructions were given about completing the second part which was left behind with the request to complete it independently and return it within a couple of weeks.

The mothers were asked to answer the questions according to their present state. The grandmothers were asked to recall the time when their daughters (the present mothers) were 10-year-olds. During the selection of measuring instruments and the questionnaires we strove as much as possible to bear this aspect in mind, by choosing measuring instruments which are global (not situation-specific), and by reminding the grandmother constantly that the questions must be answered by referring back to the time when her daughter was about 10 years old. Also, the questions of the two parts of this interview were written in the past tense to help the grandmothers to think continuously in the past. For mothers, the same questions were written in the present tense.

Variables

With the help of factor analyses a great number of variables present in the questionnaires (sometimes denoted as sub-scales) were reduced to a smaller number; for a comprehensive justification see van Zutphen (1989).

An important reason to reduce a large number of variables to a small number of factors can be found in the use of the LISREL technique. Due to the small number of respondents, the models to be analysed should be simple, with a small number of variables. In the discussion, more aspects in relation to this technique are quoted. Because every variable consists of a number of items, the new variables (factors), which are a combination of the original ones, are based on a rather large number of items, varying from twenty-three for the variable affection to ninety-one for the variable behavioural style.

These new variables (factors) were constructed by average sum scores. With the exception of the variable educational level (ranging from 1=only primary education to 8=university) the variables ranged from 1 (the characteristic concerned is present at a minimum) to 6 (the characteristic concerned is present at a maximum) and are all based on 6-point scales. The internal consistencies reported below are based on sub-scales.

Social class: the educational level of the father is often taken as indicator.

Here we chose the *educational level of the mother*, because only women were interviewed to examine their view of parenting.

Personal characteristics of the (grand)mothers: *psychological well-being* expresses the extent to which a person feels psychologically well, and a low score on this variable indicates that the person is depressive, role-restricted, incompetent and physically unhealthy. These four characteristics are the sub-scales which together form the variable psychological well-being. Reliabilities and validating results for the sub-scales are presented in de Brock, Vermulst and Gerris (1989). This variable has an internal consistency alpha coefficient of .87 for grandmothers and .86 for mothers. *Conformity* is constructed in an analogous manner. A high score indicates that parents have child-rearing attitudes which are very conformative and allow very little freedom for independent development of the child. Psychometric qualities of the three sub-scales which form this variable are described in Vermulst, Gerris, Franken and Janssens (1986) and Vermulst, Gerris and Siebenheller (1987). The internal consistency is .65 for grandmothers and .78 for mothers.

Contextual characteristics: measured by *perceived support in parenting*. A low score indicates low perceived support from the social network, a feeling of not being integrated and having little actual support. Psychometric qualities are reported in de Brock *et al.* (1989). The internal consistency is .91 and .90 for grandmothers and mothers respectively.

Parenting: a high score on the variable *restriction* indicates that parents impose many behaviour restrictions on the child by means of prohibitions and regulations; there is a high measure of control and the independent behaviour of the child will be hindered. The internal consistency of this variable is .81 for grandmothers and .69 for mothers. The variable *affection* indicates the measure to which a parent shows affective behaviour towards the child. A high score means that a warm and affective relation exists between mother and daughter. This variable consists of one sub-scale. Psychometric qualities of the sub-scales which constitute the variable restriction and the variable affection are represented in Siebenheller, Gerris and Vermulst (1986).

Child characteristics: measured by the *behavioural style* of the child. A low score indicates a difficult behaviour style and means that the child is hardly accepted, has an unpleasant mood, is depressive, withdrawn and aggressive. Psychometric qualities of the sub-scales are reported in de Brock *et al.* (1989) and Verhulst (1985). The internal consistency of this variable is .90 for both grandmothers and mothers.

It should be noted that the parenting variable *restriction* has similarities with the personal variable *conformity*. This is one of the disadvantages of the use of questionnaires: actual child-rearing behaviour in concrete rearing situations cannot be measured. In order to discriminate between items which measure attitudes (such as conformity) and items which measure (the tendency to) actual behaviour (such as restriction), the attitude items are formulated in general terms (for example, a child ought to conform to general views and rules), while the behaviour items are personally directed to the respondent (for instance, if my child is troublesome, I punish him or her). This kind of questioning will probably measure not the actual child-rearing behaviour, but the tendency to do so. The difference between an attitude and a tendency will be very small, and it is for this reason that there consists a similarity between *conformity* and *restriction*.

Results

First we examine to what degree Belsky's model holds for grandmothers, and for mothers. Then, the intergenerational model will be constructed and specific questions will be: to what extent are some characteristics transmitted from grandmother to mother; how much of the parental functioning of the mother can be explained by parental functioning of the grandmother in the past; and to what extent are there noticeable differences between grandmothers and mothers? In relation to this last question, we will particularly see if child-rearing attitudes are less conformative and child-rearing behaviour less restrictive in mothers than grandmothers.

Belsky's models constructed for grandmothers and mothers

To find out to what extent the model postulated in Figure 7.1 applies to grand-mothers and to mothers separately, LISREL VI is used (Jöreskog and Sörbom 1985). The input for the analyses is presented in Table 7.1. The results of the analyses are portrayed in Figure 7.3 (for grandmothers) and 7.4 (for mothers). The model as presented in Figure 7.3 has a goodness of fit value χ^2 (13) = 10.13, p = .683, while that in Figure 7.4 has χ^2 (13) = 5.55, p = .961. In both models, there is an excellent fit between the input correlation matrix and the correlation matrix reproduced from the significant beta weights as expressed in the nonsignificant χ^2 values. The lower χ^2, the higher the p-value and the better the fit will be. Significant relations are presented in Figures 7.3 and 7.4, which means that the t-values (to test whether beta weights deviate significantly from zero) have values above 2.

Table 7.1 Correlation matrix of the variables from the grandmothers' model (above the diagonal) and from the mothers' model (below the diagonal)

	1	2	3	4	5	6	7
1 Educational level		.18	−.38	.02	−.31	.15	.24
2 Psychological well-being	−.15		.02	.33	−.13	.25	.52
3 Conformity	−.30	.33		−.06	.78	−.16	.05
4 Perceived support	−.07	.50	.18		−.23	.41	.55
5 Restriction	−.26	.16	.86	−.02		−.33	−.13
6 Affection	.23	.15	−.30	.12	−.42		.54
7 Behavioural style child	.02	.67	.19	.41	.06	.27	

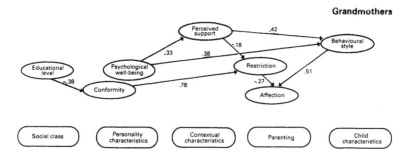

Figure 7.3 An intragenerational model of parental functioning for grandmothers

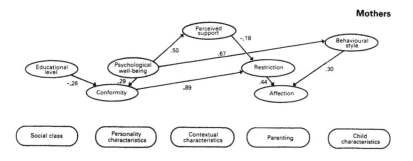

Figure 7.4 An intragenerational model of parental functioning for mothers

The negative relation of educational level with the variable *conformity* and the absence of a relation between *educational level* and *psychological well-being* is in accordance with Kohn's theory (Kohn 1963, 1976). A relation between the personality variables is not expected and is found only for mothers to a small degree. In both models, the assumed relation between *psychological well-being* and *perceived social support* is present, but the relation between *perceived social support* and *parenting* (in terms of the variable *restriction*) is not impressive. The strong relation between *conformity* and *restriction* as well as the relation between the *behavioural style* of the child and *affection* of the (grand)mother are in accordance with our expectations. The relation between the parenting variables *restriction* and *affection* shows a consistent picture in both models.

In contrast to the postulated model in Figure 7.1, a positive relation exists between *psychological well-being* of the (grand)mother and the *behavioural style* of the child in both Figures 7.3 and 7.4. Three possible explanations for this unexpected result can be given. The first explanation is that (grand)mothers, who feel psychologically well, are inclined to judge their daughter's behavioural style more positively than (grand)mothers who feel themselves psychologically unhappy. This explanation would be consistent with the widely held view that temperament as measured by questionnaire is a characteristic of the dyad rather than an individual. The second explanation is that (grand)mothers who feel psychologically unhappy radiate their mood to their children, which in turn can influence the behaviour of these children in a negative way. At first sight this influence seems much lower in the model of the grandmothers than in the model of the mothers. This could be explained by the significant relation between *perceived support* and *behavioural style* of the child for grandmothers, a relation which does not exist for mothers. Via this path there is an indirect influence (of about .14) between *psychological well-being* and *behavioural style*. The total effect (direct plus indirect) turns out to be

$$.38 + .14 = .52,$$

and does not deviate so much from the value of .67 for mothers. A third explanation has to do with an appropriate choice of variables. A parent who feels herself psychologically weak will express this discomfort in behaviour and in parenting. It is possible that this kind of specific behaviour is inadequately expressed in our variables.

The influence of *perceived social support* on the *behavioural style* of the child is not postulated in the model of Figure 7.1. This is an influence which is found with grandmothers, but not with mothers. Apparently, *perceived social support* is a mediating variable between *psychological well-being* and *behavioural style* of the child.

In summary, it appears that the model postulated in Figure 7.1 cannot be fully replicated for grandmothers and mothers. The most important deviation is the relationship of *psychological well-being* with the *behavioural style* of the child. A second important deviation is the relationship between *perceived social support* and *behavioural style* of the child for grandmothers. To find an optimal fit, the LISREL programme forces some relations between variables which are not fully supported from theoretical considerations. In addition to the explanations already mentioned for the existence of these relations, a final explanation is that the postulated model in Figure 7.1 is too simple for the description of parental functioning. Moreover, a refinement of the measuring instruments used, and other sampling designs (observations in a natural setting, independent ratings of judges, more sample subjects) can possibly explain the existence of the unexpected relations. These shortcomings are not disastrous for the determination of an intergenerational model: apart from the relationship between *perceived social support* and *behavioural style* of the child for grandmothers, no salient differences between the models of grandmothers and mothers have been found.

The intergenerational model

After the assessment of the two individual models, the intergenerational model can be developed with help of LISREL. Basically, each of the seven variables in the model of the grandmothers can influence each of the seven variables in the model of the mothers. A technical objection is that the number of parameter estimates will be very large, resulting in inaccurate parameter estimates because of the rather small sample size. With the theoretical construction of the intergenerational model it is already hypothesized that a model consisting merely of direct influences between the same variables will be the most adequate, and in this way the number of parameter estimates will be reduced considerably. One exception to the choice for direct influences is formed by connecting the behavioural style in the model of the grandmothers with the personality variables in the model of the mothers. In this case, both variables are concerned with the same person.

Such a model seems to have an excellent fit: χ^2 (71) = 75.96, p = .322; see Figure 7.5. The input for the analysis is presented in Table 7.2. In the figure, only significant relations are reported with t-values (to test whether beta weights significantly deviate from zero) greater than 2.

Table 7.2 Correlation matrix of the variables from the grandmothers' model with the variables from the mothers' model

Mothers	Grandmothers						
	1	*2*	*3*	*4*	*5*	*6*	*7*
1 Educational level	.55	.03	−.13	.14	−.14	.26	.23
2 Psychological well-being	−.10	.46	.07	.37	−.03	.21	.53
3 Conformity	−.48	.03	.50	.17	.41	−.08	.15
4 Perceived support	−.09	.01	−.11	.43	−.20	.30	.32
5 Restriction	−.43	.05	.50	.13	.45	−.10	.07
6 Affection	.14	.22	−.11	.23	−.18	.36	.18
7 Behavioural style child	.00	.19	.08	.25	−.04	.16	.45

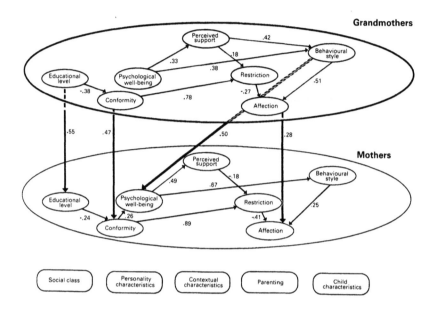

Figure 7.5 An intergenerational model of maternal functioning

It can be seen that the *educational level* of the grandmother explains to a large extent the *educational level* of the mother. The influence is equal to .55. The significant direct influence is an indication that *educational level* is an important variable in the transmission of parental functioning.

In relation to the personality variables, we see that the variable *conformity* has a significant direct influence (.47) from grandmother to mother, and is also an important variable in this transmission process. *Psychological well-being* has no direct influence, but there is an indirect influence through the *behavioural style* of the child: *psychological well-being* of the grandmother influences the *behavioural style* of the child (= the mother when she was a child), and this *behavioural style* influences the *psychological well-being* of the mother. *Psychological well-being* of the grandmothers has another indirect influence through the path from *perceived social support* to *behavioural style* of the child. The sum of these indirect effects delivers a total (indirect) influence of .25. In short, we can conclude that the two personality variables of the grandmother contribute to an explanation of the corresponding variables of the mother. The influence of *conformity* is greater than the influence of *psychological well-being*.

The *perceived social support* of the grandmother has no direct influence on the mother's *perceived social support*. Probably, the amount of *perceived social support* is directly linked to *psychological well-being*, and it is the latter which is responsible for transmission from grandmother to mother. In this way, the amount of *perceived social support* is always transmitted by a linking mechanism.

Parenting, in terms of the variables *restriction* and *affection*, also has such a linking mechanism. *Restriction* has no direct influence from grandmother to mother, but is strongly related to *conformity*. Because of this, *restriction* will automatically be induced by the variable *conformity*. *Affection* has a direct influence from grandmother to mother (.28).

The *behavioural style* of the child in the grandmothers' model has a direct significant influence on *psychological well-being* of the mother (.50): the more pleasant *behavioural style* a mother has had in her childhood the more psychologically comfortable she will feel in parenthood. The *behavioural style* of the mother's daughter is influenced indirectly by the *behavioural style* of the mother when she was a child, as *psychological well-being* is strongly connected to the *behavioural style* of the child. A significant direct influence is not present, but the total indirect effect of the *behavioural style* from the grandmothers' model to the *behavioural style* in the mothers' model equals .33.

After constructing an intergenerational model, a specific question was to what extent parental functioning of the mothers (= the seven variables in the model of the mother) can be explained by parental functioning of the grandmothers (= the seven variables in the model of the grandmother). Parental functioning of grandmothers and mothers is presented in Figures 7.3 and 7.4, and in the ellipses of Figure 7.5. For mothers, minor differences in the estimated beta weights can be seen. To what extent can the variance of the seven variables in the mothers' model be predicted from the seven variables from the grandmothers' model?

To answer this question, multiple regression analysis can be used with the grandmothers' variables as independent and the mothers' variables as dependent. Each of the seven dependent variables is predicted from the seven independent variables, and the average of the seven squared multiple correlations produces the amount of explained variance in the dependent variables (Pedhazur 1982). The multiple correlation coefficients are .61 (*educational level*), .63 (*psychological well-being*), .65 (*conformity*), .53 (*perceived social support*), .61 (*restriction*), .42 (*affection*) and .48 (*behavioural style* of the child), and the total amount of explained variance is consequently 32 per cent. We can conclude that 32 per cent of maternal parenting functioning can be explained by earlier parental functioning of the grandmother.

Differences between generations

Now we focus our attention on the extent to which differences exist between grandmothers and mothers in relation to the seven variables. Differences between grandmothers and mothers were examined using matched t-tests. The results are given in Table 7.3.

Table 7.3 Differences between grandmothers and mothers

| | Grandmothers | | Mothers | | | |
	Mean	SD	Mean	SD	T-value	P-value
Educational level	2.49	1.54	4.09	1.71	−7.67	.000
Psychological well-being	4.64	.74	4.80	.67	−1.57	.122
Conformity	3.62	.42	3.11	.51	8.10	.000
Perceived support	4.69	.93	5.15	.71	−3.84	.000
Restriction	3.73	.57	2.82	.55	11.47	.000
Affection	4.12	.51	4.47	.43	−4.82	.000
Behavioural style child	4.62	.57	4.85	.57	−2.80	.007

The mothers score significantly lower than grandmothers on *conformity* and *restriction*; the mothers' child-rearing attitudes and behaviour are less restrictive than that of the grandmothers, and they pay less attention to control and rules. Conversely, mothers score higher on *affection* with their child than do grandmothers. Additionally, mothers have a significantly higher *educational level* than the grandmothers, are higher on *perceived social support*, and perceive a more comfortable *behavioural style* than their daughters. No significant differences were found in their *psychological well-being*.

Discussion

The aim of this study was to investigate the way in which transmission of parenting variables takes place and to what extent this happens.

To start with, we examined whether the models of parental functioning for grandmothers and mothers, as theoretically represented in Figure 7.1, could be empirically replicated. The original model could not be fully replicated. Especially the relations we found between psychological well-being of the parent and behavioural style of the child (by grandmothers and mothers), and between perceived social support and behavioural style of the child (by grandmothers), are not included in the original model (see Figures 7.3 and 7.4). In spite of possible explanations for this, the relationships are not appropriate on model-theoretical grounds: the effect of personality characteristics of the (grand)mother must be mediated by behaviour and must become manifest in the interaction with the child (van IJzendoorn and Lambermon 1988). Also the relation between perceived support and behavioural style of the child must be mediated by parenting behaviour, but probably this relationship is found due to the influence of the relation between psychological well-being and behavioural style of the child. Refinement of the measuring instruments, other instruments, a different research design (such as observation in the natural home environment) and obtaining more respondents may be able to explain these relations.

Because of the fact that the models for grandmothers and mothers are generally the same, the deviations just described are not regarded as a major drawback, and the intergenerational model for transmission from grandmother to mother was constructed. The extent to which transmission occurs was determined as 32 per cent. Although this is not an insignificant percentage, still 68 per cent of the variance remains inexplicable. For that reason, the description of the mechanism behind the intergenerational transmission must be done with some caution. It can be assumed that a number of other variables not yet revealed also influence the maternal functioning.

Further study of this intergenerational model shows that two blocks of variables can be distinguished. One block includes psychological well-being, social support and behavioural style of the child; the other includes educational level, conformity and restriction. Affection plays a role in both blocks. To a large extent these two blocks can be reduced to the two personality variables psychological well-being and conformity. From this we can hypothesize that the present functioning of the mother in child-rearing will be determined mainly by psychological characteristics of the grandmother (in this case the psychological well-being) and by more or less acquired personality characteristics such as parenting values, goals and attitudes.

Concerning the established differences in level for most variables between grandmothers and mothers, the general conclusion can be drawn that there has indeed been a shift from parenting characterized by more restriction/conformity and less affection to a more permissive and affective parenting style.

A number of methodological reservations should be made about this study. It must be seen as a first step in a large-scale investigation (Vermulst et al. 1987). Firm conclusions cannot be made because of the modest size of the sample, and the fact that it was not established in a completely random manner. However, the results of this study are in line with what is found in the literature, and similar to results of research already carried out (Vermulst et al. 1986). Also the educational level of the mothers does not deviate from national data, so on this characteristic the sample can be considered as representative.

A second methodological issue concerns the use of LISREL to construct an intergenerational model in studies such as this one, where the number of respondents (here N=55 dyads) was relatively small. The maximum likelihood method used produces robust assessments with large numbers of respondents. Boomsma (1983) suggests a required minimum of 200, but Gebring and Anderson (1985) conclude that robust assessments can also be obtained with smaller numbers: these different opinions are mainly due to the complexity of the model. Testing a complex model with many parameters requires a larger number of respondents than when testing a simple model with a few parameters (Tanaka 1987). For this reason a reduction of the variables was conducted prior to the analyses by means of factor analyses. Furthermore, it is important, especially with a smaller number of respondents, that variables have a normal distribution in the scores. The disadvantageous effect of small numbers of respondents in this study is somewhat reduced as the intergenerational model is a simple model with manifest variables only, which results in the estimation of just a few parameters. Except for the variable of educational level, all the other variables in the model do have a distribution which does not significantly deviate from a normal distribution on a Kolmogorov Smirnov test.

Finally, 'retrospective bias' can certainly be an interfering factor in relation to the grandmothers' data. Grandmothers were asked to recall many facts from memory, and their answers are sure to be affected by their here-and-now situation as grandmothers. Moreover, child-rearing is not a unilateral process (Bengtson and Troll 1978). It can much better be characterized as a transactional process in which the parent influences the child, and in which the child influences the parent in return. It could very well be the case that relations between grandmaternal and maternal models will be increased because the grandmother's attitude towards parenting can no longer be regarded as detached from the mother's influence at present, even when grandmothers were explicitly asked to recall situations twenty-five years earlier.

The results of this study show that the extent to which mothers show affection to their daughters is directly related to such a parental attitude of grandmothers in the past. Affection is the only child-rearing dimension that appears to be directly transmitted in some degree from grandmothers to mothers, and so it seems that affection may play a central role in the intergenerational continuity of parenting. The assumption of Erikson (1950) that the foundation for the ability to have a warm and affective relationship with a child is formed by similar experiences in (early) childhood, where there is a warm and trustworthy relationship between the child and the mother, is supported in our study. This is even more convincing because no such relation was found with the child-rearing dimension of restriction. Apparently mothers must necessarily have experienced affection to a certain degree in childhood in order to be able to show affection to the child as a parent later, whereas with restriction such a basic condition does not apply. The level of restriction of mothers shows no direct relation with the level of restriction which grandmothers report in their former parenting attitudes.

We can only speculate about how affection is transmitted; possibly there is a learning process in the sense of transmission of an attitude via model-learning; or it may be a matter of the creation of basic conditions for an adequate socio-psychological development. In attachment theory it is supposed that the attachment biography of the parent influences the quality of the attachment relationship with the following generation. This influence is mediated by an internal working model of attachment. Such a working model is an internal representation of the mother-child relationship: what might the child expect from her environment, in view of her experiences in the past? For instance, a child with less responsive parents will construct an internal working model, in which her environment is represented as less accommodating to her needs and as rejecting her as a person in her own right (van IJzendoorn and Lambermon 1988). It is possible that this internal working model can function as a mechanism that regulates the direct transmission of affection.

Quinton and Rutter (1984) suggest that socio-economic and personality variables play an important role in the manner in which intergenerational transmission of functioning takes place (they speak of a 'linking' mechanism). We have just seen that affection is directly transferred from grandmother to mother. Our intergenerational model shows that both personality variables of the mother are indirectly affected by the personality variables of the grandmother, but that the actual intergenerational effect of this is very small. With restriction, however, this relation looks different. Restrictive parenting of mothers is largely influenced by the conformity orientation of mothers, and this orientation in turn is related to the conformity orientation of grandmothers. These orientations are also negatively related to the variables of social class in both generations. We can conclude that there is indeed a linking mechanism from one generation to another as assumed by Quinton and Rutter (1984), through the variables of social class and personality of both grandmother and mother. Restrictive behaviour is not directly transmitted from grandmothers to mothers, but indirectly through the socio-economic setting and the (partly connected) conformity orientation as a personal child-rearing attitude. A low social status and adverse social circumstances, and personal child-rearing orientations of mothers related to this which are directed at adjustment and conformity, can be transmitted from grandmother to mother. Because of their conformity orientations, mothers will subsequently treat their daughters in a rather restrictive manner. Possibly this linking mechanism can also play a role in the transmission of affective behaviour (by way of educational level, conformity and restriction), but the actual intergenerational effect here is considerably lower than with restriction.

Gerris *et al.* (1986), Kohn (1963, 1976) and Vermulst *et al.* (1986) emphasize the connection between social class and parenting through the mediation of child-rearing orientations of parents. In our model this is supported for both mothers and grandmothers. It appears that parenting (especially restriction) is determined for a substantial part by the path of social class and conformity, though it must be noted that (grand)mother's parenting is determined by conformity to a considerably larger extent than conformity in turn is determined by social class.

We may conclude that the extension of Belsky's model by the variables of social class and child-rearing orientation seems to be justified, and this certainly applies to the use of such an extended model in relation to our study of intergenerational transmission of parental functioning. The child-rearing orientation of conformity was found to be transmitted from grandmother to mother to a relatively large extent, and in both generations conformity appeared to have a negative relationship with social class.

This study supports the assumption that many parenting attitudes and their determinants are transmitted from grandmother to mother. There is also a certain amount of intergenerational continuity of parenting and parental functioning in a broader sense. The relations found between the corresponding variables in both generations, connected with differences in the level of variables between generations, suggest that transmission in child-rearing practices from generation to generation does not take place in an absolute sense. It is more a matter of relative transmission, in which differences in parenting between generations must be interpreted in terms of the dynamics of a shifting process.

References

Angenent, H. (1985) *Opvoeding en persoonlijkheidsontwikkeling*, Nijkerk: Intro.

Belsky, J. (1980) 'Child maltreatment: an ecological integration', *American Psychologist* 35: 320–35.

Belsky, J. (1984) 'The determinants of parenting: a process model', *Child Development* 55: 83–96.

Belsky, J., Hertzog, C. and Rovine, M. (1986) 'Causal analysis of multiple determinants of parenting: empirical and methodological advances', in M.E. Lamb, A.L. Brown and B. Rogoff (eds), *Advances in Developmental Psychology*, vol. 4, Hillsdale, NJ: Erlbaum.

Bengtson, V.L., Olander, E. and Haddad, A. (1976) 'The "generation gap" and aging family members: toward a conceptual model', in J.F. Gubriam (ed.), *Time, Roles and Self in Old Age*, New York: Human Services Press.

Bengtson, V.L. and Troll, L. (1978) 'Youth and their parents: feedback and intergenerational influence in socialization', in M.R. Lerner and G.B. Spanier (eds), *Child Influences on Marital and Family Interaction: a Life Span Development*, New York: Academic Press.

Block, J. (1965) *The Child Rearing Practices Report*, Berkeley, CA: Institute of Human Development.

Boomsma, A. (1983) 'On the robustness of LISREL (maximum likelihood estimation) against small sample size and nonnormality', Unpublished doctoral dissertation, University of Groningen.

Bott, E. (1971) *Family and Social Network*, New York: Free Press.

Brock, A.J.L.L. de, Vermulst, A.A. and Gerris, J.R.M. (1989) *De Nijmeegse ouderlijke stress index: een betrouwbaarheids- en validiteits onderzoek* (In preparation).

Bronson, W.C., Katten, E.S. and Livson, N. (1959) 'Patterns of authority and affection in two generations', *Journal of Abnormal and Social Psychology* 58: 143–52.

Browne, K. and Sagi, S. (1987) 'Parent–child interaction in abusing families: its possible causes and consequences', in P. Maher (ed.), *Child Abuse*, Oxford: Basil Blackwell.

Cohen, P.S. (1971) *Theorie van de samenleving*, Alphen aan den Rijn: Samson.

Cohen, S., Mermelstein, R., Kamarck, T. and Hoberman, H.M. (1985) 'Measuring the functional components of social support', in I.G. Sarason and B.R. Sarason (eds), *Social Support: Theory, Research and Applications*, Dordrecht: Martinus, pp. 73–94.

Cohler, B.J., and Grunebaum, H.U. (1981) *Mothers, Grandmothers and Daughters: Personality and Childcare in Three-Generation Families*, New York: John Wiley & Sons.

Dunham, C.C. and Bengtson, V.L. (1986) 'Conceptual and theoretical perspectives on generational relations', in N. Datan, A.L. Greene and H.W. Reese (eds), *Life Span Developmental Psychology: Intergenerational Relations*, Hillsdale, NJ: Erlbaum.

Elder, G.H., Jr. and Caspi, A. (1986) 'Problem behavior and family relationships: life course and intergenerational themes', in A.B. Sorensen, F.E. Weinert and L.R. Sherrod (eds), *Human Development and the Life Course*, Hillsdale, NJ: Erlbaum.

Elder, G.H. Jr., Downey, G. and Cross, C.E. (1986) 'Family ties and life changes: hard times and hard choices in women's lives since the 1930s', in N. Datan, A.L. Greene and H.W. Reese (eds), *Life Span Developmental Psychology: Intergenerational Relations*, Hillsdale, NJ: Erlbaum.

Erikson, E.H. (1950) *Childhood and Society*, New York: Norton.

Gallagher, B.J. (1979) 'Attitude differences across three generations: class and sex components', *Adolescence* 14: 503–16.

Gebring, D.W. and Anderson, J.C. (1985) 'The effect of sampling error and model characteristics on parameter estimation for maximum likelihood confirmatory factor analyses', *Multivariate Behavioral Research* 20: 255–71.

Gecas, V. (1979) 'The influence of social class on socialization', in W.R. Burr, R. Hill, F.J. Nye and J.L. Reiss (eds), *Contemporary Theories about the Family*, vol. 1, London: Free Press.

Gerris, J.R.M., Vermulst, A.A., Franken, W.M. and Janssens, J.M.A.M. (1986) 'Social class and parental situation perceptions as determinants of parental value orientations and behaviors', Paper presented at the Second European Conference on Developmental Psychology, Rome (Sept.), ED275413.

Ho, D.Y.F. and Kang, T.K. (1984) 'Intergenerational comparisons of child-rearing attitudes and practices in Hong Kong', *Developmental Psychology* 20: 1004–16.

Honzik, M.P. (1986) 'The role of the family in the development of mental abilities: a 50-year study', in N. Datan, A.L. Greene and H.W. Reese (eds), *Life Span Developmental Psychology*, Hillsdale, NJ: Erlbaum.

IJzendoorn, M.H. van and Lambermon, M.W.E. (1988) 'Transgenerationele overdracht van gehechtheid en verbreding van het opvoedingsmilieu', in P.P. Goudena, J.H. Groenendaal and F.A. Swets (eds) *Kind in Geding*, Louvain: Acco.

Janssens, J.M.A.M. (1986) 'Opvoeding en ontwikkeling van kinderen', in R. de Groot and J.v. Weelden (eds), *Van gisteren over morgen: een orthopedagogische overzichtsstudie*, Groningen.

Jöreskog, K.G.R. and Sörbom, P. (1985) *LISREL VI: analysis of linear structural relationships by maximum likelihood, instrumental variables and least squares models*, University of Uppsala, Sweden.

Kearl, M.C. and Hermes, M.P. (1984) 'Grandparents, grandchildren and the Kondratieff: thoughts on "period effects" in intergenerational analyses', *International Journal of Aging and Human Development* 19: 257–65.

Kohn, M.L. (1963) 'Social class and parent–child relationship: an interpretation', *American Journal of Sociology* 68: 471–81.

Kohn, M.L. (1976) 'Social class and parental values: another confirmation of the relationship: Comment on Wright and Wright', *American Sociological Review* 41: 345–58.

McLanahan, S. and Bumpass, L. (1988) 'Intergenerational consequences of family disruption', *American Journal of Sociology* 94: 130–52.

Pederson, K.K. (1969) 'Kin network research: a plea for comparability', *Journal of Marriage and the Family* 31: 271–80.

Pedhazur, E.J. (1982) *Multiple Regression in Behavioral Research: Explanation and Prediction*, New York: Holt, Rinehart & Winston.

Quinton, D. and Rutter, M. (1984) 'Parents with children in care – II. Intergenerational continuities', *Journal of Child Psychology and Psychiatry* 25: 231–50.

Rollins, B.C. and Thomas, D.L. (1979) 'Parental support, power and control techniques in the socialization of children', in W.R. Burr, R. Hill, F.J. Nye and J.L. Reis (eds), *Contemporary Theories about the Family*, vol. I, London: Free Press.

Rosnick, R.M. and Meck, N.E. (1987) 'Intergenerational relations and life-span developmental psychology', *Human Development* 30: 60–5.

Seagull, E.A.W. (1987) 'Social support and child maltreatment: a review of the evidence', *Child Abuse and Neglect* 11: 41–52.

Siebenheller, F.A., Gerris, J.R.M. and Vermulst, A.A. (1986) *De Nijmeegse Childrearing Practices Report Q-sort*, Nijmegen: Catholic University, Empirische Pedagogiek.

Staples, R. and Smith, J.W. (1954) 'Attitudes of grandmothers and mothers toward child rearing practices', *Child Development* 25: 91–7.

Stevens, J.H. (1984) 'Black grandmothers' and black adolescent mothers' knowledge about parenting', *Developmental Psychology* 20: 1017–25.

Tanaka, J.S. (1987) 'How big is big enough? Sample size and goodness of fit in structural equation models with latent variables', *Child Development* 58: 134–46.

Verhulst, F. (1985) *Mental Health in Dutch Children: an Epidemiological Study*, Proefschrift Erasmus Universiteit, Rotterdam.

Vermulst, A.A., Gerris, J.R.M. and Siebenheller, F.A. (1987) 'Opvoedingsdoelen. Bepaling van de onderliggende betekenisdimensies in het meetinstrument opvoedingsdoelen met behulp van een drietal multivariate analysetechnieken', in J.R.M. Gerris and J. van Acker (eds), *Gezin: onderzoek en hulpverlening*, Lisse: Swets & Zeitlinger.

Vermulst, A.A., Gerris, J.R.M., Franken, W.M. and Janssens, J.M.A.M. (1986) 'Determinanten van ouderlijk functioneren tegen de achtergrond van de theorie van Kohn', in J.R.M. Gerris (ed.), *Pedagogisch onderzoek in ontwikkeling*, Nijmegen: Instituut voor toegepaste sociale wetenschappen.

Zutphen, R.A.H. van (1989) *Generatieonderzoek: een studie naar overdracht van opvoedingskenmerken tussen grootmoeders en moeders*, Nijmegen: Catholic University, Department of Family Pedagogy.

The significance of grandparents for the formation of family relations

Isto Ruoppila

The child and young person grows, develops and is socialized in her or his *orientation family* (the individual's childhood family). When adult the individual will usually get married and have a child or children of his or her own in his or her *reproductive family*, where the next generation will develop and be reared. In what way and how strongly do the experiences in the orientation family later affect the new pair relation and the mother–child and father–child relation in the reproductive family? Generally, what are the relations between the orientation family and reproductive family as regards the formation of interaction in the reproductive family?

The significance of the orientation family for the achievement of different developmental tasks, especially in adolescence, has mainly been studied cross-sectionally and on the basis of information gathered from one generation, so that only its point of view has been emphasized. When the role and function of grandparents are studied, both perspectives of the interaction parts should be analysed in relation to each other.

For the socialization process the parental roles in the orientation family, its structure and interactions, have been shown to be of great importance. Especially the interactional pattern and parental attitudes in the orientation family have been analysed in relation to the interaction in the reproductive family of the next generation. In the orientation family the child and the young person acquire models of parental roles both as regards the parent–child and parent–parent relationships, models of the division of labour and child-care in the family and sex roles, all of which are interrelated. In addition to model-learning, the identification process also has an effect on role-learning in childhood and adolescence.

The relation between spouses is the axis around which other relationships in the family form. A secure, harmonious, happy family life which is characterized by a rich, open and many-sided communication between the family members and by well-functioning division of labour and child-care in the family also favours the socializing process of the younger generation. Permanent unresolved conflicts between spouses, as well as their general feeling of unhappiness, are disturbing both for the general atmosphere at home and for the acquisition of different developmental tasks connected with the parenthood of the young people

(Frommer and O'Shea 1973; Greenberg *et al*. 1959; Hill and Aldous 1969; Satir 1982; Uddenberg 1974, 1976).

In the family the child and young person learn the roles and functions of the spouses, communication and interaction between generations. Studies have been made which show how conflict-laden relationships between mother and daughter are renewed in the daughter's marriage, which signifies the importance of the mother for the daughter's development (Rautanen *et al*. 1977; Ruusuvaara 1983; Uddenberg 1974, 1976; Widholm *et al*. 1974). Much less is known about the father's significance for the son's development (Lamb 1976; Sommer 1984).

The strong connections with the orientation family and with the later behaviour of sons are especially seen in the follow-up study by Jonsson (1969, 1973), who analysed these for three successive generations. He found that unfavourable circumstances in childhood were also characteristic of an individual's parents' and grandparents' childhood. In addition, when Anderson *et al*. (1976) studied the social adaptation of these same boys later in adulthood, comparing it with that of the control group, they found a clear and strong connection between circumstances during childhood and later social adaptation.

Although there are studies which show strong associations between the family life pattern in the orientation family and the family life pattern later in the reproductive family of the next generation, very little is known about the interaction process and the most important factors contained within it as regards the continuation or discontinuation of the family life pattern. It is not only model-learning and the identification process which are of importance, but also how the young person interprets behaviour and expectations directed towards her or him. The attribution process concerning the interaction between generations has not been studied. Also the young generation has effects on the older one, whose roles are changing; for instance, when they become grandparents. These role changes can also alter the relationships between generations more generally. Grandparenthood especially can become a meaningful new resource and give new meaning and importance for ageing people. Also, the different kinds of support young parents can obtain from the older generation can help them to handle the new developmental tasks connected with parenthood. Intensive interaction between generations seems to point out that this is a very important source of psychological, social and economic support for the younger generation (Heikkinen *et al*. 1981; Tornstam *et al*. 1982). Although there are studies which give evidence of the lively interaction between generations, these give information neither on the content and significance of these interactions nor on their emotional quality. For this purpose information has to be gathered separately and independently from both generations and by methods which also allow the evaluation of the emotional quality of this interaction. This information has to be related to the living circumstances both in the orientation and in the reproductive family.

During the 1980s there have been studies at the University of Jyväskylä in Finland in which the interaction between generations and the significance of grandparenthood for grandparents themselves and for the next generation have been the main topics. In this chapter I shall focus on two particular questions: First, what is generally the amount and quality of interaction between generations, and what does this mean for the different participants? Second, and especially during the family-founding phase and later on in the young family with their first child (a) How similar are the viewpoints of grandparents and their children as regards the interaction in the orientation family and the interaction between generations? and (b) What are the relationships between the interaction in the orientation family and the interaction in the reproductive family?

The amount and quality of interaction between generations

Subjects

For the first question there are data from two representative Finnish samples of 75–84/89-year-olds. The first sample of 200 after drop-out was drawn from people born from 1898 to 1907 living in the county of Middle Finland in the town Jyväskylä and seven surrounding communities. The population of 75–84-year-olds numbered 3,972; 67 per cent of them were women, 62 per cent of the men and 18 per cent of the women were married and living with their spouse. The sample was a representative stratified random sample regarding sex and marital status, and consisted of fifty married and single people of each sex. Of the 200, 175 were living at home and 25 in institutions. The drop-out rate was 31 per cent for those living at home and zero for those in institutions: of the 78 drop-outs 14 per cent could not be reached, 23 per cent were acutely ill and in hospital, and the rest (63 per cent) refused to participate for various reasons. On the basis of the drop-out analysis the final sample was not biased as regards age, sex or place of residence. No other background data could be used for the drop-out analysis (Suutama, Salminen and Ruoppila 1988).

The second sample of 150 after drop-out was drawn from people born from 1896 to 1910 living in the county of Middle Finland in three north-western rural communities. The population of 75–89-year-olds numbered 455; 67 per cent of them were women; 53 per cent of men and 22 per cent of women were married and living with their spouse. The sample was a stratified random sample regarding sex and community, and consisted of 25 men and 25 women in each community. The drop-out rate was 15 per cent ($N = 26$). Of the 26 drop-outs 15 per cent could not be reached, 38 per cent were acutely ill and 46 per cent refused. On the basis of the drop-out analysis the final sample was not biased as regards age, sex, marital status or place of residence. No other data could be used for the drop-out analysis.

Methods

In these two studies concerning the elderly population, structured and semi-structured interviews were used for gathering anamnestic data, family, educational, vocational and social history, social activities and relationships, daily

The effects of grandparenting

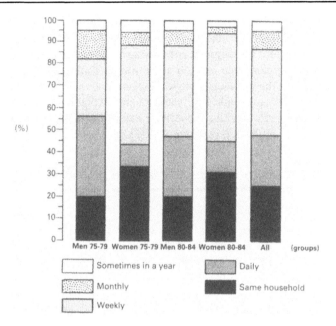

Figure 8.1 Frequency of contact with children for women and men in different age groups of the elderly having living children

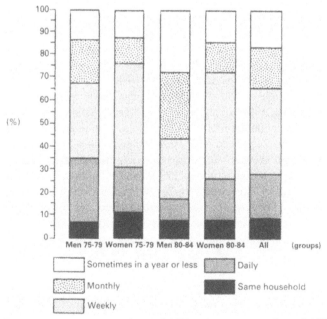

Figure 8.2 Frequency of contact with grandchildren for women and men in different age groups of the elderly having living grandchildren

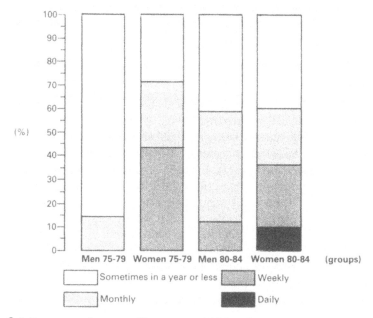

Figure 8.3 Frequency of contact with great-grandchildren for women and men in different age groups of the elderly having living great-grandchildren

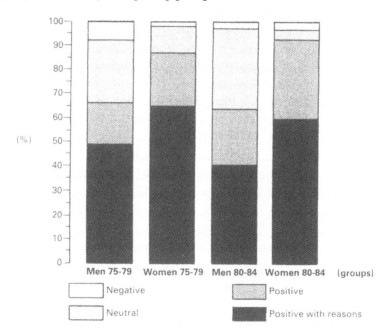

Figure 8.4 Significance of grandparenthood for women and men in different age groups of the elderly having living grandchildren

activities and interests. Data were gathered by trained psychologists at the homes of the subjects or in institutions, for those who lived there. The interviews lasted about three hours. The semi-structured part was tape-recorded for later analyses.

Results

The frequency of interaction between generations is high; about 90 per cent of those having living children reported having at least weekly contacts with them (Figure 8.1). This frequency was considerably higher than the within-generation contacts reported by the older people to their siblings. The contacts with grand-children were also quite frequent. From the first sample 44 per cent had living grandchildren, and about 70 per cent of those had at least weekly contacts with them (Figure 8.2). The contacts with great-grandchildren were much less frequent, although over 30 per cent had them at least weekly and nearly 60 per cent at least monthly (Figure 8.2). There were no great differences between women and men or between age groups as regards the frequency of contact, although men had less contact with great-grandchildren than women. The results were similar in the urban and rural samples.

All these contacts were usually regarded as easy and also sufficient. Only 5 per cent reported difficulties with contacts with their children, 10 per cent with their grandchildren and great-grandchildren. The interaction with grandchildren and great-grandchildren was felt to be very meaningful to the elderly. It was of great significance and importance to them. For a minority of about 20 per cent, for men more often than for women, grandparenthood did not seem to have any special significance (Figure 8.4). The children were very helpful to their parents in their daily activities and also often discussed their problems with them. Help and support from grandchildren were rare.

For the great majority of the Finnish elderly, interaction with younger genera-tions is frequent and satisfying; at least they report it that way in interviews (Suutama, Salminen and Ruoppila 1988).

The connections between the pattern of family life in the orientation family and in the reproductive family

Subjects

For the second question, a sample of three-generation families including young parents was obtained. Initially, we sought young pregnant women aged between 18 and at most 23 years (mean age 21 years) and awaiting their first child. The husbands/partners of the women were included in the sample: their age varied from 20 years to 36 years (mean age 25 years).

There were married couples (64 per cent, cohabiting couples (25 per cent) and single mothers (11 per cent). The subjects were chosen from two big cities, two small cities and five rural communes in Finland, representing one health centre for each centre of population. There were 115 women, fulfilling the requirements of the sample. Of these, seventy-six families (66 per cent) were willing to take part in the research on the basis of information given by the nurses.

The possible bias caused by refusals cannot be analysed because of the confidential nature of health-centre documents. Of those seventy-six families sixty-three returned the first mailed questionnaire, fifty-six families took part in the first interview, fifty-four families in the second interview and fifty families agreed to the third and (until the time of writing) the last interview. Information about the grandparents' names and addresses was sought during the first interview with the young parents. Of the 153 grandparents, 125 (82 per cent) returned a mailed questionnaire. On the basis of social background information given by the young parents there seemed to be no bias as regards the missing subjects in the grandparents' generation. When combining data from the parents and grandparents this resulted in forty-seven three-generation families, which form this sample.

The main purpose in choosing young pregnant women awaiting their first child was to study in what way and with what kind of resources these young women and their spouses could handle the many life changes they were experiencing in this phase of life. The upper age limit of 23 years for women was chosen on the basis that it is about the median age of women in Finland having their first child. The level of formal education and vocational training of the young couples or single mothers was lower than average, and they were working more often than their age mates. The seemingly high proportion of cohabiting couples (25 per cent) is typical of the life phase before marriage in Finland. In practice, most of these couples get married after their first child is born.

Methods

The information concerning the young parents was gathered for the first time during the sixth and seventh month of pregnancy by mailed questionnaires and by theme interview; the second time when the child was 3 to 4 months old by theme interview and by some personality tests (Cattell's 16 PF and a specially constructed sentence-completion test and an adjective check-list), and the third time when the child was 10 to 11 months old by theme interview. All the information from the grandparents was gathered by mailed questionnaire.

In every phase of this study both young parents (with the exception of single mothers) were interviewed separately, and they were also asked to answer the questionnaires and tests independently. Also the grandparents were asked to answer independently, which, at least on the basis of the data, they seemed to do. All the interviews were conducted at the home of the young family, and took about 1.5 hours for each subject. The interviews were tape-recorded and then coded on the basis of a content-analysis which was carried out thematically. The interviewers were four trained, female, senior students of psychology, who had already had their clinical training. The data gathered covered the developmental history of the young parents, and the relationships and the interaction within the couples and between generations. It also covered living conditions during childhood and adolescence, specifically, the family structure, socio-economic status (the parents' occupational status, length of schooling, the quality of dwelling in childhood and adolescence), parental working conditions (permanence of job, shifts of work-places and occupations, mother's working, unemployment, income), child-care arrangements, the parents' health (including psychosomatic symptoms and health habits), leisure activities and the emotional climate in the life of the family. Child-rearing was studied on the basis of the interaction between family members, the parents' interest in and control of the child's activities and the type and consistency of guidance, reward and punishment, and general child-rearing atmosphere.

Similarity of viewpoints of grandparents and their children regarding the interaction in the orientation family and the interaction between generations

The amount and quality of interaction between generations, especially during the family-founding phase, was frequent, lively and, for the great majority, good and open. After the first child was born, nearly 80 per cent of the grandparents met the young family weekly or more often, and as many of them considered this relationship to be good and open. Furthermore, the young parents themselves gave similar information about the liveliness of the interaction between generations. They experienced their own parents as important sources of social, psychological and economic support. The young parents, however, asked for prac-tical help quite seldom from their own parents; instead, they felt that the most important help was the emotional support received from them and their confidence in knowing they could get different kinds of help from grandparents in the future if and when needed.

In comparing the questionnaire and interview material gathered from the young couples and the questionnaire material from their parents, an important and also critical methodological question is how similar or how reliable the answers are and in what way perhaps the viewpoints vary from the different perspectives of parent and grandparent.

As regards the 'objective' background data, like the place of living in childhood and adolescence, and the structure of their orientation family, and also the 'sub-jective' background data, such as the emotional climate of the marriage of their parents as well as the problems in their orientation family, the answers were very or fairly similar. The extent of problems related to alcohol were rated quite simi-larly by the older and younger generations (Table 8.1). We also found that sons evaluated their relationship with their fathers more similarly than did daughters, and daughters more similarly with their mothers than did sons. The correlations are based on the mean ratings of the grandparents, from the grandfather and grand-mother when both were available; otherwise they are based on single rating, either from the grandmother or grandfather.

As regards the description of child-rearing, the viewpoints of the generations differed and the correlations between most ratings were near zero although there were some significant relationships. In Table 8.2 the ratings of the young couple have been correlated separately for the young mother and young father, not only with the rating of the grandparents as regards child-rearing but also with some other characteristics describing the relations between the child and her or his mother and father. Generally the correlations are low, but there is more agreement between the ratings of grandparents and those of their daughters than with those of their sons. Child-rearing attitudes and practices were described quite differently; the older generation remembered and evaluated having used fewer physical punishments than the younger generation had experienced, and generally the younger ones described their upbringing as having been more strict and authoritarian than the way it was described by their parents. It may be that changed norms, selectiveness of memory and the differing standards of judgement have caused these differences in ratings regarding child-rearing in the orientation family.

Table 8.1 Correlations between the ratings concerning the orientation family atmosphere given independently by the grandparents and their children (N=47); correlation coefficients (r) and significance levels (p)

Ratings of the grandparents	Ratings of young couple			
	Young mother		Young father	
	r	p	r	p
Family structure	0.86	.001	0.81	.001
Happiness in the marriage	0.44	.01	0.34	.05
Alcohol problems in the family	0.63	.001	0.74	.001
Disagreements in the family	0.51	.001	0.39	.05

Table 8.2 Correlations between the ratings concerning child-rearing given independently by the grandparents and their children (N=47); correlation coefficients (r) and significance levels (p)

Ratings of grandparents	Ratings of young couple, upbringing free v. strict			
	Young mother		Young father	
	r	p	r	p
Child-rearing (free v. strict)	0.31	.05	0.06	n.s.*
Disagreements concerning child rearing (little–much)	0.03	n.s.	0.45	.01
Use of physical punishments (no–yes)	−0.07	n.s.	0.34	.05
Mother's attitude towards child (negative–positive)	0.46	.01	−0.01	n.s.
Father's attitude towards child (negative–positive)	0.42	.05	0.05	n.s.

Note: *n.s. = not significant.

Relationships between the interaction in the orientation family and the interaction in the reproductive family of young parents

What were the family atmosphere and interaction in the orientation family and how are these related to parenthood in the reproduction family? The majority of the young parents (63 per cent of the mothers and 70 per cent of the fathers) reported having received security and attachment from both their parents in childhood. About two-thirds evaluated that their parents had had time enough for them when they were children. Both these results were in line with the information given by their own parents, especially as regards the interaction within the family when the young parent was a child. The young parents had experienced security and attachment more in whole families than in one-parent families or divorced families and more in families with no alcohol problems than those with alcohol problems. (In Finland, because of the heavy emotional loadings associated with the use of alcoholic beverages many kinds of problems inside the family are 'explained' in everyday speech by referring to the use of alcohol, and it is a socially accepted explanation for many kinds of difficulties. The use of alcohol is mainly seen as a cause and not as an effect of problems.) The feelings of security and attachment of the young mothers were associated with a harmonious mother–daughter relationship and also with the amount of activities undertaken

Table 8.3 Correlations between the interaction in the orientation family and the quality of the pair relation in the young family (N = 47); correlation coefficients (r) and significance levels (p)

| *Interaction in orientation family* | *Positive quality of pair relation* | | | |
| | *Mother* | | *Father* | |
	r	p	r	p
Mother's orientation family				
Expression of positive feelings of the mother to her husband	0.36	.05	0.05	n.s.*
Common activities of mother and daughter	0.46	.01	0.25	n.s.
Alcohol problems (no)	0.04	n.s.	0.32	.05
Disagreement between mother and daughter (little)	0.45	.01		
Father's orientation family				
Parents' common interests	0.46	.01	0.33	.05
Division of home labour (much)	0.43	.01	0.52	.001
Division of child-care (much)	0.48	.001	0.29	n.s.
Happiness of marriage	0.29	.05	0.21	n.s.
Father's positive attitude towards his son			0.45	.01
Mother's positive attitude towards her son			0.48	.001
Common activities of father and son			0.42	.01
Expression of positive feelings of mother to her husband			0.56	.001
Disagreements concerning child-rearing (little)			0.57	.001

Note: * n.s. = not significant.

together with her mother in their orientation family. The feelings of security and attachment of the young father were associated with the division of home labour and with the amount of common interests between his mother and father, with harmonious family life and with the ease with which his own father could express his positive feelings to his spouse (Table 8.3).

The more the young mother experienced her parents as having enough time for her and the more the parents had been active in different ways with her, the less the conflict between her and her mother; also, there were fewer alcohol problems according to the quality of her relation to her husband as described by the young mother. Many of the variables describing interaction in the orientation family of the young father were associated with his feelings of security and attachment in the pair relation. Especially if there had been much division of labour in the father's orientation family, good emotional relations between him and his parents, many common activities involving father and son, and good emotional relations between his parents and a few disagreements between his parents regarding child-rearing, the young father felt his relation with his wife to be good.

A conflict-ridden relationship between mother and daughter seems to lead to a situation in which the daughter looks for an early relationship with the opposite sex and wants to found her own family. Poor economic circumstances in the woman's orientation family, alcohol problems in her family and the use of physical punishments in her rearing are all associated with an early family foundation without previous planning. Conflicts between the daughter and her parents, her father's problems with alcohol and the use of physical punishments in the daughter's upbringing are also associated with young women's earlier pregnancies which ended with abortions (Table 8.4).

An emotionally warm relationship between the young mother and her own mother during childhood predicts both ease in building a security-giving relationship

Table 8.4 Interaction in the orientation family of the young mother and pregnancy planning and that of earlier pregnancies ($N = 47$); correlation coefficients (r) and significance levels (p)

Mother's orientation family	Planning of pregnancy (yes–no)		Earlier pregnancies (no–yes)	
	r	p	r	p
Mother's positive attitude towards her daughter	0.22	n.s.*	0.38	.01
Disagreements between mother and daughter (little)	0.29	.05	0.43	.01
Disagreements between father and daughter (little)	0.19	n.s.	0.50	.001
Alcohol problems (no)	0.23	n.s.	0.36	.05
Child-rearing (free–strict)	0.42	.01	0.15	n.s.
Use of physical punishments (no)	0.37	.01	0.37	.01

Note: *n.s. = not significant.

with her own child and in accepting motherhood. These findings show that the daughters are at least partly repeating their parents', and especially their mothers', problems as well as successful mother–child relationships.

Although there have been findings describing the significance of the mother–daughter relationship for the future motherhood of the daughter, the meaning of the young father's orientation family for his future fatherhood has rarely been studied (see Table 8.5). When the man's parents describe the family atmosphere in the man's childhood as harmonious and emotionally warm, happy and peaceful and when the relationship between the spouses in the orientation family was good, the young fathers also experience family life in their reproductive family as good. Especially when the man's mother has felt it easy to show positive feelings to her spouse, when she has had mutual hobbies and activities with her partner, when there have been no disagreements concerning child-rearing and no alcohol problems, it is easy for the young father to build and maintain a good and warm emotional relation to his spouse.

The child-rearing atmosphere in the man's orientation family is also of significance for the relation between spouses and for the new father–child relation. Especially if the man's father was active with his son in different ways during childhood it was easy for the young father to accept his fatherhood. The model

Table 8.5 Interaction in the husband's and the wife's orientation family and the wife's competence and feelings of motherhood (N=47); correlation coefficients (r) and significance levels (p)

	Wife's competence as a mother		Wife's positive feelings of motherhood	
	r	p	r	p
Father's orientation family				
Expression of positive feelings between mother and son	0.11	n.s.*	0.54	.001
Time given by the father to his son	0.34	.05	0.40	.01
Conflicts between father and son (no)	0.39	.01	0.08	n.s.
Expression of positive feelings between parents	0.49	.001	0.05	n.s.
Alcohol problems (no)	0.38	.01	0.32	.05
Parents' common interests	0.48	.001	0.14	n.s.
Happiness of marriage	0.26	n.s.	0.46	.01
Mother's orientation family				
Expression of positive feelings between mother and daughter	0.32	.05	−0.36	.05
Common activities of mother and daughter	0.49	.001	0.29	.05
Positive relation between father and daughter	−0.07	n.s.	−0.44	.01

Note: *n.s. = not significant.

of the father's behaviour and activities in family life can be seen having an effect on the reproductive family of the young man. If the fathers participated in household work and in child-care, the young fathers participated actively and in many different ways within the household and in child-care activities. Moreover, the young father's participation in child-rearing builds up his relation to the child, and the more he takes care of her or him the better he learns to know the child. The finding that the spouse who also takes care of the household and child-care routines feels herself happy in her relation to her husband can be explained by the fact that this participation makes it easier for the young wife to handle life changes connected with her motherhood.

The family is a functional unit in which a good mutual relationship between the spouses also creates advantageous conditions for child-care. A good relationship between the young couple is of great significance when they begin to form a parent–child relation, but the relation between spouses and the parent–child relationship have stronger connections with the fathers' than with the mothers' orientation families (see Table 8.5). Although the young father cannot be seen as only 'a second-order effector' whose significance is indirectly mediated by his spouse, the findings can be interpreted as showing that the husband functions primarily as a resource for his young wife, at least as long as she takes care of the child at home and most child-care is her responsibility. The husband's role as the mother's resource was seen, for example, in that the more he was involved in child-care the easier his wife found motherhood and the changes caused by the child in her life' (Table 8.6). Circumstances in which the husband's involvement in child-care was minimal easily became burdensome to the wife. This was indicated by the wife's many psychosomatic symptoms and her ambivalent feelings towards the child in families where the husband was not involved in child-care. In addition, the child's adjustment to the mother's return to work was more difficult in those families where the child-care and other household duties were not divided but were the woman's sole responsibility.

Although parents and their adult children had divergent views concerning

Table 8.6 Father's time used for child and wife's feelings of family atmosphere; correlation coefficients (r) and significance levels (p)

	Father's time for child (sufficient)	
	r	p
Equality within couple as regards leisure-time activities	0.54	.001
Division of child-care (much)	0.51	.001
Division of home-care (much)	0.31	.05
Father's use of alcohol (little)	0.30	.05
Positive feelings of motherhood	0.44	.02
Time enough for the pair relation/wife	0.32	.05
Time enough for the pair relation/husband	0.37	.01
Psychosomatic symptoms of the wife (little)	0.39	.01

the atmosphere of the upbringing which had characterized their parents' behaviour, the child-rearing atmosphere of the orientation family had some connections with the child-rearing methods and goals of the younger generation. A strict upbringing with the use of physical punishments for both the young mother and father meant that the young parents accepted similar child-rearing methods and were ready to use them. On the other hand, those young parents who had had a free upbringing, were themselves in favour of child-centred but not free child-rearing.

Child-rearing attitudes and methods were transmitted at least to some extent from the older generation to the younger one by those models which the young parents themselves had experienced and interpreted in a certain way. None of the young parents wanted to use completely free or *laissez-faire* child-rearing with their own child. The provision of some guidance was mostly supported at least in this phase of the life of the child. Although most young parents said that the use of physical punishment was the worst way to guide the child, it was, however, the third most commonly used way of controlling and guiding the child. Especially in this respect the upbringing which the young mother had experienced in her orientation family had connections with the way she reared her own child.

Discussion

Social interaction between the aged and their children and grandchildren is lively and frequent, but less so with great-grandchildren. This interaction was felt to be easy and meaningful. Grandparenthood was considered to be of great importance and a source of strong positive feelings, especially among women. There were considerably fewer contacts with sisters and brothers than with one's own children. There were, however, 10 to 20 per cent of grandparents who had very few contacts with their offspring.

The interaction between the young family and their parents in the family-founding phase was very intensive. It was related to the interaction and atmosphere in the orientation families of the young couples.

The relationships in the orientation family had an effect on the reproductive families in many ways, especially in young families with their first child. The transition from the family atmosphere in the orientation family to the new pair relation in the young family suggests that many models of parental interaction are acquired during childhood and early adolescence. The results concerning the mother–daughter relationship for the daughter's later relations towards her child and spouse are very similar to those of other studies which have analysed this special relationship (Carlson 1979; Conley 1979; Liljeström 1974; Mason 1975; Rautanen *et al*. 1977; Ruusuvaara 1983; Smart and Smart 1973; Tolkki-Nikkonen 1978; Uddenberg 1976; Widholm *et al*. 1974). Furthermore, the interpretations given in this chapter are in line with earlier research. The daughters repeat their parents', especially their own mothers', successes as well as problems in the social relations and interactions within the family. The much less studied father–daughter relationship also seems to be meaningful for the wife–husband relationship in the young family. The image of the father which the daughter has acquired has an effect on the generalized image of men later in life. There are, however, more and stronger connections between the mother–daughter relationship and the internal relation in the young family than between the father–daughter relationship and the pair relation.

The father–son relationship and its effects on later father–child relations as well as on the husband–wife relation has only rarely been studied (Lamb 1976; Sommer 1984). However, on the basis of the findings of this study there are many strong connections originating from the husband's orientation family with an effect on the internal relationships in his reproductive family. The emotional atmosphere between the father's parents and the models the father has given to his son, as a caretaker of different household duties and through the different activities which he has shared with his son as a child, are important influences which later guide the son's behaviour in his new role as a father.

The two indicators of family atmosphere in the orientation family – the quality of the relationship between the spouses and alcohol problems – which have strong connections with internal relationships in the young family and which were very similarly described by both generations, cannot be interpreted too narrowly; rather, they are indicators describing much more generally the quality of internal relationships in the family. It may be that the very clear occurrence of alcohol problems as a broad indicator of the family atmosphere and of the interactions between family members is especially typical to Finnish culture and cannot be generalized to other cultures with different traditions of consuming alcoholic beverages. In Finland, to mention the consumption of alcohol as a cause of various problems in the family is both a socially accepted explanation and an explanation broadly used publicly to explain many kinds of difficulties, not only in social interaction but also in other sectors of life.

In comparing the links between the young mother's orientation family and the links between the young father's orientation family to the internal relations between them in the reproductive family there seem to be more and stronger relations in the latter case (see Table 8.3). This points to the father's childhood as one important determinant for the husband–wife relation and the father–child relation, as well as indirectly for the mother–child relation, especially in young families (see Table 8.6). An experimental follow-up study by Makkonen *et al.* (1981) also showed the importance of the man's participation in child-care and household duties for the pair relation in the family and for both the mother–child and father–child relationship.

Although based on a small sample, the present findings show very clearly that the family functions as a unit which has many important internal relationships, all of which have an effect on families of later generations and on their internal relationships. This is not a new discovery, but very seldom have these relations between generations been analysed sufficiently broadly.

It may be that the transition of family models and interaction models from the orientation family to the reproductive family, which is observed quite clearly in this study, is not so clear and strong in families where parents are older and in which there is more than one child. Furthermore, older couples are more independent of their own parents than the young couples of this study. This may cause less interaction between generations and also fewer effects from the grandparents.

The results have been interpreted in terms of the orientation family as being the causal factor influencing the reproductive family. This is felt to be the most likely interpretation of the data. However, the reciprocal nature of grandparent-parent–grandchild relations, which in this report has been studied mainly retrospectively, partly prospectively, must be acknowledged.

The quite strong transition of many models of family atmosphere and family interaction from the orientation family to the reproductive family at least in young families with their first child forces a consideration of what kind of possibilities there might be to support and strengthen the transition of models evaluated as positive for internal family relations, and what kind of possibilities there might exist to break the vicious circle and to build and create new kinds of interactions in the young family. Research in which such an intervention and its effects are studied can further help to bring about an understanding of the transition process of interaction models and also the interpretation of this process, which occurs in the chain of successive generations.

References

Anderson, M. with Jonsson, G. and Kälvesten, A-L. (1976) 'Hur går det för 50-talets Stockholmspojkar? En uppföljning av 222 vanliga skolpojkar och 100 Skåpojkar', Monograph produced by the Stockholm Public Relations Office, no. 38, Stockholm: Rosenlundstryckeriet AB.

Carlson, E. (1979) 'Family background, school and early marriage', *Journal of Marriage and the Family* 41: 341–53.

Conley, M.M. (1979) 'Motivation for parenthood, need satisfaction and romantic love: a comparison between pregnant and non-pregnant teenagers', *Dissertation Abstracts International* 40(5A): 2518.

Frommer, E.A. and O'Shea, G. (1973) 'The importance of childhood experience in relation to marriage and family-building', *British Journal of Psychiatry* 123: 157–60.

Greenberg, N.H., Loesch, J.G. and Lakin, M. (1959) 'Life situations associated with the onset of pregnancy', *Psychosomatic Medicine* 21: 256–310.

Heikkinen, E., Arajärvi, R-L., Jylhä, M., Koskinen, S., Pekurinen, M. and Pohjolainen, P. (1981) *Eläkeläiset Tampereella*, Tampereen yliopisto: Kansanterveystieteen laitos, M:65.

Hill, R. and Aldous, J. (1969) 'Socialization for marriage and parenthood', in D. Goslin (ed.), *Handbook of Socialization Theory and Research*, Chicago: Rand McNally, pp. 885–950.

Jonsson, G. (1969) *Det sociala arvet*, Stockholm: Tiden-Barnängen.

Jonsson, G. (1973) *Att bryta det sociala arvet*, Stockholm: Tiden/Folksam.

Lamb, M.E. (ed.) (1976) *The Role of the Father in Child Development*, New York: John Wiley & Sons.

Liljeström, R. (1974) *Uppväxtvillkor. Samspelet mellan vuxna och barn i ett föränderligt samhälle*, Stockholm: Liberförlag.

Makkonen, T., Ruoppila, I., Rönkä, T., Timonen, S., Valvanne, L. and Österlund, K. (1981) *Operaatio perhe – Isä ja synnytys*, Mannerheimin lastensuojeluliiton julkaisu: Lapsiraportti A:34. Helsinki.

Mason, R.L. (1975) 'Differences in motivation for childrearing among childless and parental couples in a student population'. *Dissertation Abstracts International* 1976, 36(8A), 5583.

Rautanen, E., Kantero, R-L. and Widholm, O. (1977) 'Medical and social aspects of pregnancy among adolescents. Part II. Comparative study of abortions and deliveries', *Annales Chirurgiae et Gynaecologiae* 66: 122–30, Helsinki.

Ruusuvaara, L.R. (1983) 'Teenage abortions: family background, sexual experience and contraceptive use', Doctoral thesis at the University of Helsinki, Uppsala: Centraltryckeriet.

Satir, V. (1982) *Conjoint Family Therapy*, Palo Alto, CA: Science and Behavior Books.

Smart, M.S. and Smart, R.C. (1973) *Adolescents: Development and Relationships*, New York: Macmillan.

Sommer, D. (1984) *När far er hjemme – om faderrollen, faedre og spaedborn*, Copenhagen: Dansk psykologisk Forlag.

Suutama, T., Salminen, K. and Ruoppila, I. (1988) 'Physical and social functioning. Part 2', in *Living Conditions and Mental and Social Functioning of the Aged*, Helsinki: Publications of the Social Insurance Institution, Finland, M:63.

Tolkki-Nikkonen, M. (1978) *Avioliiton ensimmäinen vuosi*. Acta Universitatis Tamperensis, A:92.

Tornstam, L., Oden, B. and Svanborg, A. (eds) (1982) *Äldre i samhället förr, nu och i framtiden*. Stockholm: Liber.

Uddenberg, N. (1974) 'Reproductive adaptation in mother and daughter', *Acta Psychiatrica Scandinavica* 51: 5–115.

Uddenberg, N. (1976) 'Mother–father and daughter–male relationships: a comparison', *Archives of Sexual Behavior* 5: 69–79.

Widholm, O., Kantero, R-L. and Rautanen, E. (1974) 'Medical and social aspects of adolescent pregnancies. Part I. Adolescents applying for termination of an illegitimate pregnancy', *Acta Obstetricia et Gynecologica Scandinavica* 53: 347–52.

Part three

Theoretical perspectives

Chapter nine

Grandchildren's images of their grandparents: a psychodynamic perspective

Piergiorgio Battistelli and Alessandra Farneti

---

*I was a fief of the sun and my grandfather could enjoy me without owning
me: I was his 'wonder' because he wanted to end his days as a wonder-struck
old man; he decided to regard me as an unusual boon from fate, as a free
gift which could always be revoked: what could he have demanded of me? My
very presence satisfied him.*

J.P. Sartre, *Words* (1964)

Family structure in Italy

Among the countries represented in this book, Italy is one where the family has
undergone a transformation quite recently: from a patriarchal family, where the
women were only housewives, to a nuclear family in which mother and father
are on equal terms. Moreover, different cultural roots and great unevenness in
the process of industrialization over the various regions have produced microcosms
which are very often distinct in ideologies and habits. It is significant that there
is a higher percentage of divorce cases in the north compared to the south. It
is, therefore, particularly difficult to identify a predominant model of the Italian
family.

There has been a change in the social contract since the last world war, whereby
the family unit has normally become independent of the family of origin and freely
chooses whether or not to keep up binding emotional family ties. In this way,
the relationship between generations is no longer necessary, as it was in the
patriarchal family, but is contingent. The elderly members of the family can choose
whether they wish to take care of grandchildren or not, and grandchildren have
constant ties with their grandparents only if their parents allow it.

However, this freedom of choice is not so complete on a practical level as
it is on a conceptual one, because often the need for help conditions both the
young parents and, consequently, the grandparents. It is in this regard that studies
speak of an extended family unit, referring to the network of reciprocal assistance
that obliges families to keep up ties that can be very close. Yet the absence of
rigid social norms, which are found in tribal and patriarchal societies, makes the
situation more flexible and more closely linked to individual circumstance.

Moreover, the different stages of the family life cycle create periods when the family unit is closer and periods when it is further apart. This means that, even when grandparents are allowed to assume a close role by their children, they cannot be certain that the tie established will last. Grandparents often describe the love they feel from their grandchildren as an achievement, and it is never felt to be an inner certainty as is the love to parents. Moreover, the family is rapidly losing its function of integrating the different generations because of the continual encouragement to live most of one's time and have relationships outside the family, both in places of work and in other places where people choose to spend their free time.

Researchers in family dynamics find themselves in difficulty today, when defining duties in terms of personal relationships and family organization in an open system which is in continual evolution and which is placed both in social time as well as in family time itself. Although various approaches (systemic, developmental, behaviouristic, psychoanalytic) have helped clarify dynamics and identify the main problem areas, they have not yet been able to furnish satisfactory models to analyse a family reality that is so complex and changing (Cusinato 1988). However, the latest trend is to consider the family as a three-generational system, taking into account the influences of the family of origin on the new one and the ties that are maintained between them both on an objective as well as a subjective level.

In Italy, empirical studies on the condition of the elderly are numerous, but few of them have considered elderly people either as parents or grandparents. Interest in three-generation dynamics is recent and limited, in particular with regard to the contribution of grandparents to the psychological development of grand-children (Guidicini 1977, Novelletto 1982, Saccu and De Rysky 1983, Barletta 1984, Guaraldi and Camerini 1987). This seems strange when a recent CENSIS survey has shown that in 79 per cent of family units in Italy, the grandparent(s) either cohabit with, or live in proximity to their grandchildren, above all during the first five years of life.

If we then consider the orientation of psychological research, we see that much attention has been given over the last twenty to thirty years to the secondary figures of attachment, but that this role has been mainly identified in people outside the family unit, such as nursery school teachers. We may perhaps attribute this lack of psychological interest to the refusal to consider the position of the older members in the family because we have had them as domineering parents for too long; or to a political and ideological orientation that encourages public processes of socialization rather than private ones. Nevertheless, the meaning and richness of the relationship which grandparents may have with grandchildren have been the theme of several Italian novels, such as those by Romano (1978 and 1981), Bertin (1981) and Fonzi (1988).

Grandparents in intrafamily dynamics

Some psychoanalytical contributions have given us useful indications for our own studies on the relationship between grandparents and grandchildren, and we shall review these next.

The first are three brief publications in 1913 by Abraham, Jones and Ferenczi; all the authors focused on the male child–grandfather relationship. These authors see the (generally paternal) grandfather as an aged father figure who can be used in various ways by the child in his attempt to resolve the Oedipal conflict. The grandfather can be seen either as an old man respected by the 'omnipotent' father too, or as an old man who has to die soon. Jones in particular observed that often the children imagine themselves to be the father of their own father: 'becoming' grandfather, they reverse the real Oedipal situation whereby they completely depend on their parents. Finally, Ferenczi emphasized that grandchildren can turn their aggressive death fantasies, destined for their father, on to their paternal grandfather.

In 1945, Deutsch identified the grandmother as a figure who could be 'good' or 'bad', a 'fairy' or a 'witch', depending on her past history, on her capacity for accepting or rejecting old age, as having lived a life in which she had carried out all her duties as a woman and as a mother with various levels of satisfaction. Naturally, the good grandmother, who will also have been a good mother, will only make her daughter's relationship with her children easier and will represent a positive, gratifying figure for her grandchildren, capable of true, object love, without any narcissistic connotations.

Rapaport's observations (1957) followed these early analyses. He described identification with the grandfather right from the pre-Oedipal phases as supporting the avoidance of processes of identification with and introjection of parental figures; they can be seen as an older sibling and so become objects which are more easily attached by the child's competitive, devaluating fantasies.

In 1963, Richter proposed an interesting hypothesis, supported by clinical practice, that some parents see the equivalent of their own father or mother in their children and put into practice relational dynamics where the child–parent role is completely reversed. Demands will therefore be made on the child that are unconsciously directed at the parents, and he or she will compensate for inadequacies experienced in the past and resolve present conflicts.

More recently, Kohut (1971) referred to grandparents as 'self objects' who act as support for narcissistic investment through idealizing or fusional mirror dynamics. The child can act out fantasies of omnipotence, of fusionality and of self-idealization that would be intolerable towards the parents.

It is not possible here to describe several other interesting psychopathological views. Under certain unusual conditions, the presence of grandparents can have serious pathogenetic effects on the grandchildren; see Boszormenyi-Nagy and Spark 1973; Cahn and Weill 1972; Walsh 1978; and Geismann et al. 1980.

The grandparent–grandchild relationship

Today we can reasonably claim that the relationship between grandparents and their granchildren is important and positive for both, except in pathological cases. Yet it is very difficult to outline the exact role of grandparenthood, as it is indeed for motherhood and fatherhood too. Perhaps it is made even more difficult by the fact that there are four grandparents as against two parents.

Attempts up to now to shed light on such complex relations are still far from successful. They have often been limited to individual, partial aspects of the relationship. American researchers have made most contributions, but just because such studies are linked to a precise socio-cultural context, they need to be compared to others. Although such studies had no systematic intentions or common theoretical base, they have been able to highlight several general and differential characteristics regarding several variables, like social class, anthropological context and the age of the grandchildren. Many studies have taken into consideration the significance of grandmotherhood, the mother–daughter relationship and the continuity of corresponding educative models. The mother–daughter tie, which is consolidated and restructured when the daughter in turn becomes a mother, takes on a particularly important significance for the entire family context that seems to rotate around this central maternal axis.

In Italy, there have been a few recent contributions to the topic. Grandparenthood is often seen as a role to accept positively, a new edition of one's own fatherhood or motherhood but with new characteristics due both to the reduced involvement in the child's upbringing as well as to the different time in life when these feelings are experienced. Grandparents see the birth of a grandchild as a revitalizing event that gives them the certainty of biological continuity and thus a link to the future.

In an early explanatory, descriptive study that we carried out together with some colleagues using questionnaires and interviews (Cavallero *et al.* 1981), a notable difference was clearly observed between maternal grandparents and paternal ones and also between grandmothers and grandfathers. The relationship was seen to evolve in time, according to the different ages of the grandchildren. The maternal grandmothers stated that they had always been very close to their daughters and grandchildren and had taken an active part in the care of the child right from birth, when they substituted for the mother. The grandmothers declared that they found the situation gratifying. The paternal grandmothers referred to a greater detachment and let it be understood that this was due to the presence of the maternal grandmother, whom they possibly saw as a rival. The grandfathers declared that they had started to get involved with their grandchildren much later, towards the second year of life, when interaction was easier because the child could walk and talk. They acknowledged that they had left all the practicalities of care to the grandmother and reserved a space for play for themselves.

Surveys were then carried out to verify the grandchildren's viewpoints at different ages. The dimension that seemed to characterize the grandparent's image most was affiliative, seen as a self-centred dimension where each sought their own space in which to do something together for the sheer pleasure of doing it. However, the children also pointed out the regulative and punitive aspects of the relationship, aspects which were attributed prevalently to the grandmother, who was in fact more involved than the grandfather in the grandchild's upbringing (Battistelli *et al.* 1981).

Grandparents, parents and grandchildren

We have carried out two studies which have been prompted by the psychoanalytical hypotheses mentioned previously, with particular reference to what seemed to us to be of most importance; the hypothesis that grandparents have a part to play in the child's elaboration of Oedipal experiences. The first of these studies (Farneti and Battistelli 1985) was based on the free association made by grandchildren to forty pictures representing everyday objects and situations, with pictures of parents and grandparents. Two hundred children of both sexes aged from 4 to 7 took part. The subjects took the picture cards (illustrating, for instance, a garden or an ice-cream or a medicine or toys) from a box and had to put these cards next to the appropriate figure: mother or father or grandmother or grandfather.

The results showed a precise, constant developmental trend: in the preschool age, only slightly fewer pictures were attributed to the grandparents than to the parents. At 6 and even more at 7 years, this number tends to decrease dramatically, differing clearly from those attributed to the parents. We may thus conclude that at a younger age, the figure of grandparent is particularly rich in significance and connotation, almost reaching the parental figure in this respect. In the ages that follow, this importance is much reduced, the figure of grandparent becoming impoverished and diminishing in significance.

As regards the qualitative content, the vast majority of subjects associated with grandparents the pictures of objects which had oral connotations (feeding-bottle, sweets and so on) or play connotations (such as the park or toys). Kornhaber and Woodward (1985) found similar results in their study based on the analysis of drawings on a theme.

Once a key to reading our results had been found, their interpretation was obvious. Children reduce their affective investment towards the grandparents after they have been able to elaborate their Oedipal problems 'normally' and when they are beginning to consider their more difficult separation from parents with entry to school and to the larger social environment.

A second study (Battistelli and Costantini 1984) was based on the idea that from the content analysis of dreams, more thematic and quantitative indications can be obtained regarding children's feelings towards their grandparents. Using a suitably adapted version of Hall and Van de Castle's Scales (1966) the contents of about 150 dreams described by 5- and 6-year-olds, in which there were both parents and grandparents, were analysed. The most significant results were that in 5-year-olds' dreams, friendly actions come mainly from grandparents, while in 6-year-olds' dreams these actions are mainly attributed to the parents; and that when dreamed actions were directed towards grandparents and parents, we found, at both ages, a clear prevalence of friendly actions towards the grandparents and of aggressive actions towards the parents.

We conclude that in children's dreams, and above all in those of 5-year-olds, the grandparents' image seems to appear as the 'good' double of the parents who, as representatives of the principle of reality (physical but, above all, social and moral), alternate gratification with frustration. Rather than expressing the reality of the grandparents, probably both a little 'good' and a little 'bad', this shows the need of the child to create and conserve a 'good' internal object. This 'self-object' is therefore functional both for narcissistic investment as well as for object-ambivalence, which has not been fully accepted and elaborated. The impression of having caught a traditionally significant moment of transition between 5 and 6 years suggests that we should refer such dynamics to Oedipal separation and consider grandparents, or rather the 'couple' of grandparents, as an alternative 'scene' to that of the parental couple. It is likely that the grandparents offer themselves unconsciously in the same dimension. We therefore find ourselves agreeing, on the basis of clinical findings, with the indications given in psychoanalytical studies.

What we have not seen in our data are traces of persecutory investments towards the grandparent figures or of the competitive, devaluating dynamics regarding parents that are linked to the fantasy of generation reversal. The first (but not the only) explanation can be found in the fact that our subjects were intentionally selected without any particular mental disorder or developmental difficulty.

It can thus be noted that the widespread image of grandparents as traditionally and conventionally 'good', a sort of 'happy island' for grandchildren (Farneti and Zoli 1981), where the struggle to adapt to reality is temporarily and spatially suspended, finds its developmental explanation in the data and interpretation we propose.

Aims and hypothesis of the study

The present study starts from the assumption that, from infancy to puberty and adolescence, the place that grandparents have in their grandchildren's world becomes more and more limited and loses the connotation linked to the Oedipal dynamics that were seen in younger subjects. This hypothesis also came from an analysis of children's and teenagers' writings, in which the grandparent figure takes on different connotations according to the grandchild's age and his emotional and cognitive development. From our different studies on this theme, we could schematically assume that this relationship develops as follows: First, in children up to the age of 5 years, the grandparents are significant alternative figures to parents; they are particularly important as being more pleasant, symbiotic and manipulable than parents, and they satisfy their grandchildren's omnipotent and egocentric requirements.

Second, during school age, the child's tendency to move towards the outside world and the strengthening of the identification dynamics with his parents causes a decrease in the importance of grandparents in the family environment. Teachers are now present as alternative adult figures, and investment towards reality and society is much stronger.

Third, during puberty, rejection of adult values begins and the grandparent represents an adult world which can be despised even more easily than the parent's one, without paying any penalty. As we have seen, love for grandparents is not 'due' and it can therefore be withdrawn or given without harm.

Fourth, during the late teens, the separation process from the family, and particularly from the parent couple, is reactivated. The difference between this new separation and the previous one during the Oedipal period is that the teenager wants it and is a protagonist, while the child is forced to suffer it, creating mechanisms of defence. The teenager's new representation of the world certainly gives much emphasis to his or her own peer group, yet it also causes anxiety and insecurity which leads to an alternation of feelings and to ambivalence towards parents.

In our opinion, it is precisely because the grandparents are considered to be 'off stage', old and no longer competitive that they can then offer their grand-children affective assurance without intrusive connotations. The freedom in the relationship allows the teenager to 'use' the grandparent as he or she did during the first years of life, as a representative of an adult world with reduced strength and power.

Method

The research is based on a questionnaire of twenty-five items which aim to find out the nature of the grandchild's relationship with grandparents so far, and if there is a particularly important grandparent among them all. It was given to 475 boys and girls from three age groups, children of 8–9 years (ninety-nine boys, eighty-one girls), pre-adolescents of 12–13 years (sixty-one boys, fifty-one girls), and adolescents of 16–17 years (eighty-seven boys, ninety-six girls). The study was carried out in urban schools of various rank and order, so the social background of the children is quite mixed.

The relationship between the age and sex of the subjects and the ways in which they describe their grandparents was analysed using chi-square tests. One item of the questionnaire was made up of four pairs of opposing adjectives: nice–nasty; lively–boring; youthful–old-fashioned; open to young people's ideas–suspicious of young people. Choosing one of each adjective pair, the subjects had to describe their four grandparents. A variance analysis was carried out on these scores; the factors were the age and the sex of the subjects and the type of grandparents (MGF, MGM, PGF and PGM).

Results

The relationship with grandparents

A The time spent with grandparents

Responding to the question 'Overall, have you spent more time with maternal or paternal grandparents?', most subjects agreed that they had spent more time with maternal grandparents than with paternal ones (aged 8–9, 51.1 per cent v. 37. 7 per cent; aged 12–13, 53.6 per cent v. 35.7 per cent; aged 16–17, 58.5 per cent v. 37.2 per cent). It would seem that women today prefer, if they have the choice, to entrust their children to their own parents rather than to their parents-in-law, thus supporting a tendency which is perhaps recent, towards a maternal axis. However, it must be remembered that paternal grandparents are often older than maternal ones, as men tend to marry later. Consequently, the paternal grandparents could find it more difficult to look after their grandchildren.

B The play aspect of the relationship with grandparents

All the grandchildren declared that they play or had played (depending on their age) a lot with their grandparents, thus underlining a connotation of play in the relationship that many studies have already discovered. It is, of course, more evident at the primary school age (aged 8–9, 75.0 per cent; aged 12–13, 56.3 per cent; aged 16–17, 52.5 per cent; the age difference is very significant, $p<.001$). There is no significant difference linked to sex. Moreover, most of the subjects said that their grandparents told them a lot of stories but the girls emphasized this fact more significantly at adolescence (boys 61.0 per cent, girls 78.1 per cent; $p<.05$). We may interpret this as an indication of a tendency in the female to live and remember the relationship with their grandparents in an imaginative and intimate dimension.

C The favourite grandparent

To the question 'Do you have more fun with Grandad or Granny?', the answer was prevalently 'Granny'. At 8–9 years there were no significant differences between boys and girls, but at 12–13 years the boys chose the grandfather more than the girls (36.1 per cent v. 5.9 per cent, $p<.001$), who said they had no preference (11.4 per cent v. 49.0 per cent). At 16–17 years the preference for grandmother was stronger in the girls than the boys (61.5 per cent v. 46.0 per cent). When asked whether they felt particularly attached to one grandparent, the existence of a favourite grandparent was confirmed by most subjects regardless of age and sex (aged 7–8, 71.7 per cent boys v. 75.3 per cent girls; aged 12–13, 54.1 per cent v. 82.4 per cent; aged 16–17, 68.9 per cent v. 72.9 per cent). When we asked which grandparent is preferred, the grandmother, and in particular the maternal one, would seem to be this privileged point of reference (see Figure 9.1).

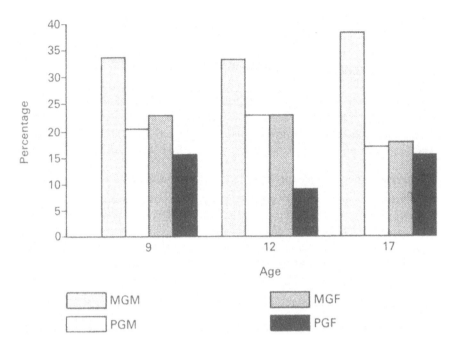

Figure 9.1 Which of your grandparents were (are) you particularly attached to?

D Comparison between grandparents and parents

Several questions in the questionnaire highlight any differences between the image of the grandparents and that of the parents. In the reply to the question 'Would you have preferred to spend time together with your parents or grandparents?', we find significant differences both by age and sex. The need to be with parents is greater in childhood, while pre-adolescents and adolescents place parents and grandparents on the same level. Moreover, at 16–17 years the girls stated a greater preference for parents than the boys ($p < .05$). The answers to three questions on more specific aspects of the relationship with parents and grandparents (presents, money and everyday problems) show the grandparents slightly behind the parents, a difference which widens with the age of the grandchildren ($p < .001$); there is some fluctuation with age in boys, while the girls show a significant tendency to distribute their attitudes evenly between parents and grandparents.

If, on the level of practical, daily problems, the grandparents seem to lose importance as the years go by, they nevertheless continue to appear to be distinctly more patient and understanding than the parents ('Do you think that grandparents are more patient with grandchildren?', 'Who do you think listens to you more, your grandparents or parents?'). This judgement, in fact, becomes firmer and firmer from childhood to adolescence (p<.001). This change seems to mirror the relative increase in conflict with the parents (p<.01), in answer to the question 'Do you argue more with your parents or grandparents?' (aged 8-9, 68.3 per cent parents v. 17.3 per cent grandparents; aged 12-13, 75.9 per cent v. 9.8 per cent; aged 16-17, 87.4 per cent v. 7.7 per cent). These data record the reawakening of conflict with parents obviously linked to the process of separation taking place and also, according to several psychoanalytic theories, to a reappearance of Oedipal dynamics. However, this phenomenon also seems to take the grandparents back to their role of idealized objects, contrasted to the parents who are more present, both positively and negatively, on the level of reality.

E Agreement between parents and grandparents and the future of grandparents

All the subjects gave a highly positive image of the three-generation family, in that significant conflicts between parents and grandparents are only rarely seen. This is undoubtedly an idealization, which also finds confirmation in the conviction that when grandparents are no longer able to look after themselves, they will live with their children or grandchildren, but be cared for mainly by the former.

Description of grandparents

The description of the grandparents' image in terms of the four adjective pairs presents several interesting aspects, despite the fact that the levels of statistical significance are generally not very high. Figure 9.2 shows the mean values summed over the four adjective pairs, on a scale from $+100$ (positive adjectives) to -100 (negative adjectives). In the variance analysis, only the effect of the variables sex of subjects and type of grandparent get anywhere near the probability level of .10.

We believe that such a poor differentiation may be attributed to the fact that the number of adjectives available to the subjects was very low and the meaning of these adjectives, with a predominantly evaluative connotation (such as nice or nasty), was very generic. In this way, a generically positive evaluation on the part of almost all the subjects and towards all four grandparents may have hidden possibly differentiated connotations.

Having noted this, it is interesting that in a more analytical comparison between the four grandparents, and between the various ages and two sexes of the subjects, using t-tests, we found six significant results in the 8-9-year-olds, two significant differences in the 12-13-year-olds and no significant differences in the 16-17-year-old subjects. This trend in the results seems to describe a process of progressive homogenization of the figures of the four grandparents under a generic connotation of a positive type. More particularly, it is the figure of the two maternal grandparents who, as their grandchildren grow older, progressively lose their positive valency until they are largely assimilated with the paternal ones (on the other hand, the level of evaluation of the latter remains more or less constant). Such a trend may perhaps be interpreted as an indicator of the progressive

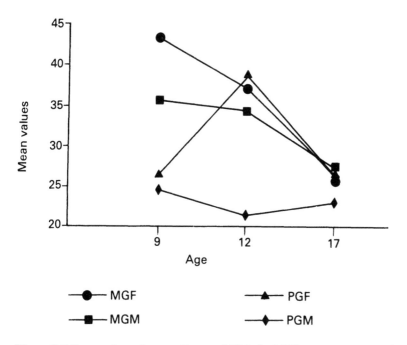

Figure 9.2 Image of grandparents for grandchildren of different ages; mean values over four adjective pairs

detachment of children in the 'maternage' area, or investment with the mother's side of the family. In this way, if the lack of differentiation on a statistical level between grandparents for age and sex of the grandchildren is interpreted as we propose above, it confirms the hypothesis of a progressive loss of specific, important significance for pre-adolescent and adolescent grandchildren in comparison to the period of childhood.

Conclusions

From our results, there would appear to be a contradiction. We can see that from an analysis of the relations with grandparents, a mainly very positive image emerges of the relationship, especially with the maternal grandparents and most of all with the maternal grandmother. On the other hand, the judgement that comes from the attribution of adjectives clearly shows a change from the 8–9-year-old group to the 16–17-year-old group. From an initial significant distinction between maternal and paternal grandparents in favour of the former, there is a progressive levelling-out where maternal and paternal grandparents are placed together in an increasingly less positive judgement.

The first result confirms what has emerged from other studies, both by us as well as by other authors (Robins and Tomanec 1962, Hoffman 1979–80). Attachment, above all to maternal grandparents, not only persists but gets stronger with time and seems to have deep roots in early infant experiences and in the habits of the relationship. However, such an attachment does not stop the adolescent, as he or she grows up, from distinguishing between the affective tie and the judgement of personal characteristics of grandparents who have, in the meanwhile, also grown older.

Children may find it difficult to distinguish their feelings of attachment from their representation of reality. Just as parents seem still to be omnipotent and omniscient because they are loved, so the grandparents cannot have characteristics of old people because they belong to the familiar world. On the contrary, for adolescents a more realistic judgement of their grandparents' characteristics and their relative secondariness in real terms does not prevent them from keeping the grandparent image, on the level of affective attachment, as a support for the ambivalence and precariousness of the process of separation that is taking place. However, this separation presents distinctive characteristics compared to the separations experienced in earlier childhood in that we are dealing with an actively sought-for and desired separation and with the prospect of taking on adult status.

For these reasons, the support given by grandparents to the adolescent seems to have a connotation that in some ways is the opposite to the role they have for the young child. In fact, a teenager can feel adult and protective towards his grandparents who are weaker but always available, receiving in exchange the sanction of the status if not of adult, at least no longer of a child. On the other hand, the parents very often live through this separation and the consequent acquisition of adult status by their offspring with great ambivalence. It may be maintained, in this case too, that the grandparents have a 'transitional object role' towards the adolescent grandchild. In fact they are an object which, because he or she is ready to be protected, 'protects the protector' in turn, in a deeper sense, from anxieties and hesitations of the separation process, confirming at the same time the vitality of old attachment ties. In this interpretation, we can find once more in adolescence, the connotation of maternage rather than paternage, of a 'maternal code' rather than a 'paternal' one (Fornari 1981) adopted by grandparenthood and expressed with greatest evidence by the maternal grandmother (Battistelli *et al.* 1983; Guaraldi and Camerini 1987).

References

Abraham, K. (1913/1948) *Selected Papers on Psychoanalysis*, London: Hogarth Press.
Barletta, G. (1984) *Nonni e nipoti. Significato di una relazione*, Turin: SEI.
Battistelli, P., Cavallero, P. and Farneti, A. (1981) 'La relazione nonno–nipote nella dinamica familiare', *Atti XVIII Congresso degli Psicologi Italiani, Acireale 1979*

4: 234–47, Palermo: Edikronos.

Battistelli, P., Cavallero, P., Farneti, A. and Zoli, P. (1983) 'I nonni: alcuni ipotesi preliminari', *Psicologia Italiana* 1: 8–13.

Battistelli, P. and Costantini, L. (1984) 'L'immagine dei nonni nei contenuti onirici manifesti', *Studi urbinati*, special number: 159–84.

Bertin, M. (1981) *Dimensione nonna*, Bologna: Cappelli.

Boszormenyi-Nagi, I. and Spark, G. M. (1973) *Invisible Loyalties: Reciprocity in Intergenerational Family Therapy*, New York: Harper & Row.

Cahn, R. and Weill, D. (1972) 'Du role pathogène de certaines grandmères d'enfants psychotiques', *Revue de Neuropsychiatrie Infantile* 20: 23–32.

Cavallero, P., Battistelli, P. and Farneti, A. (1981) 'Atteggiamento dei nonni nei confronti del proprio ruolo e del nuovo nucleo familiare', *Atti XVIII Congresso degli Psicologi Italiani, Acireale 1979* 4: 257–64, Palermo: Edikronos.

Cusinato, M. (1988) *Psicologia delle relazioni familiari*, Bologna: Il Mulino.

Deutsch, H. (1945) *The Psychology of Women*, New York: Grune & Stratton.

Farneti, A. and Battistelli, P. (1985) 'La rappresentazione dei nonni in età prescolare e scolare', *II Congresso Nazionale della Divisione Psicologia dello Sviluppo*, Urbino (6–8 Oct.).

Farneti, A. and Battistelli, P. (1988) 'Nonni e nipoti. Orientamenti delle ricerca europea sui processi intergenerazionali', *Età Evolutiva* 33: 60–103.

Farneti, A. and Zoli, P. (1981) 'I nonni. Un'isola felice', *Infanzia* 3: 5–8.

Ferenczi, S. (1913/1964) *Bausteine zur Psychonalise. Band I: Theorie*, Berne: Verlag Hans Huber AG.

Fonzi, A. (1988) *Un amore senza Edipo*, Turin: Edizioni Gruppo Abele.

Fornari, F. (1981) *Il codice vivente*, Turin: Boringhieri.

Geismann, P., Geismann, C., Amar, M. and Dumerc, C. (1980) 'Les grands-parents des enfants psychotiques', *Neuropsychiatrie de l'Enfance* 3: 89–91.

Guaraldi, G.P. and Camerini, G.B. (1987) 'Età evolutiva e terza età: l'importanza di essere nonni', *Bambino Incompiuto* 2: 85–95.

Guidicini, P. (1977) *La condizione anziana oggi*, Milan: F. Angeli.

Hall, C.S. and Van De Castle, R.L. (1966) *The Content Analysis of Dreams*, New York: Appleton Century Crofts.

Hoffman, E. (1979–80) 'Young adults' relations with their grandparents: an exploratory study', *International Journal of Aging and Human Development* 10: 299–310.

Jones, E. (1913/1948) 'The phantasy of the reversal of the generations', in *Papers on Psychoanalysis*, London: Balliere Tindall & Cox.

Kornhaber, A.M. and Woodward, K.L. (1985) *Grandparents - grandchildren: the vital connection*, New Brunswick, NJ: Transaction Books.

Kohut, H. (1971) *The Analysis of the Self*, London: Hogarth Press.

Novelletto, A. (1982) 'Il ruolo dei nonni nello sviluppo psichico normale e patologico', *Neuropsichiatria Infantile* 246: 269–82.

Parsons, T. and Bales, R.F. (1955) *Family, Socialization and Interaction Process*, Glencoe, IL: Free Press.

Rapaport, E.A. (1957) 'The grandparent syndrome', *Psychoanalytic Quarterly* 27: 518–37.

Richter, H.E. (1963) *Eltern, Kind und Neurose*, Stuttgart: Ernst Klett Verlag.

Robins, L.N. and Tomanec, M. (1962) 'Closeness to blood relatives outside the immediate family', *Marriage and Family Living* 24: 340–46.

Romano, L. (1978) *L'ospite*, Turin: Einaudi.

Romano, L. (1981) *L'inseparable*, Turin: Einaudi.

Saccu, C. and De Rysky, M. (1983) 'L'approccio multigenerazionale in terapia familiare', *Neuropsichiatria Infantile* 264/265: 380–87.

Walsh, F.W. (1978) 'Concurrent grandparent death and birth of schizophrenic offspring: an intriguing finding', *Family Process* 17: 457–63.

Chapter ten

An evolutionary perspective on grandparent–grandchild relationships

Martin Sherer Smith

Like other highly social mammals, humans evolved to nurture kin, particularly offspring. However, recent theories of social evolution suggest that humans evolved kin investment dispositions that are more complex than a general tendency to derive satisfaction from raising children (Alexander 1979, 1987; Daly and Wilson 1983, 1988a; Trivers 1985). A contemporary evolutionary perspective suggests that humans probably evolved to discriminate in their solicitude towards kin, based on factors including degree of relatedness, certainty of relatedness, access to resources and reproductive value (MacDonald 1988a, b; Smith 1987, 1988).

Natural selection has produced organisms that attempt to reproduce the maximum number of copies of their genes, or maximize genetic 'fitness'. Like other animals, humans evolved adaptations that enhance reproductive fitness. An example is extensive parental care. Like all mammalian females, human females have been selected to be highly parental. Human males have also been selected to display considerable parental investment, perhaps because aspects of human evolutionary ecology made direct paternal investment adaptive (Daly and Wilson 1983). Human males are more parental than other males in great ape species, and it is likely that evolution selected human males who enjoyed direct contact with their offspring. However, there are some evolutionary factors that selected human males to be somewhat less interested in direct parental investment than human females, in spite of the comparatively high level of parenting behaviour in both sexes. One such factor is paternal uncertainty.

The certainty of relatedness to putative kin is expected to have shaped evolved dispositions towards kin investment. Among non-human animals, a high degree of male parenting behaviour generally occurs in monogamous species where there is little chance of a male's mate conceiving offspring by another male. Many animals also demonstrate considerable within-species variation in paternal investment as a function of paternal uncertainty in individual cases (Daly and Wilson 1983).

Human paternity is rarely certain. Human fathers can seldom be sure that their ostensible offspring are actually their own; there is always a possibility that their spouse has been impregnated by another man. In some cultures, this situation is

157

not uncommon. Among the !Kung hunter-gatherers of Southern Africa, up to 5 per cent of the 'fathers' believe themselves to be the natural fathers of offspring when this is not the case (Harpending, cited in Trivers 1972). In contrast, women in all cultures are generally certain that their offspring are their own. Evolutionary psychologists believe paternal uncertainty is among the factors that have had the cumulative effect of selecting men to be somewhat less interested than women in direct parental investment.

This reasoning leads to the simple prediction that human mothers will display more parenting behaviour than fathers. This is the case in all known human cultures; although the degree of sex differences in parenting varies across cultures, mothers are more involved in child-care than fathers (Lamb 1981; Parke and Tinsley 1984). Of course, there are biological factors apart from paternal uncertainty that undoubtedly were associated with the evolution of sex differences in parenting behaviour, the most obvious of which is the female's role in suckling infants. The grandparental relationship, however, is unconfounded by such functional constraints, and therefore a more interesting set of predictions relating paternal uncertainty and kin investment can be generated for grandparents (Barash 1982; Dawkins 1976). Grandparents are predicted to invest more in the offspring of their daughters, because they can be more assured that uterine grandchildren will be related to them, whereas they cannot always be certain of their sons' offspring. Furthermore, grandmothers will invest more in grandchildren than grand-fathers, because a grandmother can be sure that her own offspring, male or female, are her own, whereas grandfathers cannot be certain of their paternity. These two predictions considered together generate a third prediction, that grandparents will invest in grandchildren in the descending order: (1) maternal grandmothers; (2) paternal grandmothers and maternal grandfathers; (3) paternal grandfathers (see Figure 10.1). A maternal grandmother is expected to invest more because she can be sure that she is the mother of her daughter, and that her daughter is the mother of her grandchildren. Paternal grandmothers and maternal grandfathers are predicted to invest equally in grandchildren, because both groups experience one generational link of uncertainty regarding their genetic relatedness. A paternal grandfather is expected to invest least, because he cannot be sure that he fathered his son, nor that his son fathered his grandchildren.

Although no previous study has directly examined these predictions, a number have reported findings that are congruent with them. Troll and colleagues (Troll, Miller and Atchley 1979; Troll 1983) and Hagestad (1984) summarize research that suggests that daughters are a stronger link in the grandparenting relationship than are sons. Robins and Tomanec (1962) reported that American undergraduates felt closer to their maternal than their paternal grandparents. Farber (1971) and Matthews and Sprey (1985) reported similar findings, but looked at feelings toward all four grandparental categories, and found that feelings of closeness followed the predicted order. Kahana and Kahana (1970) asked children in three age groups to pick their favourite grandparents. Preference generally followed the predicted order, although the differences were clearest among the youngest children.

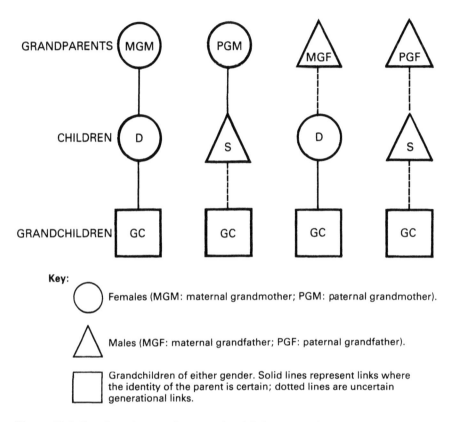

Figure 10.1 Certain and uncertain generational links among three generations

Forty-two per cent of 4- and 5-year-olds preferred their maternal grandmother, whereas paternal grandmothers and maternal grandfathers were each preferred by 16 per cent. Only 5 per cent of the young children preferred their paternal grandfather.

These studies assessed the grandparent bond from the perspective of the grandchild, and although it is interesting that grandchildren's preferences for their grandparents follow the order predicted for grandparental investment, it is grandparents' feelings for grandchildren that are most relevant to the present hypotheses. I could locate only two studies that addressed this issue. Hagestad and Speicher (1981) examined grandparents' reported attempts to influence grandchildren, and their results followed the order predicted in this study: maternal grandmothers reported the most attempts to influence grandchildren, paternal grandfathers the fewest, with the other two grandparental groups intermediate. Hagestad and Speicher found particularly strong relationships in same-sex lineages (for example, grandmother–daughter–granddaughter). Neugarten and Weinstein (1964) interviewed grandparents as to the apparent personal significance of the grandparent role. For grandmothers the most significant aspect of grandparenting was 'biological renewal and/or continuity', judged to be of primary importance for 41 per cent of grandmothers. This was much less important for grandfathers, being the most important facet of the grandparent role for only 23 per cent. This result supports the reasoning underlying the present study's hypotheses: that mothers, and grandmothers in particular, behave more nurturantly toward their descendants because in our evolutionary past females could be more certain of their relatedness to descendants than could males. Grandmothers can be assured that they have been 'renewed biologically' and that their lineage is indeed 'continuous'.

Although there is some support in the literature for this study's predictions, few previous studies are directly relevant. The present study was specifically designed to determine if North American grandparents behave in a way that is consistent with the hypothesized predictions from kin selection theory.

Method

Sample and procedure

The sample consisted of Canadian grandparents, primarily from the Toronto and Vancouver areas, who volunteered to complete a questionnaire on the amount of time they spent with their grandchildren. Grandparents were recruited through community organizations such as Canadian Legion branches, or through newspaper and radio solicitations.

The questionnaire asked grandparents to list their gender and age as well as those of their children and grandchildren. They were also asked to indicate if their children or grandchildren were adopted or step-children, how far they lived from each grandchild, and how much time they spent in the company of each grandchild. Respondents completed the questionnaires at home and returned them by post. They had the option of identifying themselves on the questionnaire or remaining anonymous.

Volunteers returned 816 questionnaires. A total of 115 responses were excluded from the analysis because they did not include the sex of the grandparents or children, the distance from the grandparent's home to the children's home, or a codable description of time spent with grandchildren. A further 114 responses were excluded from the analyses because it was possible that some characteristic of the grandparents or their descendants might have obscured a clearer test of the hypotheses. Responses excluded for this reason included those where one or more of the grandparent's children were separated or divorced, where grandparents lived in the same home as their grandchildren, or where the mean age of the grandchildren was greater than 18 years. Grandparents with divorced children were excluded because mothers usually receive custody of children after divorce, thereby limiting the paternal grandparents' access to their divorced son's children, and biasing grandparental investment toward daughters' children. Grandparents living with their grandchildren were excluded because cohabitation makes extensive grandparent–grandchild interaction almost unavoidable, removing much of the grandparent's choice of interaction time. Because grandmothers more often live with their children than grandfathers, and grandparents more often live with their daughters than their sons, data from live-in grandparents would be biased in favour of the research hypotheses. Grandparents with older grandchildren were excluded because qualitatively different and attenuated patterns of kin investment are expected with older grandchildren, especially with those who are no longer living with their parents. After excluding these cases the responses of the remaining 587 respondents were coded and analysed.

Coded variables

The following eight variables were coded for each grandparent.

Grandparent age: age in years of respondent.

Children's age: mean age in years of the grandparent's offspring who were parents. In this report, the first generation is referred to as grandparents, the second generation as children, and the third generation as grandchildren. Because the focus of this study was investment in grandchildren, the grandparents were not asked to provide information on the time they spent with their childless offspring, and the Children's age and Number of children variables did not include childless offspring in the calculations.

Grandchildren's age: mean age in years of the respondent's grandchildren.

Number of children: number of the respondent's offspring who were parents.

Number of grandchildren: number of the respondent's grandchildren.

Distance from grandchildren: a score from 1 to 6 indicating the mean distance separating the homes of the grandparent and his or her grandchildren. Distance codes were:

1 Living in the same home as the grandparents. (Grandparents with grandchildren in this category were excluded from analysis, as discussed above.)
2 Living within walking distance.
3 Living in the same city.
4 Living within 100 miles.
5 Living within 400 miles.
6 Living further than 400 miles.

The distance values for all of a grandparent's grandchildren were summed and divided by the number of grandchildren to provide the value for this variable.

Total time. The total amount of time grandparents spent with all their grandchildren, in hours per month. The time that the grandparent spent with each grandchild was coded according to coding rules (available from the author), and then the time was totalled for all grandchildren. If a grandparent spent 20 hours per month with a particular sibship of three grandchildren, then only 20 hours (not 3 x 20 hours) were counted toward Total time.

Average time. Mean time that grandparents spent with each of their grandchildren. Average time = Total time divided by Number of grandchildren.

Grandparents were divided into two categories and the data were analysed separately for each category. Grandparents who had grandchildren via children of only one sex (that is, via daughters or sons, but not via both) comprised the unilineal group (N = 394; 294 grandmothers, 100 grandfathers). Grandparents who had grandchildren via both sons and daughters comprised the bilineal group (N = 193; 145 grandmothers, 48 grandfathers). This division was useful on logical grounds, because the bilineal grandparents could choose to spend time with either daughter's children or son's children, whereas unilineal grandparents did not have this choice.

For bilineal grandparents there were also two sub-categories of Average Time calculated:

Average uterine time: The mean time spent with daughter's children.
Average agnatic time: The mean time spent with son's children.

Results

The results are presented in four sections: for the entire sample, for the unilineal group, for the bilineal group, and then comparisons among the four grandparental subgroups of Figure 10.1.

Entire sample

Table 10.1 lists the mean values for the entire sample, and then separately for grandmothers and grandfathers. Because respondents occasionally omitted some information, the sample for some variables is less than the overall total. The minimum information necessary to be included in the analysis were sex of the grandparent and children, distance from grandchildren, and time with grandchildren; therefore the sample is complete for these variables.

The average grandparent in the sample was 58.9 years old, and had two children who were 31.8 years old. He or she had 3.8 grandchildren with a mean age of 6.5 years, and lived within 100 miles of them. The average grandparent spent a total of 62.0 hours per month in the company of all his or her grandchildren, and averaged 22.4 hours per month with each grandchild.

More than three times as many grandmothers as grandfathers returned a usable questionnaire. Grandmothers and grandfathers did not differ significantly on most of the variables (Table 10.1). Grandmothers spent more total time with their grandchildren than did grandfathers: 66.0 hours to 50.3 hours. Grandmothers also spent more time with each grandchild (23.3 v. 19.7 hours) but the difference was not significant. Correlations among the variables for the entire sample are shown in Table 10.2.

Table 10.1 Means, standard deviations and grandmother/grandfather comparisons for all variables (see text for explanation)

Variable	All grandparents M±SD	Grandmothers M±SD	Grandfathers M±SD	GM/GF difference (P)[a]
Average time	22.4±30.7	23.3±30.7	19.7±30.5	n.s.
Total time	62.0±71.4	66.0±75.1	50.3±58.0	<.05 (BF)
Number of children	1.9± 1.1	1.9± 1.2	1.8± 1.0	n.s.
Number of grandchildren	3.8± 2.8	3.9± 3.0	3.4± 2.4	n.s.
Grandparent age	58.9± 7.4	58.2± 7.4	61.2± 7.1	<.01
Children's age	31.8± 5.5	32.0± 5.5	31.4± 4.8	n.s.
Grandchildren's age	6.4± 4.2	6.5± 4.2	6.1± 4.3	n.s.
Distance from grandchildren	3.9± 1.1	3.9± 1.1	3.9± 1.2	n.s.

Note: For all grandparents N = 525 to 587; for grandmothers N = 396 to 439; for grandfathers N = 129 to 148. N varies due to missing data for some variables.
[a] Difference tested with analysis of variance. Where variances in the groups differed significantly the Brown-Forsythe analysis of variance was used (designated BF in table).

Table 10.2 Correlations among grandparenting variables

Variable	1	2	3	4	5	6	7
1 Average time							
2 Total time	.55[†]						
3 Number of children	−.17[†]	.38[†]					
4 Number of grandchildren	−.23[†]	.38[†]	.88[†]				
5 Grandparent age	−.18[†]	−.03	.10*	.22[†]			
6 Children's age	−.22[†]	−.02	.10*	.25[†]	.70[†]		
7 Grandchildren's age	−.21[†]	−.07	.22[†]	.38[†]	.54[†]	.68[†]	
8 Distance from grandchildren	−.32[†]	−.18[†]	.17[†]	.15[†]	.06	.07	.06

Note:
Ns for correlations ranged from 523 to 587.
$*p<.05.$ $†p<.01.$

Unilineal grandparents

Table 10.3 lists the Unilineal group data. Grandmothers in this group spent an average of 26.6 hours per month with each grandchild, whereas grandfathers spent 25.1 hours. This difference was not significant. However, because grandmothers had more grandchildren than grandfathers (2.7 versus 2.3), grandmothers did spend significantly more total time with their grandchildren.

Unilineal grandparents with grandchildren via daughters (uterine grandparents) did spend more time with each of those grandchildren than did grandparents with grandchildren via sons (agnatic grandparents), 28.4 versus 21.0 hours. Uterine grandparents also spent more total time with all grandchildren, 56.8 versus 42.8 hours.

Table 10.3 Means, standard deviations, grandmother/grandfather and uterine/agnatic comparisons: unilineal grandparents

Variable	All unilineal grandparents M±SD	Unilineal grandmothers M±SD	Unilineal grandfathers M±SD	GM/GF difference (P)[a]
Average time	25.7±35.2	26.6±34.9	25.1±35.9	n.s.
Total time	51.6±66.8	55.7±72.2	39.7±45.5	< .05 (BF)
Number of children	1.3± 0.6	1.4± 0.7	1.3± 0.5	n.s.
Number of grandchildren	2.6± 1.8	2.7± 1.9	2.3± 1.4	< .05 (BF)
Grandparent age	58.6± 7.6	57.8± 7.4	60.9± 7.5	< .01
Children's age	31.5± 5.5	31.7± 5.7	30.9± 4.6	n.s.
Grandchildren's age	6.0± 4.4	6.1± 4.3	5.7± 4.5	n.s.
Distance from grandchildren	3.7± 1.1	3.8± 1.1	3.7± 1.2	n.s.

Variable		Uterine grandparents M±SD	Agnatic grandparents M±SD	U/A difference (P)[a]
Average time		28.4±38.6	21.0±27.9	< .05 (BF)
Total time		56.8± 7.6	42.8±46.2	< .05 (BF)
Number of children		1.4± 0.6	1.4± 0.6	n.s.
Number of grandchildren		2.6± 1.9	2.7± 1.6	n.s.
Grandparent age		58.1± 7.7	59.5± 7.3	n.s.
Children's age		30.8± 5.6	32.7± 4.9	< .01
Grandchildren's age		6.3± 4.7	5.4± 3.8	< .05 (BF)
Distance from grandchildren		3.7± 1.1	3.8± 1.2	n.s.

Note:
For all unilineal grandparents N=347 to 394; for grandmothers N=263 to 294; for grandfathers N=84 to 100; for uterine grandparents N=219 to 248; for agnatic grandparents N=127 to 146. N varies due to missing data for some variables.
[a]Difference tested with analysis of variance. Where variances in the groups differed significantly, the Brown-Forsythe analysis of variance was used (designated BF in table).

It is possible that this difference in time variables might be related to factors other than the sex of children. One possible confounding variable is the distance that grandparents lived from their children. Table 10.2 shows that there is a correlation between distance and time; unsurprisingly, the further grandparents live from grandchildren, the less time they spend with them. If the uterine and agnatic grandparents differed on distance from grandchildren, the time differences might be partly attributable to that variable. However, grandmothers lived the same average distance from grandchildren as grandfathers, and there were also no distance differences between uterine and agnatic grandparents. Controlling for distance from grandchildren in an analysis of covariance (ANCOVA) did not significantly affect the time differences among the unilineal grandparent groups.

Another possible confounding variable is number of grandchildren. Table 10.2 indicates that grandparents with more grandchildren spent more total time with them, and less time with each individual grandchild, than grandparents with fewer grandchildren. However, Table 10.3 indicates that uterine and agnatic grandparents have the same number of grandchildren, so it is unlikely that number of grandchildren accounts for the time differences between these groups. An ANCOVA confirms this. Grandmothers and grandfathers, however, do differ on number of grandchildren: 2.7 versus 2.3. It is therefore possible that number of grandchildren might be accounting for some of the total time difference between grandmothers and grandfathers. An ANCOVA supports this: when number of grandchildren is controlled, the adjusted means for grandmothers and grandfathers are 54.3 and 43.9 hours respectively, compared to the unadjusted means of 55.7 and 39.7 hours (Table 10.3). The difference between the adjusted means is not significant:

$$F(1,391) = 2.04, p = .15.$$

In contrast, controlling for number of grandchildren increased the average time difference between grandmothers and grandfathers, since average time and number of grandchildren are negatively correlated. With number of grandchildren controlled, the adjusted means for the grandmother/grandfather comparison were 27.1 and 21.6 hours respectively, compared to the unadjusted means of 26.6 and 23.1 hours. However, the difference between the adjusted means was still not significant.

The final possible confounding variable examined was grandparent age, which did not correlate with total time but correlates negatively with average time. Agnatic grandparents were not significantly older than uterine grandparents, but grandfathers were significantly older than grandmothers. When grandparent age was controlled in an ANCOVA, the average time difference between grandmothers and grandfathers disappeared.

When all three possibly confounding variables (distance from grandchildren, number of grandchildren, grandparent age) were controlled simultaneously, the grandmother/grandfather difference on average time increases slightly, but the difference between the adjusted means was still not significant:

$$F(1,378) = 1.22, p. = .27.$$

Controlling for the same three variables had more of an effect on the total time comparison, but in the other direction: the difference between grandmothers and grandfathers decreased, and was not statistically significant. Controlling the same three variables had little effect on the comparison between uterine and agnatic grandparents.

To summarize the unilineal group findings: uterine grandparents spent more time with their daughter's children than agnatic grandparents spent with their son's children. They spent more time with individual grandchildren, and also more total time with all their grandchildren. These differences are not attributable to the effects of variables such as distance from grandchildren, number of grandchildren and grandparent age. In comparison, grandmothers and grandfathers did not differ much on the time they spent with grandchildren, and the differences that did emerge decreased when extraneous variables were controlled.

Bilineal grandparents

Results were similar for the bilineal grandparents (Table 10.4). Bilineal grandparents had more than twice as many grandchildren as did unilineal grandparents. They spent more total time with all their grandchildren, and less with each individual grandchild, and they lived further from their grandchildren. The ages of the grandparents, children and grandchildren were similar in the two groups.

Table 10.4 Means, standard deviations, grandmother/grandfather and uterine/agnatic comparisons: bilineal grandparents

Variable	All bilineal grandparents M±SD	Bilineal grandmothers M±SD	Bilineal grandfathers M±SD	GM/GF difference (P)[a]
Average time	15.7±16.5	16.6±17.9	12.8±10.9	n.s.
Total time	83.2±75.9	86.7±76.6	72.6±73.6	n.s.
Number of children	2.9± 1.2	2.9± 1.2	2.9± 1.0	n.s.
Number of grandchildren	6.0± 3.2	6.1± 3.4	5.6± 2.6	n.s.
Grandparent age	59.5± 7.2	58.8± 7.4	61.7± 6.3	< .05
Children's age	32.4± 5.0	32.4± 4.9	32.3± 5.1	n.s.
Grandchildren's age	7.3± 3.7	7.4± 3.7	7.1± 3.6	n.s.
Distance from grandchildren	4.1± 0.9	4.0± 0.9	4.4± 0.8	< .05

Variable	Uterine lineage M±SD	Agnatic lineage M±SD	U/A difference (P)[a]
Average time	19.4±26.5	13.6±19.3	< .01
Total time	48.3±51.5	34.4±50.2	< .01
Number of children	1.5± 0.8	1.4± 0.7	n.s.
Number of grandchildren	3.2± 2.4	2.8± 1.7	< .01
Grandparent's age	- -	- -	-
Children's age	32.0± 5.9	32.5± 5.5	n.s.
Grandchildren's age	7.5± 4.5	6.4± 4.2	< .01
Distance from grandchildren	4.1± 1.2	4.1± 1.2	n.s.

Note:
For all bilineal grandparents N = 170 to193; for grandmothers N = 130 to 145; for grandfathers N = 40 to 48; for uterine and agnatic lineages N = 170 to 193. N varies due to missing data for some variables.

Although bilineal grandmothers spent both more average time and total time with their grandchildren than did bilineal grandfathers, neither difference was significant at the .05 level (Table 10.4). However, unlike the unilineal situation, bilineal grandmothers lived closer to their grandchildren than did bilineal grandfathers and, as in the unilineal case, grandfathers were older than grandmothers. When these variables were controlled in an ANCOVA, the time differences between grandmothers and grandfathers became even smaller.

In contrast, bilineal grandparents spent significantly more average time and total time with their daughter's children (uterine grandchildren) than with their son's children (agnatic grandchildren). Bilineal grandparents lived no closer to their uterine grandchildren, however, so distance does not account for the difference. Uterine and agnatic descendants did differ on two variables aside from the time measure: number of grandchildren and grandchildren's age. Grandparents

166

had more uterine grandchildren who were older than their agnatic counterparts. Controlling for these two variables in an ANCOVA did not affect the time comparisons, and the difference remained significant.

To summarize, the bilineal grandparent data generally corroborated the patterns reported in the unilineal group. Although grandmothers spent more time with grandchildren than grandfathers did in both groups, these differences were generally not significant and became even less pronounced when potentially confounding variables were controlled. Grandparents spent more time with daughter's children than son's children in both groups, and the difference could not be attributed to differences on any of the other variables.

Grandparental subgroups

The final hypothesis was that grandparent investment would follow the descending order: (1) maternal grandmothers; (2) paternal grandmothers, maternal grandfathers; (3) paternal grandfathers. Table 10.5 displays the mean average time values for these grandparental sub-groups separately for unilineal and bilineal grandparents. These values follow the predicted order, although the unpredicted similarity between grandmother and grandfather investment reported above was reflected in the sub-group values: for instance, in the unilineal group, the average time of maternal grandfathers was more similar to maternal grandmothes than to paternal grandmothers, contrary to the prediction. However, the ordinal position of the sub-groups was as predicted, although the relative position of the two intermediate sub-groups was not.

The wide variation among the sub-groups in number of cases and variances rendered tests of significance problematic for detecting meaningful differences. The preponderance of grandmothers meant that differences involving grandmother sub-groups were more likely to be statistically significant than differences of similar magnitude involving grandfathers. In both unilineal and bilineal groups, maternal grandmothers differed significantly from paternal grandfathers. Maternal grandmothers also differed from paternal grandmothers. None of the other average

Table 10.5 Grandparent sub-groups: average time with grandchildren

		Uterine grandmothers	*Agnatic grandmothers*	*Uterine grandfathers*	*Agnatic grandfathers*	*Total*
Unilineal grandparents	M	29.3	22.1	26.0	17.4	25.7
	SD	37.3	30.3	42.2	17.5	35.2
	N	182	112	66	34	394
Bilineal grandparents	M	20.3	14.1	16.8	12.4	16.5
	SD	26.3	20.3	27.1	16.2	22.8
	N	145	145	48	48	193

Note: Each unilineal grandparent is represented in only one of the four grandparent-sex by child-sex subgroups, whereas each bilineal grandparent is represented in both the uterine and agnatic categories. M = mean, SD = standard deviation, N = number of subjects.

Table 10.6 Significance levels for sub-group comparisons

		Agnatic grandmothers	Uterine grandfathers	Agnatic grandfathers
Unilineal grandparents	Uterine grandmothers	n.s. (BF)	n.s.	†(BF)
	Agnatic grandmothers		n.s.	n.s.
	Uterine grandfathers			n.s.
Bilineal grandparents	Uterine grandmothers	†(RM)	n.s.	*(RM)
	Agnatic grandmothers		n.s.	n.s.
	Uterine grandfathers			n.s.

Note:
Significance tests are conventional one-way analyses of variance except where the variance of the comparison groups differed significantly, in which cases Brown-Forsythe analyses of variances were used (designated BF). Repeated measures analyses of variance are designated RM.
$*p < .05.$ $†p < .01.$

time pairwise comparisons in either group produced significant differences (Table 10.6). As in the previous analyses, where controlling for possibly confounding variables had any effect on the average time sub-group comparisons, the effect was in the direction of increasing predicted differences, although in none of the comparisons did unadjusted non-significant comparisons achieve significance at the .05 level after controlling for extraneous covariates.

To summarize, the order of the grandparent sub-groups on average time was generally as predicted, although the absence of a pronounced grandmother/grand-father difference influenced the order of the sub-groups. The comparatively small number of grandfathers may have contributed to the lack of statistical significance in some of the predicted differences.

Discussion

Validity of the results

Two basic questions address the validity of the results. First, how representative is the sample; that is, to what degree does the sample resemble the population of all grandparents in North America? Second, how accurate is the information that the respondents provided regarding the time they spend with their grandchildren?

It is difficult to determine the representativeness of the sample, because few data have been published on the demography of grandparenthood. Nevertheless, there are several things we can assume about the sample, based on knowledge of volunteer responses to questionnaires (Rosenthal and Rosnow 1975). The sample is likely to be better educated and wealthier than the population of grandparents. They are likely to have more grandchildren, spend more time with them, and enjoy them more than non-responders. Because women tend to return question-naires more than men, grandmothers are probably disproportionately represented compared to the population. However, although these factors mean the sample is not entirely representative of the population in terms of education, sex ratio and interest in grandchildren, there is little reason to suspect that these factors should greatly distort the comparisons of interest: whether grandparental interest in grandchildren is influenced by the sex of the grandparents and children.

Regarding the accuracy of this kind of questionnaire data, self-reports are often inaccurate, and respondents often reply in a way that they believe corresponds to what the investigator wants, or in a way that preserves the respondent's self-image (Silverman 1977). However, self-reports appear to be more distorted if they involve attitudes or socially disapproved behaviour. Information regarding relatively straightforward and socially approved behaviour such as that requested here is generally more accurate. Although it is likely that the respondents varied in the accuracy with which their self-reported time with grandchildren corresponded with their actual behaviour, there is again little reason to suspect that such inaccuracies systematically biased the results. It is more likely that the substantial noise in the data would make the hypothesized differences more difficult to discern.

Validity would have been improved by randomly selecting grandparents from the population, rather than utilizing self-selected volunteers, and by actually monitoring grandparental interaction in the home. However, instituting these procedures was impossible under the constraints of this investigation, and would have meant decreasing the sample size. The potential threats to validity notwithstanding, it is likely that the results retain a considerable degree of validity and that the reported differences do correspond to similar differences in the population of North American grandparents.

Why was the sex-of-child-effect greater than the sex-of-grandparent effect?

The reasoning underlying the hypotheses implied that grandmother investment should exceed grandfather investment by the same proportion that investment in daughters' children exceeded investment in sons' children. That is because both predictions are based on the same phenomenon: the probability that males are actually fathers of their putative offspring. Why, then, was there only an equivocal difference between the time grandmothers and grandfathers spent with offspring, while the preferences for daughters' offspring was much greater?

Among the factors that may have contributed to the equivocal difference between grandmothers and grandfathers were the criteria for excluding cases from analysis. The fact that grandparents who were cohabiting with their grandchildren were excluded probably decreased the grandmother/grandfather difference since live-in grandparents generally invest heavily in their grandchildren, and a majority of live-in grandparents are women. Similarly, the exclusion of families where divorce was reported probably decreased the average grandmother time figures, because mothers generally receive custody after divorce, and, following divorce in the grandparent generation, this could lead to a closeness between mother and children that would influence investment towards grandchildren.

169

Another factor to consider in understanding the unexpected similarity of grandmother and grandfather investment is that grandparents often visit their grandchildren as part of a grandparent couple. In these cases, the most interested spouse (hypothesized here as the grandmother) might 'pull along' the less interested partner, and the reported interaction time would be equal. The questionnaire did not provide sufficient information to examine this possibility thoroughly, as it did not ask grandparent couples to identify themselves, nor did it enquire as to current marital status or circumstances of the grandparent visits. However, by matching grandmothers and grandfathers on details of grandchild sex/age constellations, it was possible to nominate likely couples from among the respondents. Only sixteen possible couples were thus discerned, and the results remained substantially the same when the grandparent couples were excluded from the analysis.

Although it is possible that sample selection criteria or other factors might account for part of the unexpected similarity between the degree of grandmother and grandfather investment, a reconsideration of the premises of the hypotheses provides another possible explanation. The original premises may have been incomplete because they failed to consider whether grandfathers had any fitness-maximizing alternatives to investing in their grandchildren. It is obviously true that a male's probability of being related to his putative descendants does not change as he ages. However, what may change is the inclusive fitness return from engaging in behaviours other than investing in lineal descendants. For instance, a younger man has a number of alternatives to investing in his putative offspring for increasing his inclusive fitness. One such possibility, which is not so much an alternative as a variation of 'direct' investment, is to work outside the family in order to supply the resources necessary to maximize the viability of his offspring. This is the pattern followed by most males in modern industrial societies. Accrual of resources by the male increases his fitness in at least two ways. Resources sustain his offspring, and his wife, who usually cares for his offspring. Resources increase his ability to sustain sexual relationships with more than one woman, thereby potentiating more children with the additional partners. This pattern is formally sanctioned in polygynous societies, and also occurs to some degree in cultures that are ostensibly monogamous. Therefore a major fitness alternative for males to investing in one's own putative offspring has been to initiate additional sexual relationships that, in natural environments, would often result in additional offspring for the male. Yet another alternative to offspring investment is to invest in kin other than offspring, particularly in sister's children. This pattern is formalized in avuncular relationships that are normative in some cultures (Alexander 1979; van den Berghe 1979).

Therefore 'direct' investment by way of time with offspring was not the only way in which males could increase their inclusive fitness in our evolutionary past. It is likely that males evolved to derive emotional rewards from several types of fitness-related activities, including the following:

1 investing 'indirectly' in offspring by accruing resources that ensure their viability;
2 investing 'directly' by spending time nurturing, protecting and teaching offspring;
3 investing in relatives other than offspring, primarily siblings, nephews, nieces and grandchildren;
4 sustaining sexual relationships with more than one woman.

These various options differ in their fitness effects depending on the male's circumstances, and one factor would reliably influence the success of a particular option is the age of the male. It is likely that the benefits of pursuing strategies besides investment in lineal descendants becomes less profitable with age. For instance, grandfathers may be less able than when they were younger to attract and maintain an extra mate. The same investment of time, energy and resources might yield a better inclusive fitness return by being focused on grandchildren. Therefore, although grandfathers become no more likely to be related to their descendants when they are older than when they are younger, the diminishing returns of alternative fitness-enhancing strategies may dispose them to invest almost as much in grandchildren as do grandmothers. In terms of inclusive fitness, investing in an uncertain pay-off is better than not investing at all.

The diminishing returns for grandfathers' alternative fitness options would not be expected to lessen the bias towards daughters' children. All grandparents, including grandfathers, have a higher probability of being related to their daughters' children than to their sons' children, and if either sex has a choice of grandchildren to invest in, their inclusive fitness would benefit by biasing towards daughters' children, at any point in their lifespan.

This consideration of the changing benefits of alternative fitness options throughout a male's lifespan renders the results more explicable in terms of inclusive fitness theory. Support for the possibility that males' fitness-enhancing strategies become more focused on nurturance of kin rather than on alternative options comes from a study of the development of psychological characteristics across the lifespan. Feldman, Biringen and Nash (1981) found that although young and middle-aged mothers rated themselves as more tender and compassionate than did fathers of the same ages, there were no differences in how grandmothers and grandfathers rated themselves on the same characteristics. While female self-ratings on these characteristics remained stable throughout the adult lifespan, males showed a steady rise in tenderness and compassion as they got older, peaking at grandparenthood. And these researchers believe that tenderness and compassion are more closely linked to child-care activities than any of the other characteristics they measured.

It is not likely that humans evolved to strive consciously towards producing as many descendants as possible. It is likely that people evolved to value and pursue those activities that led to more descendants during our evolutionary past (Symons 1987). Natural selection may have designed males to manifest the changes in tenderness and compassion reported by Feldman *et al.*, and these developmental patterns might well be part of an evolved system of emotional rewards that changes predictably across the lifespan. Although cultural factors probably also influence these changes, it is nevertheless quite possible that natural selection shaped men and women to differ in their socio-emotional development across the lifespan to the same extent that they differ physically and endocrinologically.

Measurement of human kin investment

An evolutionary perspective views all organismic activity, including human social behaviour, as having evolved in order to facilitate the reproduction of the genes that comprise individuals (Hamilton 1964). Activities that promote the survival of an individual's genes in a conspecific are referred to as 'kin investment', of which parental investment in offspring is the most basic. Kin investment refers to behaviours (and other investment) that facilitate the survival and reproduction of kin. In highly social mammals, adult care is necessary for the survival of offspring. Kin must provide nourishment, protection and tuition in survival and social skills. The latter aspect is particularly important in complexly social mammals such as humans. With some exceptions, such as bequests (Smith, Kish and Crawford 1987), human kin investment requires expenditures of time in order to be effective, and therefore the amount of time that grandparents spend with grandchildren is probably a good rough measure of the degree of kin investment. Tinsley and Parke (1984, 1987) reported that greater grandparental contact with infants was associated with higher scores on the Bayley Scales of Infant Development, and this finding suggests a relationship between grandparental investment and grandchildren's successful development.

Although the genetic interests of close relatives are more congruent than any other conspecifics, they are still not identical. So conflicts of interest can be expected even among close kin, especially where resources are limited. Behaviour patterns that contribute maximally to a parent's inclusive fitness may not be entirely in the best genetic interests of the offspring, and similarly, there may be circumstances where the genetic interests of siblings conflict. This issue has been discussed by Alexander (1979, 1987), Daly and Wilson (1983, 1988b) and Trivers (1985). These theorists suggest we should not expect humans to have evolved to be unreservedly altruistic towards anyone, even grandchildren, but rather to distribute solicitude according to its likely effects on the altruist's inclusive fitness.

Ultimately what activities constitute human kin investment is an empirical question, to be addressed by assessing exactly which behaviours that adults display towards children contribute to the children's eventual reproductive success. Addressing these kinds of questions necessitates a synthesis of ideas and data from evolutionary biology, developmental psychology and behavioural economics.

Mechanisms mediating kin investment dispositions

Unlike some animals, humans probably have not evolved physiological 'detectors' that measure degree of relatedness, and influence our behaviour accordingly (Porter 1987; Wells 1987). However, we do appear to express a more flexible kin investment disposition: something like 'behave altruistically towards people you grew up with and with whom you spend the most time'. Evolved kin investment dispositions are expected to be mediated through our emotions; through our feelings of love and nurturance towards our children, siblings and parents, and the milder forms of those emotions that we feel towards more distant kin such as nephews, nieces and grandchildren. The anger and frustration that is often directed towards relatives may also reflect fitness-maximising dispositions; as mentioned above, relatedness does not preclude conflict of interest.

The preference towards daughters' children reported in this research is also probably mediated through systematic variation in emotional bonds. Presumably, grandparents spend more time with daughters' children because they enjoy being with them more, although that explanation was not examined in this research. This preference might result if grandparents favoured grandchildren who resembled them more in appearance and personality (see Leek and Smith, this volume). This is because some putative grandchildren via sons might not share any genes with the grandparents, and therefore the average resemblance with a son's putative children is likely to be less than with a daughter's children. There is also the possibility that grandparents are disposed to prefer daughters' children regardless of the perceived similarity between themselves and the grandchildren. Such possible kin investment dispositions would be flexible and manifested as conscious cognitions and emotions of considerable subtlety and complexity, and they would be moderated by cultural norms and individual life histories.

Non-evolutionary explanations for preference for daughters' children

If evolved kin investment dispositions do play a role in the preference for daughters' children, it is unlikely that they are the only factor accounting for this preference. Some researchers have suggested that the emotional bond between mothers and daughters may be uniquely strong and enduring, but this possibility would not explain why grandfathers' preferences for daughters' children were as strong as that of grandmothers.

A more plausible alternative explanation is that daughters are at home with the grandchildren more than sons, and grandparents probably feel more comfortable visiting with their daughter and grandchildren than with their daughter-in-law and grandchildren. To examine this possibility, future research should compare grandparental visiting patterns in families where both parents worked full-time with those in which either the mother or father was a full-time homemaker. To find a preference for daughters' children in a sample where both parents were in the home for equal amounts of time would provide stronger evidence for the possibility of an evolved bias towards daughters' children. Further research should also examine in more detail the grandparents' feelings about their grandchildren, and the circumstances surrounding their visits.

It is important to note that evolved kin investment dispositions undoubtedly interact with environmental factors to produce observable patterns of family interactions. An evolutionary perspective on family interactions should not be construed as excluding other explanations of family behaviour. Evolutionary psychology provides another level of explanation in multi-level models of family interactions and social development (Belsky, Lerner and Spanier 1984; Cairns 1979; Parke and Lewis 1981).

Summary and conclusion

This research indicates that grandparents spend more time with their daughter's children than with their son's children. It also discovered that grandmothers and grandfathers do not differ much in the time spent with grandchildren. These data do not answer the question of whether evolved kin investment dispositions influenced these patterns. However, the results are congruent with one model of how natural selection may have shaped discriminative solicitude towards kin. This study adds to the growing body of empirical research in evolutionary psychology (for example, Buss 1988, 1989; Cosmides 1989; Daly and Wilson 1988a, 1988b), and suggests that social evolutionary theory may provide important insights into the development of social relationships across the lifespan.

Acknowledgements

I thank Martin Daly, Bob Ley, Irwin Silverman, Janet Strayer and Margo Wilson for comments on earlier versions of this chapter. This research was supported by the Social Sciences and Humanities Research Council of Canada.

References

Alexander, R.D. (1979) *Darwinism and Human Affairs*, Seattle: University of Washington Press.

Alexander, R.D. (1987) *The Biology of Moral Systems*, New York: Aldine de Gruyter.

Barash, D.P. (1982) *Sociobiology and Behavior* (2nd edn), New York: Elsevier.

Belsky, J., Lerner, R.M. and Spanier, G.B. (1984) *The Child in the Family*, Reading, M.A.: Addison-Wesley.

Brown, M.B. and Forsythe, A.B. (1974) 'The small sample behavior of some statistics which test the equality of several means', *Technometrics* 16: 129–32.

Buss, D.M. (1988) 'The evolution of human intrasexual competition: tactics of mate attraction', *Journal of Personality and Social Psychology* 54: 616–28.

Buss, D.M. (1989) 'Sex differences in mate preferences: evolutionary hypotheses tested in 37 cultures', *Behavioural and Brain Sciences* 12: 1–49.

Cairns, R.B. (1979) *Social Development: the Origins and Plasticity of Interchanges*,

San Francisco: Freeman.

Cosmides, L. (1989) 'The logic of social exchange: has natural selection shaped how humans reason?', *Cognition* 31: 187–276.

Daly, M. and Wilson, M. (1983) *Sex, Evolution and Behavior* (2nd edn), Boston: Willard Grant Press.

Daly, M. and Wilson, M. (1987) 'Evolutionary psychology and family violence', in C.B. Crawford, M.S. Smith and D. Krebs (eds), *Sociobiology and Psychology: Ideas, Issues and Applications*, Hillsdale, NJ: Erlbaum.

Daly, M. and Wilson, M. (1988a) *Homicide*, New York: Aldine de Gruyter.

Daly, M. and Wilson, M. (1988b) 'Evolutionary social psychology and family violence', *Science* 242: 519–24.

Dawkins, R. (1976) *The Selfish Gene*, New York: Oxford University Press.

Farber, B. (1971) *Kinship and Class: a Midwestern Study*, New York: Basic Books.

Feldman, S.S., Biringen, Z.C. and Nash, S.C. (1981) 'Fluctuations of sex-related self-attributions as a function of stage of family life cycle', *Developmental Psychology* 17: 24–35.

Hagestad, G.O. (1984) 'Continuity and connectedness', in V.L. Bengtson and J. Robertson (eds), *Grandparenthood: Traditional and Emergent Perspectives*, Beverly Hills, CA: Sage.

Hagestad, G.O. and Speicher, G.O. (1981) 'Grandparents and family influence: views of three generations', Paper presented at the Society for Research in Child Development Meeting, Boston.

Hamilton, W.D. (1964) 'The genetical evolution of social behaviour: I and II', *Journal of Theoretical Biology* 7: 1–52.

Kahana, B. and Kahana, E. (1970) 'Grandparenthood from the perspective of the developing grandchild', *Developmental Psychology* 3: 98–105.

Lamb, M.E. (ed.) (1981) *The Role of the Father in Child Development* (2nd edn), New York: John Wiley & Sons.

MacDonald, K. (ed.) (1988a) *Sociobiological Perspectives on Human Development*, New York: Springer-Verlag.

MacDonald, K. (1988b) *Social and Personality Development: an Evolutionary Synthesis*, New York: Plenum.

Matthews, S.H. and Sprey, J. (1985) 'Adolescents' relationships with grandparents: an empirical contribution to conceptual clarification', *Journal of Gerontology* 40: 621–26.

Neugarten, B.L. and Weinstein, K.K. (1964) 'The changing American grandparent', *Journal of Marriage and the Family* 26: 118–24.

Parke, R.D. and Lewis, N.G. (1981) 'The family in context: a multilevel interactional model of child abuse', in R.W. Henderson (ed.), *Parent–child Interaction: Theory, Research and Prospects*, New York: Academic Press.

Parke, R.D. and Tinsley, B.R. (1984) 'Fatherhood: historical and contemporary perspectives', in K.A. McCluskey and H.W. Reese (eds), *Life-span Developmental Psychology: Historical and Generational Effects*, New York: Academic Press.

Porter, R. (1987) 'Kin recognition: functions and mediating mechanisms', in C.B. Crawford, M.S. Smith and D. Krebs (eds), *Sociobiology and Psychology: Ideas, Issues and Applications*, Hillsdale, NJ: Erlbaum.

Robins, L.N. and Tomanec, M. (1962) 'Closeness to blood relatives outside the immediate family', *Marriage and Family Living* 24:340–46.

Rosenthal, R. and Rosnow, R.L. (1975) *The Volunteer Subject*, New York: John Wiley & Sons.

Silverman, I. (1977) *The Human Subject in the Psychological Laboratory*, New York: Pergamon.

Smith, M.S. (1987) 'Evolution and developmental psychology: toward a sociobiology of human development', in C.B. Crawford, M.S. Smith and D. Krebs (eds), *Sociobiology and Psychology: Ideas, Issues and Applications*, Hillsdale, NJ: Erlbaum.

Smith, M.S. (1988) 'Research in developmental sociobiology: parenting and family behavior', in K. MacDonald (ed.) *Sociobiological Perspectives on Human Development*, New York: Springer-Verlag.

Smith, M.S., Kish, B.J. and Crawford, C.B. (1987) 'Inheritance of wealth as human kin investment', *Ethology and Sociobiology* 8: 92–104.

Symons, D. (1987) 'If we're all Darwinians, what's the fuss about?', in C.B. Crawford, M.S. Smith and D. Krebs (eds), *Sociobiology and Psychology: Ideas, Issues and Applications*, Hillsdale, NJ: Erlbaum.

Tinsley, B.J. and Parke, R.D. (1984) 'Grandparents as support and socialization agents', in M. Lewis (ed.), *Beyond the Dyad*, New York: Plenum.

Tinsley, B.J. and Parke, R.D. (1987) 'Grandparents as interactive and social support agents for families with young infants', *International Journal of Aging and Human Development* 25: 259–77.

Trivers, R.L. (1972) 'Parental investment and sexual selection', in B. Campbell (ed.), *Sexual Selection and the Descent of Man*, Chicago: Aldine.

Trivers, R.L. (1974) 'Parent–offspring conflict', *American Zoologist* 14: 249–64.

Trivers, R.L. (1985) *Social Evolution*, Menlo Park, CA: Benjamin/Cummings.

Troll, L.E. (1983) 'Grandparents: the family watchdogs', in T.H. Brubaker (ed.), *Family Relations and Aging*, Beverly Hills, CA: Sage.

Troll, L.E., Miller, S.J. and Atchley, R.C. (1979) *Families in Later Life*, Belmont, CA: Wadsworth.

Van den Berghe, P.L. (1979) *Human Family Systems: an Evolutionary View*, New York: Elsevier.

Wells, P.A. (1987) 'Kin recognition in humans', in D.J.C. Fletcher and C.D. Michener (eds), *Kin Recognition in Animals*, New York: John Wiley & Sons.

Chapter eleven

Cooperation and conflict in three-generation families

Maria Leek and Peter K. Smith

Many causal factors can be invoked to understand or explain behaviour. Some will be very immediate or 'proximal' factors; these will include the immediate motivation for behaviour; for example, love of a grandchild, if we are trying to understand helping behaviour in grandparent–grandchild relations. Lying behind these may be factors due to learning and experience and, in the human case, societal norms and cultural tradition. Further levels of explanation still may lie in our evolutionary history, in the reasons why certain kinds of predispositions and learning mechanisms have been selected; for example, why we readily form attachments to people whom we know well. These can be called 'distal' factors.

In this chapter we attempt two things. First, we outline some of the arguments from evolutionary biology which may be particularly relevant to understanding human grandparenthood. Second, we describe some attempts at modelling the influence of a number of causal factors, distal and proximal, on reported grandparental behaviour to children and grandchildren.

Evolutionary biology and grandparenthood

Evolutionary strategies may be predicted to lie behind certain patterns in grandparent behaviour and in the behaviour adopted by other members of the extended family towards the grandparents. This approach, which we will call the 'sociobiological approach', has often been criticized when applied to the human case; it is argued that human behaviour is essentially too complex to be encompassed by the mechanisms of natural selection. However, the strength of this argument remains an empirical question and, granted the importance of non-genetic factors in the human case, the potential gains to be made by linking cultural and biological explanations are sufficiently great to justify exploring sociobiological reasoning further. This is not to suggest that non-biological explanations of the behavioural patterns are invalid; rather, that they are most usefully seen as the proximal causes of behavioural strategies, the distal causes of which require an evolutionary perspective for a full explanation (see also M.S. Smith, this volume).

Why should *grandparents* be of interest to sociobiologists? The essence of sociobiology is to explain behaviour in terms of the differential transmission of gene types. It is not immediately clear why grandparental behaviour provides relevant subject matter for this. After all, many grandparents, especially grandmothers, tend to be past hope of child-bearing and thus of increasing their direct genetic contribution to future generations. However, Hamilton's (1964) theory of 'inclusive fitness' states that individuals are selected not simply to maximise their own genetic contribution to the next generation, but also to promote the reproductive opportunities of those who share their genes. Besides providing a coherent sociobiological rationale for such behaviours as altruism and conflict, this also provides an explanation for the human tendency to live well past the age at which reproduction is feasible, a tendency which does not appear in most other animal species. This extension of the lifespan makes grandparenthood of particular interest to sociobiology.

What lifespan expectancies might be selected for in different species? One evolutionary strategy would be for individuals to possess body clocks which curtailed their existence once reproduction ceased to be viable. In this way, the risk of actually harming one's existing offspring – for example, by consuming limited resources – would be reduced. In fact, this strategy does seem to be the one adopted by many organisms. In some species, however, including our own, in which parents invest much time and energy in offspring ('K' selection, MacArthur and Wilson 1967) a more subtle tactic has been developed, in which older individuals who are less likely to reproduce continue to invest time and energy in promoting the well-being and ultimately the reproductive success of their offspring.

In the human case this tactic is exemplified in the phenomenon of the menopause, where reproductive opportunities have entirely ceased. This strategy, apparently disastrous for the individual's own future reproductive success, may be explained if females have been selected to terminate their own reproductive efforts once these become of low value. For older mothers the genetic 'gain' of having more offspring is reduced by the greater chances of having a handicapped child, or dying in childbirth and hence leaving an offspring without the protection it needs for survival. With age this 'gain' comes to be exceeded by the 'gain' in an alternative strategy; that of enhancing the well-being and hence reproductive opportunities of one's existing children and existing and future grandchildren. The benefits of this alternative strategy are particularly great in K-selected species, in which the elderly can provide useful care and support for the young.

The above argument also applies in essence to the male case. The older male's chances of successful reproduction are lessened by decreased fertility, the tendency of females to prefer more able and attractive partners, and the increased risk of having handicapped offspring which he shares with the female. Consequently, the older male might also be expected to shift towards the alternative strategy of supporting the reproductive efforts of his offspring. The argument is less strong than in the female case, since the male does not bear children and thus need not incur the direct costs attached to any future reproduction; also the benefits of the alternative strategy are diminished by any uncertainty about his genetic relatedness to his grandchildren. Perhaps as a consequence, the shift to the alternative non-reproductive strategy is less final in males, with no 'menopause' *per se*.

In summary, the sociobiological rationale behind grandparenthood is that we stay alive in order to reproduce vicariously through the efforts of our offspring. On this basis, we can predict a number of patterns which should be observable both in terms of grandparental behaviour and the behaviour of offspring towards their (often) unreproductive elders. Some of these will be outlined and the extent to which our empirical work supports them will be examined. First, the methods followed for data collection are reviewed.

The grandparent sample

Grandparents were recruited by way of advertisements in local newspapers, posters in day centres and contacts in various clubs and organizations. The sample of sixty-five grandparents had a mean age of 68.4 years for females (N=47) and 64.6 years for males (N=18). Most were still married, and regarded themselves as healthy. They were split between the lower and upper middle classes, and tended not to have attended school past the age of fifteen or sixteen. In all they had 144 children, of mean age 32.0 years; of the children ninety-four were or had been married (children's spouses); and there were 175 grandchildren, of mean age 12.1 years. Grandparents reported an average of about nine close friends.

Perceived role as a grandparent

Grandparents were asked to give their subjective opinions of the grandparental role, by asking them to place in rank order the five following statements (taken from Crawford 1981) in terms of how well they matched their own feelings. These statements represent the five styles of grandparenthood identified by Neugarten and Weinstein (1964):

A   Having a grandchild means living on into the future.
B   Having a grandchild means a chance to be a better grandfather/mother than I was a father/mother.
C   Having a grandchild means that I will be able to help him/her.
D   Having a grandchild means that he/she may achieve in life what I failed to achieve.
E   Having a grandchild means very little to me.

The median responses show that statement *A* was given the highest rank, statement *C* came second, statements *D* and *B* ranked equally at third place, and statement *E* was decisively placed in last position, with only one respondent ranking it higher than fourth place. The high priority of 'living on into the future' and being 'able to help him/her' in the views of the grandparents are certainly consistent with the broad sociobiological perspective outlined above.

The grandparent questionnaire

The questionnaire provides an economic means of obtaining data on interactions within the three-generation family. Although questionnaire data do present problems of response validity, this is less so if, as here, the interest is in the grandparents' subjective perceptions of the situation rather than any objective truth. The questionnaire we developed in fact covered a number of different issues, including child-rearing practices and sibling conflict, but the discussion concentrates on patterns of altruism and disagreement, these being particularly relevant to the sociobiological arguments presented.

The questionnaire items asked subjects to express their feelings towards each other member of their extended family and close friends, in terms of the following outcome variables (see also Table 11.1): frequency of help, and value of help, both given and received; feelings of altruism or unselfishness towards them; frequency of disagreements and seriousness of disagreements. It also included

Table 11.1 Hierarchical nature of variables

Distal variables	Age of grandparent (chronological age) Sex of grandparent (male = 0, female = 1) Personality similarity Physical similarity Age of (grand)child (chronological age) Sex of (grand)child (male = 0, female = 1) Socio-economic status (1 = high to 5 = low) Dependence on grand(child)

Proximal variables	Contact
	    frequency
	    duration
	    indirect
	    desire for
	Reciprocation
	    help received frequency
	    help received value
	    altruism feelings received
	Affect
	    liking
	    sociability
	    involvement

Outcome variables	Help
	    frequency
	    value
	    altruism feelings
	Disagreement
	    frequency
	    seriousness

Note: All variables are measured on 7-point rating scales unless otherwise specified.

questions about physical similarity and personality similarity; dependence; contact; and affect. These all comprised seven-point rating scales. There were also open-ended questions relating to roles and relationships within the family.

The questionnaire was given during a directed interview, but later a postal questionnaire was also used. Analyses revealed no significant difference between the distribution of responses given in the interview setting and via the postal questionnaire, so the results presented derive from the combined sample.

Predictions from sociobiological theory

In sociobiological terms, altruism (here mainly referred to as 'help') and conflict (here mainly referred to as 'disagreement') are expected to be influenced by a number of factors. We discuss in particular degree of relatedness, certainty of relatedness and reproductive value. In the following sections the implications for altruism are drawn out; implications for conflict will normally be the inverse of these.

Degree of relatedness

The traditional view of relatedness is illustrated by considering the branches of a family tree: with each additional branch connecting actor and recipient, the value of the relatedness coefficient between them decreases geometrically. This is a rather simplistic model of the very complex nature of genetic relatedness; however, it provides a straightforward method of categorizing relationships within the extended family, which we employ in the present context. Following Hamilton's (1964) basic model, altruism should decrease from children (relatedness of 0.5), to grandchildren (relatedness of 0.25), to non-relatives (in this sample close friends and children's spouses; relatedness of 0.0). (Although human subjects are aware of degrees of relatedness, the above reasoning does not imply that they use this information *consciously* to mediate altruism and conflict, even if empirically their behaviour were found to follow the predicted pattern.)

Certainty of relatedness

Whatever the cultural degree of relatedness may be, as socially defined by (for example) using the terms 'son' or 'granddaughter', this may not correspond to genetic relatedness with absolute certainty. One reason for this is that the socially defined father is not (short of genetic fingerprinting information) absolutely certain that he is the genetic father. Altruism would be expected to decrease as relatedness certainty decreases. In this study the predictive powers of two measures of relatedness certainty were examined.

Paternity certainty

As elaborated by M.S. Smith (this volume), a male would be uncertain of his relationships with any of his children, whereas a female would normally be quite certain of her relatedness since she gives birth to the infant. Thus the highest certainty of relatedness is expected for maternal grandmothers, with less for maternal grandfather and paternal grandmother (one uncertain link), and least for paternal grandfather (two uncertain links). This model relies on cues external to any provided by the offspring themselves.

Perceived similarity

Another model assesses certainty of relatedness, but independently of pedigree or family ties. This is phenotypic matching, a particular form of which is known as 'genetic similarity theory' (Rushton, Russell and Wells 1984). The individual is seen as assessing degree of genetic similarity on the basis of perceived phenotypic resemblance. Recognition of the individual as genetically similar relies on cues displayed by the individual, rather than on properties ascribed by virtue of external circumstance. Unlike the paternity certainty model, it predicts that non-relatives will also have their degree of similarity assessed.

Two measures of similarity of others to them as perceived by the grandparents were used: (1) personality similarity (covering personality and temperament), and (2) physical similarity (in appearance). It would be predicted by genetic similarity theory that altruism would increase with greater assessed similarity, even within one relationship class such as children or grandchildren.

Reproductive value (of child or grandchild)

This concept refers to the 'value' of the individual in terms of the likelihood that they will reproduce in future. Altruism should (other things being equal) be directed to individuals of greater reproductive value. The two mediators of this variable considered are (1) age of (grand)child, and (2) sex of (grand)child.

Age of (grand)child is important because investment should follow the reproductive curve determined by it; greater resources being given to those approaching the age at which reproduction becomes likely and resource investment decreasing as the individual moves further away from this optimum point.

Sex of (grand)child is also of importance, but in a more complex way. Males have a greater base-line potential for gene propagation than females, but male reproductive success is more variable than female success since females are in effect the limiting resource (Trivers and Willard 1973). Thus families with more resources would be expected to display a preference for helping male offspring (with extra investment ensuring that the male is successful in terms of reproductive competition), while those with fewer resources would be expected to help female offspring more, since even the least successful females will have a greater chance of mating than an unsuccessful male (Dickemann 1979). In order to examine this, we examined sex of (grand)child in relation to socio-economic status as a measure of resource availability.

The individual's ability to make use of the factors cited above in choosing an optimal behaviour pattern depends both on the accuracy of his or her knowledge base and on any constraints imposed by the environment (including the actions of other individuals). Furthermore, it is likely to be the case that any programming of our behaviour is flexible in the sense that any general 'rule' is open to modification by particular circumstance. For this and other reasons a perfect match between behaviour in the real world and behaviour as modelled by sociobiological theories is not expected.

Results

Degree of relatedness

Table 11.2 indicates the spread of responses to the outcome variables. All three measures of altruism (frequency of help, value of help and feelings of altruism) vary by category of relatedness in the way that sociobiological theorists would predict. Patterns of help for children's spouses and close friends match one another quite closely and are lower than those for grandchildren, which in turn are lower than those for children. In general, there was a close fit between these findings about help and altruism, and those expected by kin selection theory; such a general finding was also obtained by Essock-Vitale and McGuire (1985) in a study of white US families.

The findings for frequency of disagreement and for the seriousness of disgreements occurring do not fit so well with the sociobiological model. Table 11.2 indicates that in both cases disagreements follow the rank order: child > child's spouse > grandchild > close friend. Thus it appears that grandparents are more restrained in relations with non-family members and with younger relatives. The fact that patterns of disagreement appear to be further removed from relatedness than do patterns of help may be explained by the different end results attributable to the behaviours. It is likely, for example, that close friends (who are no doubt socially valuable to the older individual) would be more quickly offended by a series of disagreements than would family members who have been acquainted with the individual for a much longer time.

Table 11.2 Mean values of help and disagreement variables for grandparents to children, grandchildren, in-laws and friends

	Help frequency	Help value	Altruism feelings	Disagree frequency	Disagree seriousness
Grandparent to children	4.47	5.31	6.06	2.77	2.58
Grandparent to grandchildren	4.17	5.18	5.96	1.89	1.79
Grandparent to children's spouses	3.53	4.68	5.41	2.12	2.11
Grandparent to close friends	3.46	4.71	5.38	1.51	1.63

Certainty of relatedness

Paternity certainty

There were few differences between the patterns of help and disagreement shown by male and female grandparents. T-tests indicated no significant differences in the mean values reported by grandmothers and grandfathers in relation to four of the five outcome variables for behaviour towards grandchildren. However, the value of help given to grandchildren by grandmothers was greater than that reported by grandfathers (a mean of 5.35 for females as opposed to 4.73 for males, $p < 0.002$), as would be expected given the greater certainty of relatedness grandmothers have over grandfathers.

A further analysis was made by sex and lineage and is shown in Table 11.3. One-way ANOVAs were carried out for each of the five outcome measures, but none was significant. MGMs do score highest on frequency of help and value of help, in agreement with sociobiological predictions; but on a model such as M.S. Smith's (this volume) one would expect more significant discrimination for the other outcome variables and amongst the other types of grandparent. Only one of the five outcome variables (that for value of help) yields results entirely in the direction predicted.

Table 11.3 Mean values of help and disagreement variables for four types of grandparents

	Help frequency	*Help value*	*Altruism feelings*	*Disagree frequency*	*Disagree seriousness*
Maternal grandmother (N=44)	4.56	5.67	5.76	1.87	1.87
Paternal grandmother (N=40)	3.89	5.47	6.29	1.46	1.48
Maternal grandfather (N=18)	4.12	4.62	5.56	2.80	2.21
Paternal grandfather (N=15)	4.17	4.50	6.25	2.00	2.33

In fact, of all the variables considered in our analyses, the only one we found to covary directly and significantly with certainty of relatedness was that of contact. This has important implications for M.S. Smith's study because there contact was the only variable measured. As in our results certainty failed to mediate more direct measurements of the behaviour considered by M.S. Smith, it may be the case that his alternative 'culture-based' explanation of his findings is the more accurate – that is, that uterine grandchildren are visited more frequently because females tend to be the individuals staying at home with the children, and grandparents feel more comfortable visiting their own daughter than someone else's. As M.S. Smith has suggested, this point can only be elucidated further by means of empirical research.

Although there is some indication of paternity certainty being taken into account, the patterns of help and disagreement in this sample do not provide strong support for a direct influence of certainty on altruism or conflict. This may simply be the result of males in our society feeling highly confident in their paternity.

Table 11.4 Correlates of help and conflict: grandparents to children (only correlations significant beyond p<.01 are shown)

	Help frequency	Help value	Altruism feelings	Disagree frequency	Disagree seriousness
Age of grandparent					
Sex of grandparent					
Personality similarity		0.26	0.36	−0.25	−0.22
Physical similarity					
Age of child	−0.22			−0.29	
Sex of child				0.33	
Socio-economic status					0.23
Dependence	0.21	0.23			
Contact frequency	0.56	0.46			
Contact duration	0.24				
Contact indirect		0.25			
Contact desire	−0.29		0.31		
Help received frequency	0.36	0.25			
Help received value		0.36	0.31		
Altruism feelings received			0.67	−0.35	−0.31
Affect: liking		0.29	0.62	−0.46	−0.44
Affect: sociability		0.28	0.53	−0.25	−0.31
Affect: involvement	0.39	0.43	0.28		

Table 11.5 Correlates of help and conflict: grandparents to grandchildren (only correlations significant beyond p<.01 are shown)

	Help frequency	Help value	Altruism feelings	Disagree frequency	Disagree seriousness
Age of grandparent					
Sex of grandparent		0.24	−0.28	−0.33	
Personality similarity		0.21			
Physical similarity					
Age of grandchild			−0.23		
Sex of grandchild		−0.27			
Socio-economic status	−0.22	0.22	0.29		0.29
Dependence				0.24	
Contact frequency	0.50	0.28			
Contact duration	0.33	0.30			
Contact indirect	0.32			0.32	
Contact desire		0.25			
Help received frequency				0.25	0.35
Help received value					
Altruism feelings received			0.35		
Affect: liking		0.26	0.57		
Affect: sociability		0.23	0.56		
Affect: involvement		0.46	0.50		

Because this particular male sample was also very small it is possible that we selected males who happened to be more confident in their paternity than the true 'average male' in the population.

Perceived similarity

Correlations with these (and subsequent) variables are shown in Table 11.4 (from grandparents to children) and Table 11.5 (from grandparents to grandchildren). Because of the large number of correlations calculated, only those significant at the p<.01 level or higher are shown.

At this level there were no significant correlations of perceived physical similarity with any outcome measure. Personality similarity, however, correlated significantly with the value of help given to children and also with feelings of altruism towards them (Table 11.4). Furthermore, disagreements with children perceived as more similar in this way were both less frequent and less serious. With regard to grandchildren, the relationship is less clear-cut (Table 11.5), with personality similarity being linked to value of help but not to the other measures of help or disagreement.

This disparity in the importance of personality similarity to children, and to grandchildren, could be explained in a number of ways. Two possible explanations are that either similarity is a problematic judgement when considering individuals separated from oneself by a large age gap, or that similarity is most important for individuals of maximum reproductive value. These ideas are highly speculative and there is a need for further empirical work to separate out the factors actually involved.

The finding that any effects of similarity on interpersonal behaviour were produced by judgements relating to personality and temperament, rather than to physical appearance, whilst needing replication, does deserve some comment. From the viewpoint of proximal mediators of behaviour, this finding might be explained by the greater satisfaction to be obtained from associating with others who possess similar feelings and ways of behaving to oneself, which would not necessarily follow from any physical similarity. From the more distal, sociobiological viewpoint it might be explained by the greater number of genes involved in personality structures as opposed to physical attributes. Similarity on a trait involving a large number of genes gives a greater indication of overall relatedness than similarity on a trait requiring only one or two genes. The proximal and distal views can be linked if we consider personality in the light of a collection of behavioural strategies; it could be argued that matching for similar strategies in others is a central mechanism operating in 'inclusive fitness' and therefore this aspect of similarity would be expected to be of considerable importance.

The correlational data indicate that personality similarity is of some significance in terms of the determination of help and disagreement. If so, then perhaps grandparents were targeting their behaviour to benefit genetically similar others. However, only perceived similarity was measured, leaving unanswered the interesting question of whether perceived similarity is indeed a reflection of genetic similarity. A subset of families is now being tested to match perceived similarity and expressed preferences to genetic similarity based on blood antigen analysis.

Reproductive value

Age of (grand)child

The age of child and age of grandchild did correlate with some outcome variables, though such findings are difficult to interpret sociobiologically without fitting the data to a reproductive cycle curve. Increased age of child correlates with a decrease in both frequency of help and frequency of disagreement. Increased age of grand-children decreases feelings of altruism.

Sex of (grand)child

Grandparents appeared to have greater frequency of disagreements with female children than with male children. Male grandchildren were perceived as receiving greater value of help than that given to female grandchildren. The main sociobiological predictions relate to hypothesized interactions between sex of (grand)child and socio-economic status.

To test these, t-tests were carried out for each of the five outcome variables, between male and female grandchildren, separately for high socio-economic status (first two levels), and for low socio-economic status (last two levels). None of these t-tests were significant; of the ten t-tests carried out, only three were in the right direction.

These results will be discussed further after reporting the results obtained with a wide range of variables, in the next section.

Modelling behaviour within the extended family

In this section an attempt is made to examine the causal influences of various factors on our outcome measures of help and disagreement. Included are sex of grandparent, and perceived similarity to (grand)child, and age and sex of (grand)child; as discussed earlier, these are of interest to sociobiological theorists, amongst others. A number of other variables, summarized in Table 11.1, are also used.

We have organized most of our analyses and resultant model fitting by splitting the variables into three components. The first comprises the group of variables which we regard as *distal* predictors of behaviour. The second comprises those variables which might be seen as more *proximal*; for example, frequency of contact and liking. The third comprises our outcome measures of help and disagreement. Although the variables have been split this way, we do not suggest that these boundaries are absolute. In addition, the distal/proximal distinction does not coincide with the biological/cultural distinction. For example, although we place reciprocation under the heading of a proximal variable, it could as easily be seen as having importance in the context of a purely sociobiological model.

Distal variables

In addition to the variables discussed above, age of grandparent was introduced, and two indirect measures of access to resources (by grandparent): first, the socio-economic status (SES) group of the grandparent, which is taken as a measure of the likelihood that the grandparent will have sufficient resources to distribute. It would be expected that with lower SES the frequency of help would be less, but not necessarily its value (perceived), nor feelings of altruism. Second, the dependence the grandparent feels on the recipient of his or her actions; this is taken as a measure of the freedom with which the grandparent can distribute any resources which he or she controls. A grandparent might for example feel some constraint in resource allocation if they were more socially dependent on one child than another.

Proximal variables

The distal factors outlined above may be expected to operate in an indirect manner by way of the more apparent features of interaction such as emotional response and desire for contact. Of these more immediate predictors of interpersonal behaviour, those considered here are contact, reciprocation and affect.

Contact

Contact is likely to be an important determinant of how much help you can give to your relatives and how likely you are to argue with them. Klatzky (1971), and Frankel and DeWit (1989) have found that distance accounts for most of the variation in frequency of contact between relatives. The effect of contact may thus be viewed as purely opportunistic; an alternative interpretation is that individuals indirectly target their altruistic and conflict responses by choosing to live near and associate more with some individuals than with others. The measures were (1) frequency of contact, (2) duration of contact, (3) indirect contact (that is, frequency of letters, phone calls) and (4) desire for contact.

Reciprocation

It is to be expected that willingness to help another will be mediated by their attitude towards returning such help. In sociobiological terms, the importance of reciprocation should be greater when the actor is considering the responses of an individual who is not genetically similar to themselves. In cultural terms the response to non-reciprocation could be seen in terms of the frustration or anger produced by having one's gestures of friendship ignored or rebuffed. We measured first, the frequency of help received; second, the value of help received; and third, perceived feelings of altruism received, from children and grandchildren.

Affect

Whatever actions we carry out are to some extent mediated both by our feelings towards the recipient of our actions and the feelings we assume them to hold regarding ourselves. On this basis we decided to assess the part played by feelings of (1) liking, (2) sociability, and (3) involvement, in determining the grandparent's level of altruism and conflict towards children and grandchildren, using both the grandparent's view of the recipient and the grandparent's view of how the recipient perceived her or him.

Results

Factors affecting help and disagreement

The predictive power of the variables was analysed in two stages. First, we looked at the importance of each variable independently (see Tables 11.4 and 11.5).

Distal variables

Results for sex of grandparent, perceived similarity, and age and sex of grand-child, have been discussed above. There were no significant correlations with age of grandparent.

Socio-economic status appeared to be a more important variable in terms of behaviour to grandchildren than to children. For children, the only measure relevant to SES was the seriousness of disagreement, this being reported as greater amongst grandparents of lower SES. For grandchildren, feelings of altruism and the value of help given were both greater in the case of low SES grandparents whilst, as would be predicted on the basis of resource availability, frequency of help decreased in these groups. It is possible that lower SES grandparents are coping with the cognitive dissonance induced by their inability to help grand-children as much as they would like to or feel they ought to, by placing greater emphasis on their feelings of altruism and the value of their help than on the actual frequency of its occurrence.

Socioeconomic status may be regarded as a measure of resource control; the dependence of the grandparents on their children and grandchildren can be regarded as a measure of how free they are to distribute any resources they do hold. For this account to be valid, it is important that grandparents regard dependence not in terms of financial dependence (in which case we would simply have a second measure of resource control) but rather in terms of how necessary the recipient is to them in the sense of emotional or social support. The data given in Table 11.4 suggest that the grandparents are indeed considering dependence in this way; it correlates with frequency of help and value of help to children. It is consistent with these data that grandparents are somewhat constrained in their distribution of resources by the need to avoid alienating individuals on whom they depend for emotional support. An alternative account would be that grand-parents are most dependent for emotional support on those to whom they are most emotionally attached and thus to those whom they would in any case favour in

189

the allocation of resources. This is not supported by our data, however, since there is no significant correlation between dependence and any of the three measures of affect, either for children or grandchildren.

Proximal variables

Contact emerges as a powerful correlate of help, if not of disagreement. It is measures of actual help (frequency of help and value of help), rather than feelings of altruism, which correlate significantly. This suggests that grandparents help most those children and grandchildren whom they actually see most often. This may not correspond with their expressed wishes, as is supported by the finding that the measures of contact which appeared to matter most were those of actual rather than of desired contact.

Reciprocation appeared as an important variable in the case of children. Frequency of help received from children linked strongly both with frequency of help and value of help given. Similarly, value of help received linked both with value of help given and with feelings of altruism. The latter in its turn correlated very strongly with the level of altruistic feelings perceived to be held by the child towards the grandparent and in addition appeared to correlate with a reduction both in the frequency of disagreements and their seriousness.

Reciprocation seems to be an important aspect of grandparents' relations with their children (as would be expected by both sociobiological and cultural theories). It is not so important for grandparents' relations with grandchildren in our sample; perhaps because many grandchildren were not yet at an age where they could reciprocate effectively.

The three measures of affect are fairly similar in their pattern of correlations. In the case of both children and grandchildren, affect emerges as a powerful correlate of both the value of help, and feelings of altruism (whereas frequency of help relates most to contact). In addition, for children only, affect relates negatively to measures of disagreement.

Model fitting

As a second stage in the analyses, we looked at the strength of various composite models comprising groups of variables split into the distal and proximal categories (see Tables 11.6 and 11.7). We were then in a position to develop a composite model of the processes involved, with greater explanatory power than each modifier considered independently.

This type of composite model was attempted for each of the measures of help and disagreement, by fitting a series of regression models to the data. Separate models were used for the proximal and distal variables, and all initial models comprised the variables significantly correlated with the measure in question. The particular technique used was stepwise regression. The significance levels cited in Tables 11.6 and 11.7 are t-values derived from the standardized beta coefficients. These coefficients can be taken as adequately representing the *relative* importance of each variable within a given model as a mediator of the factor being considered, since they have been constrained to normality to nullify the effect of variance. The value of R squared is also adjusted, to indicate the likely fit of each model to the population at large rather than simply to this particular sample.

Table 11.6 Regression analyses: grandparents to children

Variable	Adjusted R squared	Beta	t
Help frequency	(Distal)		
Dependence	0.13	0.19	0.03
Age of child	0.10	−0.33	0.0002
	(Proximal)		
Contact frequency	0.28	0.42	0.000
Help frequency received	0.40	0.36	0.000
Help value	(Distal)		
Dependence	0.04	0.23	0.02
	(Proximal)		
Contact frequency	0.35	0.25	0.009
Affect: involvement	0.22	0.35	0.003
Help value received	0.30	0.27	0.004
Altruism feelings	(Distal)		
Socio-economic status	0.09	0.33	0.01
	(Proximal)		
Altruism feelings received	0.46	0.37	0.0001
Affect: liking	0.37	0.38	0.0001
Help value received	0.48	0.17	0.04
Disagreement frequency	(Distal)		
Age of child	−0.24	0.48	0.02
Sex of child	0.22	0.35	0.03
	(Proximal)		
Affect: liking	0.15	−0.39	0.000
Disagreement seriousness	(Distal)		
Personality similarity	0.20	−0.49	0.02
	(Proximal)		
Affect: liking	0.15	−0.39	0.000

It is to be expected that proximal variables will show a stronger fit to the data in absolute terms than will distal variables, given that the latter are to be seen as operating via these more immediate factors. From the final analyses produced, it can indeed be seen that in all but two cases the proximal variables provided a stronger fit to the data than the distal variables. (The two exceptions both related to grandparental disagreement.) This does not, however, imply that the distal account is of no value. Although in relative terms the proximal analysis provides the most powerful predictive tool, a complete account would require both types of variable to be present.

Table 11.7 Regression analyses: grandparents to grandchildren

Variable	Adjusted R squared	Beta	t
Help frequency	(Proximal)		
Contact frequency	0.24	0.48	0.0000
Contact: indirect	0.32	0.30	0.0002
Help value	(Distal)		
Grandparent sex	0.12	0.37	0.01
	(Proximal)		
Contact frequency	0.22	0.47	0.001
Contact desire	0.13	0.45	0.001
Altruism feelings	(Distal)		
Socio-economic status	0.09	0.33	0.01
	(Proximal)		
Affect: sociability	0.44	0.45	0.000
Affect: involvement	0.59	0.27	0.0001
Altruism feelings received	0.61	0.16	0.04
Disagreement frequency	(Distal)		
Grandparent sex	0.19	−0.46	0.0004
	(Proximal)		
Contact: indirect	0.74	0.32	0.002

Taking the analysis of proximal data first, it can be seen that in the case of grandparents to their children, a reasonable account can be provided for measures of help, in terms of reciprocation, affect and contact. The emphasis on reciprocation is present for all the measures of help and altruism. Contact is important for actual help (frequency of help and value of help), while affect is important for value of help and feelings of altruism.

In the case of grandparents to grandchildren, actual help (frequency of help and value of help) depends very much on opportunities for contact. Interestingly, as in the case of grandparents to children, feelings of altruism are dependent not on opportunity for contact but on a mixture of affect and perceived reciprocation.

The fit of the models to measures of disagreement is less satisfactory. Liking is an important variable in terms of the frequency of disagreement between grandparents and grandchildren. Indirect contact is a powerful predictor for the frequency of disagreement with grandchildren.

The distal models show a poorer fit, but dependence relates to frequency of help and value of help given to children, while personality similarity and seriousness of disagreement show an inverse relationship. Sex of grandparent (female) relates to greater value of help as well as lesser frequency of disagreements to grandchildren.

We intend to continue our analysis of the present data by providing a path analytic model for the behaviours considered.

Conclusion

The sociobiological approach to grandparenthood suggests that grandparents act so as to further the propagation of their genes indirectly, by means of the reproductive efforts of their descendants. The predictions following from such a model suggest a number of patterns which should be observed in the behaviour of grandparents within the family context. In this chapter, we have attempted to outline what some of these predictions might be, and the extent to which they match the empirical data we have obtained.

Degree of relatedness does correlate in the ways predicted, with measures of help and altruism. So far as certainty of relatedness is concerned, the evidence is rather mixed; there is some, but rather weak, evidence for the importance of paternity certainty; there is better evidence supporting the influence of similarity in personality/temperament, but not of similarity in physical appearance. For reproductive value, there appears to be rather little interaction between sex of (grand)child and socio-economic status, although some of the results are in the predicted direction. Overall, it must be said that the success of the predictions is very modest, apart from those for degree of relatedness, which are, however, least unique to sociobiology. The results for personality similarity seem the most promising to pursue further.

We have also emphasized the need to consider both proximal and distal factors in providing a full account of behaviour within the extended family, and suggest that a useful way forward is to combine the two types of model. Proximal factors such as contact, reciprocation, and affect, do indeed seem to be important predictors of measures of help given by grandparents to their children and grandchildren. They were found to be rather less good predictors of measures of disagreement. Distal variables may be considered as the ultimate mediators of behaviour which are more directly moderated by proximal factors such as emotional response. Overall, the influence of the distal variables we examined was less marked than that of the proximal factors, but some significant associations were found for all the variables considered, except for grandparental age, and perceived physical similarity. A combined model taking full account of both proximal and distal factors, and elaborated by path analysis, may make it easier to provide a reasonably complete account of the complex patterns of cooperation and conflict observable between generations.

Acknowledgement

Maria Leek has been supported by a grant from the Science and Engineering Research Council, U.K., which is gratefully acknowledged.

References

Crawford, M. (1981) 'Not disengaged: grandparents in literature and reality, an empirical study in role satisfaction', *The Sociological Review* 29: 499–519.

Dickemann, M. (1979) 'Female infanticide, reproductive strategies and social stratification: a preliminary model', in N.A. Chagnon and W. Irons (eds), *Evolutionary Biology and Human Social Behaviour: an Anthropological Perspective*, North Scituate, MA: Duxbury Press, pp. 321–67.

Essock-Vitale, S.M. and McGuire, M.T. (1985) 'Women's lives viewed from an evolutionary perspective. II. Patterns of helping', *Ethology and Sociobiology* 6: 155–73.

Frankel, B.G. and DeWit, D.J. (1989) 'Geographic distance and intergenerational contact: an empirical examination of the relationship', *Journal of Aging Studies* 3: 139–62.

Hamilton, W.D. (1964) 'The genetical theory of social behaviour. 1 and 11', *Journal of Theoretical Biology* 12: 12–45.

Klatzky, S.R. (1971) *Patterns of Contact with Relatives*, Washington, DC, American Sociological Association, Rose Monograph Series.

MacArthur, R.H. and Wilson, E.O. (1967) *The Theory of Island Biogeography*, Princeton, NJ: Princeton University Press.

Neugarten, B.L. and Weinstein, K.J. (1964) 'The changing American grandparent', *Journal of Marriage and the Family* 39: 199–204.

Rushton, J.P., Russell, R.J.H. and Wells, P.A. (1984) 'Genetic similarity theory: beyond kin selection', *Behaviour Genetics* 14: 179–93.

Trivers, R.L. and Willard D.E. (1973) 'Natural selection of parental ability to vary the sex ratio of offspring', *Science* 179: 90–2.

Name index

Abraham, K. 145
Ainsworth, M.D.S. 11, 90, 92
Albrecht, R. 6, 22
Aldous, J. 124
Alexander, R.D. 170, 172
Ambrus, V.J. 5
Anderson, J.C. 117
Anderson, M. 124
Angenent, H. 100
Apostel, U. 32, 33, 42, 46
Apple, D. 6
Arend, R. 90
Aronson, E. 55
Atchley, R.C. 158

Bachtold, L.M. 72
Baldwin, W. 85
Bales, G.G. 24, 96
Baltes, P.B. 12
Bandura, A. 95
Baranowski, M.D. 86
Barash, D.P. 158
Barer, B.M. 8, 11
Barletta, G. 144
Battistelli, P. 6, 7, 10, 11, 12, 143, 147, 154
Bayley, N. 90, 91, 92, 93, 172
Belsky, J. 100, 103, 104, 105, 106, 107, 174
Benedek, T. 21, 23, 25
Bengtson, V.L. 7, 8, 9, 21, 22, 23, 24, 29, 32, 101, 118
Benn, R. 2, 9, 10, 11, 85, 92
Benn, R.K. 92
Berger, P. 21
Bertin, M. 144
Biller, H.B. 86
Biringen, Z.C. 171, 172
Birren, J.E. 12
Blackwelder, D.E. 6, 7, 11
Blakeslee, S. 74
Blanchard, R.W. 86
Blieszner, R. 1
Block, J. 86

Block, J.H. 86
Boomsma, A. 117
Borden, B. 3
Borzi, P.C. 74
Boszormenyi-Nagy, I. 33, 145
Bott, E. 103
Brem-Graser, L. 38
Brock, A.J.L.L. de 2, 9, 10, 100, 109
Brooks-Gunn, J. 85
Brown, G.W. 9
Brown, M.B. 163
Browne, K. 102
Buholz, M. 69
Buhr, M. 35, 37, 42, 44, 47
Bumpass, L. 102
Burroughes, J. 5
Burton, L.M. 7, 8, 9
Buss, D.M. 174

Cahn, R. 145
Cain, V. 85
Cairns, R.B. 174
Camerini, G.B. 144, 154
Campbell, V. 69
Carlson, E. 136
Carroll, V. 72
Cartwright, D.S. 90
Cassirer, E. 52
Caspi, A. 102
Castle, R.L. van de 147
Cavallero, P. 146
Cherlin, A.J. 10, 23, 68, 69, 70, 73, 74, 75, 76
Clavan, S. 19, 24, 70
Clayton, V. 12
Coe, R.M. 25
Cohen, P.S. 101
Cohler, B.J. 56, 69, 75, 100, 101, 103
Colletta, N.D. 72
Conley, M.M. 136
Cosmides, L. 174
Costantini, L. 147

Subject index